CHRISTIANS MUST HEED JESUS

HARUN YAHYA (ADNAN OKTAR)

Harun Yahya and His Works

Now writing under the pen-name of HARUN YAHYA, Adnan Oktar was born in Ankara in 1956. Having completed his primary and secondary education in Ankara, he studied fine arts at Istanbul's Mimar Sinan University and philosophy at Istanbul University. Since the 1980s, he has published many books on political, scientific, and faith-related issues. Harun Yahya is well-known as the author of important works disclosing the imposture of evolutionists, their invalid claims, and the dark liaisons between Darwinism and such bloody ideologies as fascism and communism.

Harun Yahya's works, translated into 73 different languages, constitute a collection for a total of more than 55,000 pages with 40,000 illustrations.

His pen-name is a composite of the names Harun (Aaron) and Yahya (John), in memory of the two esteemed Prophets who fought against their peoples' lack of faith. The Prophet's seal on his books' covers is symbolic and is linked to their contents. It represents the Qur'an (the Final Scripture) and Prophet Muhammad (saas), last of the prophets. Under the guidance of the Qur'an and the Sunnah (teachings of the Prophet [saas]), the author makes it his purpose to disprove each fundamental tenet of irreligious ideologies and to have the "last word," so as to completely silence the objections raised against religion. He uses the seal of the final Prophet (saas), who attained ultimate wisdom and moral perfection, as a sign of his intention to offer the last word.

All of Harun Yahya's works share one single goal: to convey the Qur'an's message, encourage readers to consider basic faith-related issues such as God's existence and unity and the Hereafter;

3

and to expose irreligious systems' feeble foundations and perverted ideologies.

Harun Yahya enjoys a wide readership in many countries, from India to America, England to Indonesia, Poland to Bosnia, Spain to Brazil, Malaysia to Italy, France to Bulgaria and Russia. Some of his books are available in English, French, German, Spanish, Italian, Portuguese, Urdu, Arabic, Albanian, Chinese, Swahili, Hausa, Dhivehi (spoken in Maldives), Russian, Serbo-Croat (Bosnian), Polish, Malay, Uygur Turkish, Indonesian, Bengali, Danish and Swedish.

Greatly appreciated all around the world, these works have been instrumental in many people recovering faith in God and gaining deeper insights into their faith. His books' wisdom and sincerity, together with a distinct style that's easy to understand, directly affect anyone who reads them. Those who seriously consider these books, can no longer advocate atheism or any other perverted ideology or materialistic philosophy, since these books are characterized by rapid effectiveness, definite results, and irrefutability. Even if they continue to do so, it will be only a sentimental insistence, since these books refute such ideologies from their very foundations. All contemporary movements of denial are now ideologically defeated, thanks to the books written by Harun Yahya.

This is no doubt a result of the Qur'an's wisdom and lucidity. The author modestly intends to serve as a means in humanity's search for God's right path. No material gain is sought in the publication of these works.

Those who encourage others to read these books, to open their minds and hearts and guide them to become more devoted servants of God, render an invaluable service.

Meanwhile, it would only be a waste of time and energy to propagate other books that create confusion in people's minds, lead them into ideological confusion, and that clearly have no strong and precise effects in removing the doubts in people's hearts, as also verified from previous experience. It is impossible for books

4

devised to emphasize the author's literary power rather than the noble goal of saving people from loss of faith, to have such a great effect. Those who doubt this can readily see that the sole aim of Harun Yahya's books is to overcome disbelief and to disseminate the Qur'an's moral values. The success and impact of this service are manifested in the readers' conviction.

One point should be kept in mind: The main reason for the continuing cruelty, conflict, and other ordeals endured by the vast majority of people is the ideological prevalence of disbelief. This can be ended only with the ideological defeat of disbelief and by conveying the wonders of creation and Qur'anic morality so that people can live by it. Considering the state of the world today, leading into a downward spiral of violence, corruption and conflict, clearly this service must be provided speedily and effectively, or it may be too late.

In this effort, the books of Harun Yahya assume a leading role. By the will of God, these books will be a means through which people in the twenty-first century will attain the peace, justice, and happiness promised in the Qur'an.

To the Reader

- A special chapter is assigned to the collapse of the theory of evolution because this theory constitutes the basis of all anti-spiritual philosophies. Since Darwinism rejects the fact of creation—and therefore, God's existence—over the last 150 years it has caused many people to abandon their faith or fall into doubt. It is therefore an imperative service, a very important duty to show everyone that this theory is a deception. Since some readers may find the opportunity to read only one of our books, we think it appropriate to devote a chapter to summarize this subject.

- All the author's books explain faith-related issues in light of Qur'anic verses, and invite readers to learn God's words and to live by them. All the subjects concerning God's verses are explained so as to leave no doubt or room for questions in the reader's mind. The books' sincere, plain, and fluent style ensures that everyone of every age and from every social group can easily understand them. Thanks to their effective, lucid narrative, they can be read at one sitting. Even those who rigorously reject spirituality are influenced by the facts these books document and cannot refute the truthfulness of their contents.

- This and all the other books by the author can be read individually, or discussed in a group. Readers eager to profit from the books will find discussion very useful, letting them relate their reflections and experiences to one another.

- In addition, it will be a great service to Islam to contribute to the publication and reading of these books, written solely for the pleasure of God. The author's books are all extremely convincing. For this reason, to communicate true religion to others, one of the most effective methods is encouraging them to read these books.

• We hope the reader will look through the reviews of his other books at the back of this book. His rich source material on faith-related issues is very useful, and a pleasure to read.

• In these books, unlike some other books, you will not find the author's personal views, explanations based on dubious sources, styles that are unobservant of the respect and reverence due to sacred subjects, nor hopeless, pessimistic arguments that create doubts in the mind and deviations in the heart.

Contents

FOREWORD CHRISTIANS MUST HEED JESUS THE MESSIAH

Why Is It Essential to Properly Grasp the Purpose of This Book?

There is a very important fact that we want our Christian brothers who read this book to understand: this book was not written in order to criticize our Christian brothers, to disparage them, to completely invalidate the Gospel or to do away with Christianity.

As revealed in verse 136 of 2nd Chapter of the Koran, Muslims say, "We have faith in God and what has been sent down to us and what was sent down to Abraham and Ishmael and Isaac and Jacob and the Tribes, and what Moses and Jesus were given, and what all the Prophets were given by their Lord. We do not differentiate between any of them." Therefore, in the same way as Christians, Muslims also have an obligation to abide by the true commands in the Gospel and to praise its wise words.

In the same way that he is a Muslim, a Muslim is also a true follower of Abraham, of Noah, of Moses and of Jesus. He recognizes, loves and praises all the prophets. Muslims and

Christians are together awaiting the coming of Jesus (pbuh) in the End Times, in which we are now living. At the same time, as required by Islam, a religion of peace and love, true Muslims have a duty to love and watch over and protect Christians and Jews, described as the People of the Book in the Koran.

There are many verses in the Koran in which Jesus (pbuh), Hazrat Mary, Christians and the Jews are praised. Although a number of false beliefs that were added onto Christianity only subsequently are corrected in the Koran, the Koran confirms that the true Gospel is a Divine text revealed by God. **Christians and Jews enjoy a special status as the "People of the Book" in the Koran and are Muslims' allies against irreligion.**

Muslims therefore have a duty to call on the People of the Book to adhere to the true, uncorrupted Torah and Gospel, to show them the way, to ensure they become more devout and sincere and to call on them to believe in God, the One and Only. This is exceedingly important in terms of establishing brotherhood, union and unity among those who believe in God.

The purpose of the information in this book addressed to our Christian brothers is to act as an invitation to sincerity and the truth, in other words, the Koran. It is also to free Christians from false practices and superstitious additions to their faith that appear nowhere in the Gospel revealed to Jesus and **to make them true Christians who abide by the commandments of the true Gospel.**

As Muslims, it is also our desire for we also want Christians to become true believers. Our duty, as revealed by God in the Koran is to **"enjoin the right and forbid the wrong"** (Koran, 3:104) and to call on the People of the Book to believe in the Oneness of God (Koran, 3:64). These require that we lead them away from errors that some of our Christian brothers have unknowingly fallen into and show them the truth. It is therefore a matter of the greatest importance for Christians to be warned against these dangers, like all other believers, and to be invited to adhere to the true commands revealed by God and to abide by logic and reason.

This book deals with beliefs that entered Christianity, a true faith, over the course of the years and which the Koran warns against. As the verses telling of these errors are set out, evidence will be produced from the Gospel, Christians' own holy book, to do away with these. As with all beliefs, there may be Christians who look at matters from a radical perspective, who insist on these false beliefs we have mentioned and who harbor a prejudiced view of the Koran. Our advice to our Christian brothers in question is to read what is presented in this book in an objective manner and to evaluate what they read rationally and from an entirely new perspective. This will not lead them astray from what is commanded in the Gospel. On the contrary – by God's leave – it will be instrumental in their approaching the Gospel more honestly and obeying it in a more perfect manner.

Surely God is beyond all those expressions in this book that are in any way disrespectful of Him.

In the name of God, All-Merciful, Most Merciful

Say: 'He is God, Absolute Oneness, God, the Everlasting Sustainer of all. He has not given birth and was not born. And no one is comparable to Him.'
(Koran, 112:1-4)

INTRODUCTION: CHRISTIANITY IS ACTUALLY A MONOTHEISTIC FAITH

The Christian religion that was born among Jews living in the Holy Land was the result of sincere Jews living by the law of the Prophet Moses (pbuh) choosing to follow Jesus. The distinguishing feature of the Jews who followed Jesus is that they believed in God as the one and only god.

However, this monotheistic belief changed after the ascension of Jesus and the spread of Christianity into pagan lands. Jesus began being regarded as divine due to the belief in the Trinity that was subsequently made part of Christianity (surely God is beyond that). Christians espousing that superstitious belief claimed that Almighty God took human form and incarnated himself in Jesus, and disseminated that belief.

Belief in the Trinity – surely God is beyond that – is used in the sense of a belief in a tripartite God – "Father, Son and Holy Ghost." Led and supported by the Roman Emperor Constantine of the time, various people who wished to modify Christian belief pointed to the references to "the son of God" that appear in the Torah and the Gospel as evidence. They claimed that Jesus was quite literally the son of God and ascribed divine status to him. However, the references to "the son of God" in the Torah and the Gospel are a metaphorical expression of the fact that all sincere believers are God's beloved servants. This is made clear in The Gospel According to Matthew - *"Blessed are the peacemakers, for they will be called children of God."* (Matthew, 5:9). The reference to Jesus means the same thing. The term "son" in the Gospel means that he is a beloved servant of God and not that he is the actual son of God (surely God is beyond that).

This false and quite dangerous belief that was added onto Christianity at a later date and intended to destroy monotheistic belief gradually became the main precondition and article of faith in Christianity. Indeed, people who rejected the dogma were even regarded as having abandoned the Church. Under the leadership of certain priests advocating the Trinity, attempts were made to impose the dogma on Christianity through force and compulsion. Anyone rejecting belief in the Trinity was severely punished, exiled from their homelands or even killed. [For more detail on the subject see *Jesus (pbuh) Is Not the Son of God, But His Prophet, Adnan Oktar, www.bookglobal.com*]

It needs to be emphasized that the belief in the Trinity, or the "three in one" as some Christians put it, that was later added onto Christianity **appears neither in the Torah nor the Gospel.** The word Trinity does not appear in the Gospel, even though it is still regarded as an article of faith. However, this belief imposed as dogma and that seeks to portray Jesus as the son of God is a major error and danger. The majority of our Christian brothers are unaware of the scale of this danger, which God describes as follows in the Koran:

> **They say, "The All-Merciful has a son." They have devised <u>a monstrous thing</u>. <u>The heavens are all but rent apart and the Earth split open and the mountains brought crashing down</u>, at their ascription of a son to the All-Merciful! <u>It is not fitting for the All-Merciful to have a son.</u> There is no one in the heavens and Earth who will not come to the All-Merciful <u>as a servant.</u> (Koran, 19:88-93)**

God describes this effrontery as something that will cause the Earth to split open and the mountains to come crashing down. Sincere Christians must be aware of this great danger that so angers God. They need to see that belief in the Trinity, which was added onto the Gospel centuries later and was imposed despite all the objections in a climate of great strife, is completely incompatible with the true Gospel. They need to free themselves from their dogmas and look at matters rationally.

Of course, saying "see the danger" may not be enough for some Christians who have been taught solely the idea of the Trinity throughout their lives. That is why the idea of the Trinity and other subjects that entered Christianity only later need to be clarified in the light of the words of the Gospel and all the evidence. This evidence is set out in the pages that follow. The statements that follow concerning the Trinity are examined in three separate sections.

The first section consists of historical information proving that the idea of the Trinity was included in the Gospel and Christianity at a later date. This section will also discuss how the concept of the Trinity has no basis in the Torah.

The second section is intended to encourage sincere Christians to reflect and see certain truths in the light of passages from the Gospel and verses from the Koran. When our Christian brothers read these words they will see why a true believer must not believe in the Trinity and that this can have no place in the law of God.

The third section discusses a truth that will change the lives of all rational people of good conscience. That is the true nature of matter. The concept of representation will be fully understood in the light of the information provided about the true nature of matter and the ideological basis on which the Trinity rests will be completely demolished.

The Koran Confirms All the Earlier Books. The People of the Book Also Are Responsible toward the Koran

Before moving on to discuss this, one very important point needs to be emphasized. In addition to the Gospel, evidence is also provided from the Koran in order that various matters be properly understood. The reason for this is that **the Koran is the book of Christians and Jews, as well as of Muslims.**

The Koran is the last holy scripture. It has been protected, and there are therefore no discrepancies or inconsistencies in it. As God reveals to our Prophet (pbuh): **"We will cause you to recite so that you do not forget –"** (Koran, 87:6). God also reveals in verses that He protects the Koran - **"it truly is a Noble Koran in a well-protected Book."** (Koran, 56:77-78)

The Koran is pure revelation. It bestows peace and light, in the same way as the uncorrupted parts of the Torah and the Gospel. Anyone looking through the eyes of reason and conscience will immediately see this. They will see this as soon as they read the Koran. There is no need for any other evidence. No conscience can withstand the beauty and truth of the Koran. Anyone who reads the Koran and sees its extraordinary language, its superb clarity, the way it so perfectly addresses the conscience and the soul, the honesty of its statements, its warmth, its perfect evidence and the absence of any discrepancies will immediately form a firm opinion regarding it. It is totally obviously a Divine text. Almighty God has also confirmed this with numerous amazing miracles unique to the Koran. (For more detail see *The Miracles of the Koran 1-2, Adnan Oktar, www.bookglobal.net*)

There is an important fact that Christians need to know about the Koran: The Koran was not sent down to invalidate the scriptures before it. <u>On the contrary, the Koran was sent down in order to corroborate the true passages in the Torah and the</u>

Gospel and to show people the truth. It is therefore unlawful for a Muslim to deny the existence of true books before the Koran. (Some Muslims may claim the opposite, but these are people with a radical mindset, lacking in knowledge about the Koran and therefore about the essence of Islam. The explanations given here are based on verses of the Koran, not on the supposed logic of the radicals in question.) The revelation in the Koran requires that Muslims recognize and genuinely love all the prophets. In the same way that the Prophet Muhammad (pbuh) is our prophet, so are the Prophets Moses (pbuh) and Jesus (pbuh). As commanded in the Koran, it is impossible to discriminate between them:

> **Say, "We have faith in God and what has been sent down to us and what was sent down to Abraham and Ishmael and Isaac and Jacob and the Tribes, and what Moses and Jesus were given, and what all the prophets were given by their Lord. We do not differentiate between any of them. We are Muslims submitted to Him." (Koran, 2:136)**

Therefore, a Muslim is at the same time also **a true follower of Moses and a true follower of Jesus.** Again according to the Koran, a Muslim must obey those parts of the Torah and the Gospel that are compatible with the Koran.

Since the Koran confirms all previous scriptures and prophets, **true Judaism and true Christianity are existing in the Koran.** True Judaism and true Christianity are therefore only possible by recognizing the Koran and becoming a follower of the Prophet Muhammad. For that reason, **not only Muslims but also all Jews and all Christians have a responsibility toward the Koran.**

God states in one verse how He has sent the Koran as light and a clear sign for the People of the Book, that is Christians and Jews:

> **People of the Book! Our Messenger has come to you, making clear to you much of the Book that you have kept concealed, and passing over a lot. A Light has come to you from God and a Clear Book. (Koran, 5:15)**

18

The fact that the Koran was sent to confirm the Torah and the Gospel is expressed as follows:

> **Say, "Anyone who is the enemy of Gabriel should know that it <u>was he who brought it down upon your heart, by God's authority, confirming what came before, and as guidance and good news for the</u> believers." (Koran, 2:97)**

> **He has sent down the Book to you with truth, confirming what was there before it. And He sent down the Torah and the Gospel. (Koran, 3:3)**

These verses make it clear that the Koran was sent down to confirm Jews' and Christians' own books and to show them what is right and wrong, a book in which they can find the most perfect clarification of everything. Another verse of the Koran reveals how Jews and Christians must also obey the Koran:

> **<u>You who have been given the Book [Jews and Christians]! Have faith in what We have sent down confirming what is with you [the Torah and the Gospel]</u>, before We obliterate faces, turning them inside out, or We curse you as We cursed the Companions of the Sabbath. God's command is always carried out. (Koran, 4:47)**

Another verse is addressed to the People of Book who insist on adhering to their own books despite being invited to obey the Koran, and they are reminded that the Koran was sent down to confirm their own scriptures:

> **When they are told, "Have faith in what God has sent down," they say, "Our faith is in what was sent down to us," and they reject anything beyond that, even though <u>it [the Koran] is the truth, confirming what they have</u>... (Koran, 2:91)**

Almighty God also reveals in verses that the Torah and the Gospel used to be a source of wisdom, but that the true source of wisdom is now the Koran, which confirms the true passages in all other scriptures:

> **He has sent down the Book to you with truth, confirming what was there before it. And He sent down the Torah and the Gospel, previously, as guidance for mankind, and He has sent down the Furqan [the Koran, the One that discriminates between what is right and wrong].** Those who reject God's signs will have a terrible punishment. God is Almighty, Exactor of Revenge. (Koran, 3:3-4)

This feature is again set out in another verse of the Koran, which also reveals that the Koran contains explanations of all kinds and is a guide for true believers:

> There is instruction in their stories for people of intelligence. **This is not a narration which has been invented but confirmation of all that came before, a clarification of everything,** and a guidance and a mercy for people who have faith. (Koran, 12:111)

God addresses Jews as follows in the Koran:

> **Have faith in what I have sent down [the Koran], confirming what is with you [the Torah].** Do not be the first to reject it and do not sell My signs for a paltry price. Have fear of Me alone. (Koran, 2:41)

Our Christian brothers must not misinterpret this point: **None of the above passages ask any Christian to abandon his devotion to the Gospel and Jesus.** It is unlawful for a Muslim to ask such a thing. In our religion, anyone who denies Jesus or the Gospel has renounced the faith. The call here is one made for Christians to understand the Koran, to believe in the Koran and to believe in the evidence given them by the Koran. It is a call made so that Christians can be more perfect Christians and so they can love Jesus more. Because only if a Christian becomes a follower of Muhammad and believes that the Koran is a true book can he properly understand his own faith and fully love Jesus.

Our Christian brothers must note the following point: **Obeying the Koran and believing in the Prophet Muhammad will not deprive Christians of Jesus. On the contrary, it will bring them even closer to this blessed prophet.** Someone who reads and accepts the Koran will become both a perfect Christian, and a perfect Jew, and a perfect follower of Joseph and a perfect follower of Noah and of Abraham and of Muhammad. He will accept all the prophets and embrace them and thus become an immaculate believer. **The existence of the Koran, which shows them the truth and confirms their own books and which is a great source of guidance for them, and the fact that it has never changed, is also a great blessing for the People of the Book.**

Indeed, in one verse God speaks of the existence of the People of the Book who adhere to the Koran and tells them of a reward in His Presence in the hereafter:

> <u>Among the people of the Book there are some who have faith in God and in what has been sent down to you and what was sent down to them</u>, **and who are humble before God. They do not sell God's signs for a paltry price. Such people will have their reward with their Lord. And God is swift at reckoning. (Koran, 3:199)**

The evidence from the Koran should be evaluated in the light of these facts in the chapters that follow.

Hadiths of Our Prophet (pbuh) That Encourage the Reading of the True Torah

Muslim related: "Abu Hurairah witnessed the Prophet say; 'The Prophet Muhammad said that the People of the Book read the Torah in Hebrew and translated it into Arabic for the Muslims'." (Mishkat al- Masabih, 1st chapter, part 6, p. 42)

"Al-Hafiz al-Zahabi relates that Abdullah ibn Salam who converted from Judaism to Islam came to the Prophet (pbuh) and said, "(Yesterday evening) I read the Koran and the Torah." He replied, "Read one in one evening and the other in another evening." (Al-Thalabi, Al-Iman al-Thalabi Tathkarar al-Huffadh, Vol. 1, p. 27)

"Abdullah Ibn al-Amr, one of the Prophet Muhammad's (pbuh) close followers, would frequently read the Torah. One night he dreamed he held honey in one hand and oil in the other, and would sometimes eat from the honey and sometimes from the oil. Abdullah Ibn al-Amr described his dream to the Prophet Muhammad. The Prophet interpreted his dream as referring to two books, and to his sometimes reading the Torah and sometimes the Koran." (Bukhari, Vol. 6, hadith 987, p. 439)

From Abu Said al-Khudri: We asked the Prophet (pbuh), "O Prophet of God! Can we relate things from the people of Israel? He replied; "Yes, you can relate things from the people of Israel, there is no harm in that. If you relate something from them, know that they have even more interesting knowledge." (Hanbal, Musnad, 111/12, hadith no:11034)

From Abdullah Ibn al-Amr; The Messenger of God said, "You can relate things from the people of Israel, there is no harm in that." (Hanbal, Musnad, 11/159, hadith no: 6486)

CHAPTER 1: ACCORDING TO HISTORICAL SOURCES, THE GOSPEL HAS BEEN CORRUPTED OVER TIME

Christians Will Not Have Abandoned Their Faith by Admitting the Possibility That the Gospel Has Changed

Many of our Christian brothers overreact on the subject of the Gospel having changed over time and never accept any such idea.

They regard this as a sort of "renunciation of their faith": It is of course understandable for Christians to react against claims that their faith has become corrupted. However, in order to establish whether this is something that should never be mentioned and whether it might represent a renunciation of faith they need to reflect a little, look at the history of Christianity and reexamine all these in the light of the Gospel.

It is important to reiterate that the Gospel is also sacred to us as Muslims. We therefore have no desire for it to have been changed and misinterpreted. Yet this has happened, as we are told of it in the Koran. We therefore need to look at the evidence for this distortion and at historic events. Of course, this does not mean discounting the Gospel entirely. The original of the Gospel has been preserved down to the present day. It is currently concealed, and will be absolutely discovered by God's will. The important thing, therefore, is to evaluate the Gospel in the light of the Koran in order to identify its true pronouncements and to think in a manner compatible with reason and good conscience.

However, there is one other matter needing to be known and reflected upon regarding the four Gospels currently used by our Christian brothers:

What you will be reading in this book is not deductions or claims made by Muslims. <u>On the contrary, what the book says is all based on Christians' own sources.</u>

Material concerning the history of Christianity that has previously been set out in detail in our book *Jesus (pbuh) Is Not the Son of God, But a Prophet of God* is merely set out here under brief headings as a reminder:

The Spread of Christianity and the Origin of the Belief in the Trinity according to Christian sources

- When we look at the earliest Christian documents and communities we see that Jesus (pbuh) **taught nothing different to**

24

the Prophet Moses (pbuh) or the Prophet Muhammad (pbuh) on the subject of the existence and oneness of God.

- After Jesus, Christianity was spread by the disciples. They preached in places where monotheistic beliefs prevailed, particularly the Middle East, Jerusalem, Antioch and Urfa [Edessa]. Since these regions are those where prophets appeared, **they turned to Christianity very quickly since the inhabitants were already familiar with monotheistic belief.**

- The belief in the Trinity, which did not exist before, finally appeared long after Jesus as Christianity spread to regions where Greco-Roman paganism predominated.

- The reason is that the Christians who had converted from paganism in regions such as Alexandria in Egypt, Greece, Italy and Anatolia began to build a Christianity under the influence of their former beliefs that they called the Trinity.

How did paganism prepare the ground for belief in the Trinity?

Throughout the course of history, pagans have always regarded three idols as superior to all the others. They regarded the greatest of these as the Father, the second as the Mother and the third as the Son. Some examples are as follows:

l The concept of a trinity appears in Indian paganism in the form of Brahma, Vishnu and Shiva.

l The Koran also refers to the idea of a trinity in Arab paganism: **"Have you really considered al-Lat and al-'Uzza and Manat, the third, the other one?"** (Koran, 53:19-20)

l Belief in a tripartite god was widespread in pre-Christian Syria and the surrounding area.

l Osiris (Father), Isis (Mother) and Horus (Son) also represented a **tripartite deity** in ancient Egyptian paganism.

ǀ **Mithraism was also a superstition involving three deities** in Persian paganism. This was widespread in ancient Anatolia and Europe, including the Roman Empire.

ǀ Trinitarian belief was also present in Roman and Greek paganism. Zeus, Hera and Apollo were the three predominant gods of ancient Greece. The idea of the trinity is known to have entered Christianity from Greek and Roman paganism.

ǀ There are many father and son gods in Greek mythology. Plato even formulated this trinity and suggested that **the gods have a son called "logos" (the word) and a daughter called "sophos" (knowledge). One of the words used to refer to Jesus in Christianity is "logos."**

The American professor of theology Dr. Paul R. Eddy noted this and made the following comments on the subject in a paper *"Was Early Christianity Corrupted by Hellenism?":*

> *The ancient world, as far back as Babylonia, the worship of pagan gods grouped in threes, or triads, was common. That influence was also prevalent in Egypt, Greece, and Rome in the centuries before, during, and after Christ. After the death of the apostles, such pagan beliefs began to invade Christianity. . . . While [Plato] did not teach the Trinity in its present form, his philosophies paved the way for it. (Dr. Paul R. Eddy, "Was Early Christianity Corrupted by 'Hellenism'?", http://www.xmark.com/focus/Pages/hellenism.html)*

The general belief in paganism, especially in Greek and Roman paganism, was that the greatest of the three gods married a mortal woman and that she gave birth to a male child, who was also a god or quite often, a demigod.

ǀ Belief in a child god born to a mortal woman bears a very close similarity to the present day Christian belief in the Trinity.

Ancient Greek philosophers fabricated the idea of god through logical deductions from the physical world. However, they were unable to fathom how a god they regarded as unchanging and

eternal could create finite and changing entities. For that reason, they attempted to explain the formation of the universe through a **material entity.**

Accordingly they maintained that, as a child is born to a mother and a father, so there must have been intermediaries between the gods and the entities for the universe to come into being; in other words, hierarchical divine entities. The senior god in this hierarchy was responsible for authority and creation, while the others were responsible for matters involving the world of space and time, and secondary deities covered sundry matters such as punishment and reward.

These supposed gods and godlike entities were generally defined as a "three-in-one entity," beginning with the most important. Therefore, belief in a trinity or a tripartite deity is a widespread idea that emerged in pagan times.

William Varner says that the perspective of the Gentiles [a term used in the Gospel to refer to non-Jews; it is also used for the Romans in the time of Jesus] who heard the preaching of Jesus was shaped in the light of these ideas. He goes on to say:

> *Their idea of a son of God was rooted deeply in polytheistic thought and was, therefore, difficult to transform into the monotheistic message of Jesus and His apostles. (William C. Varner, "Jesus the Son of God," http://www.foigm.org/IMG/sonofgod.htm)*

Similarities between belief in the Trinity and the character of Dionysus in Greek mythology

Statements about Jesus (pbuh) by believers in the Trinity bear uncanny similarities to the character of the pagan deity Dionysus in Greek mythology (Bacchus in Latin), the worship of whom is estimated to have persisted until around the Fourth Century AD:

27

| Dionysus **is a mortal god, the son of an immortal deity father Zeus.**

| Dionysus was born to a **mortal mother** by the name of Semele.

| **He was killed by mortals.**

| He was sent to the world as **a savior.**

| Dionysus **was resurrected in physical form after his death.**

| Although Dionysus was semi-divine, he **lived among people in human form and shared people's weaknesses.**

| Dionysus permitted himself to be caught and put to death **as a sacrifice of his own free will.**

| Followers of Dionysus in ancient Greece **ate meat and drank wine** in remembrance of and to give thanks to him. They regarded this as **eating the flesh and drinking the blood** of Dionysus and imagined that this drew them closer to him. This pagan ritual, a precursor to the doctrine of transubstantiation, is applied to Jesus (pbuh) in a most interesting way in The Gospel According to St. John:

*Jesus said to them, "Very truly I tell you, **unless you eat the flesh of the Son of Man and drink his blood,** you have no life in you. **Whoever eats my flesh and drinks my blood has eternal life,** and I will raise them up at the last day. **For my flesh is real food and my blood is real drink. Whoever eats my flesh and drinks my blood remains in me, and I in them."** (John 6: 53-56)*

| In another passage, Jesus gives the disciples wine to drink by his own hand and tells them to regard this as his blood:

*While they were eating, Jesus took bread, and when he had given thanks, he broke it and gave it to his disciples, saying, "Take and eat; **this is my body."** (Matthew 26: 26)*

*Then he took a cup, and when he had given thanks, he gave it to them, saying, "Drink from it, all of you. **This is my blood** of the covenant, which is poured out for many for the forgiveness of sins." (Matthew 26: 27-28)*

How was the belief in the Trinity that developed parallel to pagan belief disseminated?

Ⅰ Christian historians and theologians are agreed that the idea of the Trinity was first disseminated by St. Paul. The accuracy of this is confirmed by historical documents and by Paul's letters in the Gospels.

Ⅰ **Paul was not a disciple of Jesus.** Not only was he not a disciple, he was originally fiercely opposed to him in life. Four years after the ascension of Jesus he claimed to have seen a sudden vision and declared himself to be a follower, thus entering the first Christian community.

Ⅰ Paul's aim was to be able to spread Christianity to the West. In order to do that he sent numerous letters to various regions in the West, 14 of which appear in the Gospel as "immutable" sacred texts known as the Pauline Letters.

Ⅰ Paul was a Roman citizen who, in addition to the Aramaic and Hebrew spoken by the Jews, **also spoke very good Greek. He was well acquainted with the Romans and was well aware of the policies needing to be adopted against them.**

Ⅰ In order to be able to spread his ideas to the West, Paul therefore **established a Christian dogma ideally suited to the pagan beliefs in the region** (there is of course a possibility that his expositions were misinterpreted by the pagan society in question). He adopted the concepts of the

Father and the Son to Roman pagan beliefs, establishing a concept similar to that of the belief in a tripartite deity consisting of a father and son in that pagan system. It is highly likely that he did thus in the hope that it would be easier for Christianity to spread in that form.

I The terms **"father" and "son" appear frequently in his letters that appear in the Gospel.**

I This pagan belief added onto Christianity **spread easily through the region** – since it was eminently compatible with the West's pagan views. As Western Rome and Byzantium gradually grew materially and politically stronger, a policy of repression of the monotheistic conception in eastern Christianity appeared. Attempts were made to eliminate eastern Christian monotheism, attempts which were to a large extent successful.

Gospel texts established through "majority vote" in the councils

I The Trinity was first officially made part of Christianity by **the Council of Nicaea in 325 AD**. This council took place with the participation of the Roman Emperor Constantine.

The council was held for the following reasons:

a The Roman Empire's expansion into lands where Christianity had spread.

a Tensions had arisen between pagans and Christians because of that expansion and the Empire faced the threat of being divided into two.

a The idea that a new belief, a synthesis between the old pagan faith and the new Christianity, was needed if the Empire was not to be divided in two, and for preparatory work to be done on this.

I As we have seen, it was assumed that conflict in pagan lands could only be avoided if Christianity were changed. This council that met in Nicaea decided that the solution to internal conflict was for **the idea of the Trinity to be added to the Gospel. That decision was duly implemented.**

I The four Gospels espousing the idea of the Trinity were declared to be completely reliable at the council.

I Apart from a few preserved handwritten manuscripts, other gospels espousing strictly monotheistic belief were denounced as "heretical" and **burned.**

I Those people who espoused monotheism were condemned for holding heretical beliefs. **The punishment for heresy was burning at the stake.**

I **Excommunication** is a sanction first applied against the opponents of the Trinity. The Papacy and Roman and Byzantine politicians inflicted various punishments, including burning at the stake, on opponents of the Trinity and supporters of monotheism. The courts known as the Inquisition were also set up for that purpose.

I The monotheistic Arian movement, started by the Alexandrian priest Arius on the basis of early and trustworthy writings, was highly influential in that period. However, this development alarmed the **Romans, who burned the Library of Alexandria and the documents and books it contained in 411.**

The "religious dogma" established by the Church and how Christians were compelled to adhere to it

I It was Trinitarian Christians who imposed a new meaning on the word "dogma."

| In brief, religious dogma means that the *"Christian religion can only be formulated by the Papacy or Church authorities, and it is obligatory to believe in it in just that form."*

| To put it another way, it is impossible for a Christian to decide what or what not to believe on the basis of the Holy Book. **The Church decides what he may or may not believe.**

| For example, if someone says, "I reject the Trinity and believe that God is the One and Only Creator, and that Jesus is the servant of God, not His son," then **he is no longer a Christian, strictly speaking.** No matter how much he has reached this conclusion from the holy books he has read and his own investigations and in the light of his own reason, conscience, conceptual abilities and mental capacities, the Church **will still not regard him as a Christian.**

| In order to be regarded as a "Christian," a person has to close his eyes to the truth shown him by his conscience, mind and experience and **adopt the idea of the three-in-one deity, defined as the Father, Son and Holy Ghost, as imposed by the Church.**

| **The shape of the belief was formulated in this form by the Church and a Christian is obliged to believe in it in that form.**

| That is what is meant by religious dogma, or **religious imposition**, to put it another way.

| That is the sole reason why a great many Christians are so devoted to the idea of the Trinity. Since the Church and the Papacy were shaped according to the structure of the Roman Empire, the Church was also the source of the idea of the Trinity. That is why regarding the Gospel has having been altered or rejecting the Trinity is regarded as **"abandoning the faith."**

| Yet all these pretexts for "excommunication" emerged hundreds of years after Jesus **and were invented by the Church. Many of our Christian brothers are totally unaware of all this.**

As is clear from above, the Papacy and the Church obviously possessed greater authority than a holy book. And that is the case still, despite the Reformation, meaning a return to the holy book, and the Protestant movement.

The belief in the Trinity that was subsequently added to Christianity in a number of stages

I **"The Trinity"** appears in no sacred text. It appears nowhere, either as a name or a teaching, in the sacred teachings of Christianity – or any other true religion. Christians themselves admit this.

I Belief in the Trinity was fabricated and made part of Christianity in gradual stages. These can be summarized as follows:

a The idea of the divinity of Jesus was agreed at the Council of Nicaea in 325,

a Claims regarding the divinity of the Holy Ghost were accepted at the First Council of Constantinople in 381, and

a The idea that Jesus had two natures, one human and one divine, was agreed at the Council of Chalcedon in 451.

I Although the belief in the Trinity assumed a specific form at the First Council of Constantinople in 381, there was still no agreement regarding the elements of the Trinity and the relationship between them.

I Apart from a reference in the Gospel According to Matthew to baptism "in the name of the Father, Son and Holy Spirit," **no sacred text contains a single reference in which the Holy Spirit is mentioned together with the Father and Son, the first two elements of the Trinity.**

l Indeed, the Gospel contains no references or indications regarding the divinity of the Holy Spirit. On the contrary, various Christian sources state that the term refers to the angel Gabriel, as also stated in the Koran.

l The term "baptizing them in the name of the Father and of the Son and of the Holy Spirit" **was added** to Matthew 28:18-20 at the end of the Fourth Century in order to establish compatibility with the idea of the Trinity.

l The doctrine of the Trinity, which was made official in the Fourth Century, **was added** to the text written in the First Century. In this way, this text was made compatible with the order of the council. With these subsequent additions, **a text which originally espoused monotheism, was turned into one pointing to the doctrine of the Trinity.**

l Just about everyone held a different opinion on the subject. That is why everyone accused everyone else of error, heresy and apostasy. Even people who shared the same belief in the Trinity held different opinions regarding it.

The Church's final decree regarding the Trinity: "The Trinity is not a matter for reason and logic; there is no need for you to reflect on and understand it"

l The subject of the Trinity was constantly reshaped by a succession of councils, ongoing study and new decrees. Various passages in the Gospel were re-interpreted; **passages that had one been rejected were suddenly declared to be trustworthy and added to the Gospel, while others were removed.**

34

| In this extraordinarily contradictory environment, **the Church tried to shape itself in the light of new suggestions and objections** in order not to have to give way on the doctrine of the Trinity.

| **The arguments and discrepancies regarding the Trinity remain unresolved to this day.** The final decree on the subject was issued by the Council of Florence in 1443. The council did not manage to eliminate the contradictions and inconsistencies on the subject, however, and the arguments persisted for a long time thereafter.

| The First Vatican Council, summoned by the Papacy in 1868-1870 with the aim of putting an end to these endless disputes, [fully 1,870 years after Jesus] decreed that **the Trinity is not a matter for reason and logic, but a mystery and an article of faith.** (Const. "De fide, cath", IV)

| To put it another way, the insoluble dilemma of the Trinity was simply declared by the Church to be a "mystery," in order to eliminate opponents and their justified objections as required by logic, reason and the genuine verses of the Gospel. The message being sent out, in other words, was **"There is no need for you to think about this anymore!"**

This subject will be considered in greater detail in the pages that follow.

The "additions and removals" officially carried out by the Church, to the four Gospels while asserting their unchanging nature

| The oldest handwritten copies of the holy texts regarded as canonical date back to the Third Century. In other words, **these**

were written three hundred years after Jesus. In fact, **there are differences in the texts and expressions** in all the sacred texts.

I Indeed, the texts refer to **events and people from long after** the earliest dates these are considered to have been written.

I **The oldest copy of the Gospel According to John dates back to approximately 200 AD, and there are more than 10,000 different texts of that particular gospel alone. The number of major differences among these 10,000 different copies is around 200,000.**

I In order to avoid confusion, **footnotes are often provided for the various gospels.** These contain the following expression "According to other ancient authorities, this word or sentence should not appear" or "other ancient authorities have read this as..." or "other ancient authorities omitted the following words..."

I The Revised Standard version of the Holy Bible (*New York, Glasgow 1971*) refers to Jesus as "the son of God" in the first sentence of the Gospel According to Mark. There then follows a footnote, saying **"other ancient authorities did not include the term (the son of God)."**

I The four canonical Gospels contain major discrepancies and differences. But this variation is not limited to the Gospels in question alone. **There are also major differences between the oldest handwritten and printed copies of each of these Gospels.**

I During the preparation of the standard version of the Gospel, say According to Matthew, **selections were made based on the differences, and extra and missing passages in the previously printed manuscripts.** It is therefore impossible to be sure which terms should be regarded as true and valid.

I **Various sentences in the final part of the Gospel According to Mark had to be removed in order for the Gospel to be agreed at the Council of Nicaea** because those expressions were diametrically opposed to the doctrine of the Trinity.

36

I Various passages were taken from the works of the other authors of the Gospels and a concluding paragraph to the Gospel According to Mark was prepared on that basis.

I All passages describing Jesus as the Messiah of the Jews were removed from the Gospel According to John. This was replaced with a superhuman figure of Jesus.

(Prof. Dr. Mehmet Bayrakdar, The Trinity, a Christian Dogma, Ankara School Publications, September 2007, p. 163)

The text of the Gospel According to John is accepted to have been written in 110 AD; it is generally considered to be the oldest of the canonical Gospel. This means that the disciple John must have lived for at least 140-150 years, which is highly unlikely. In addition, the fact that the text of John contains information from much later times also casts doubt on whether the disciple John was really the author of the Gospel.

The other Gospels emphasized that Jesus is the Messiah of the Jews, is descended from the line of the Prophet David (pbuh) and will liberate Israel. **However, all Judaic concepts that would displease Hellenic Christians were removed from the Gospel According to John.** The influence of Greek philosophy in the Gospel According to John is very obvious.

I Various other Gospels and passages from these Gospels that would later be dismissed by the Church as fabrications were for a long time thought of as valid. These were accepted for a long time, and anyone claiming they were false was promptly excommunicated.

I For example, **in the Fourth Century one Christian sect recognized 23 books in the Gospel, while a few centuries later that same sect recognized 27.**

New sects that emerged due to contradictions, illogicalities and

discrepancies regarding the Trinity

I Following the decision to include the Holy Spirit as one member of the three-in-one, the debates and disagreements over the Trinity increased still further.

I As a result of these debates, the idea emerged that the Holy Spirit should appear both from the Father and from the Son. **The concept of filioque, meaning "from the son," was thus added to the doctrine of the Trinity.**

I For that reason, and because of other problems that arose later, **the Church of Rome divided into two parts, Catholic and Orthodox, in 1054.**

I The Catholic Church, which accepted filioque (as well as the Protestant Church that would later break away from it) **believed that the Holy Spirit emerged from both the Father and the Son**, making the already confusing belief in the Trinity even more complex.

I **The Orthodox Church, which rejected filioque, maintains that the Holy Spirit comes from the Father alone.** The greatest disagreement between the two churches, and which has come down to the present day, regarding the Trinity involves filioque.

I Therefore, **the Holy Spirit was recognized as divine by the advocates of the Trinity 56 years after the recognition of the divinity of the Son.**

To summarize the actions taken to resolve the confusion over the Trinity: (surely God is beyond this) The explicit and official recognition of the divine status of Jesus stems from the decision of the **Council of Nicaea in 325** and the divine status of the Holy Spirit from **the Council of Constantinople in 381.** The dual nature of Jesus, one part divine and one part human, was raised at the **councils of Ephesus in 431 and Chalcedon in 451**, and the question of filioque, the Holy Spirit coming from Jesus was discussed at the **councils held in Toledo in 447 and 589** and was resolved at the Council of Constantinople. This brief summary here reveals that further confusion was loaded onto Christianity at every council.

To reiterate, all the information provided above is based on documentation and other evidence from Christian, not Muslim, historians and theologians. This provides essential information on how Christianity developed and how the Gospel assumed its present form. These are fundamental historical details proving that the belief in the Trinity has no place in the true Gospel.

What someone needs to do after seeing all this evidence is to seek to understand the truth by reflecting and using logic, analyzing the Gospel in view of all these historical data. In order to pursue this logical inquiry, the following questions should be considered in the light of reason and good conscience:

| Each Divine scripture sent down to each faith is unique. How is it possible **for there to be four separate Gospels in Christianity and for each one to be considered valid by itself?**

| If each of the four books is true, **then how did the inconsistencies between them, the serious gaps of meaning and major discrepancies of the historical data all come about?**

| How could a true book sent down to a true faith **have been identified "by majority vote" from among books espousing different beliefs?**

| Why were those Gospels and early manuscripts espousing monotheism that did not receive a majority vote **burned and destroyed?**

| Why were people who espoused monotheism **sentenced to death? And what was the reason for that opposition and savagery?**

| The four Gospels and the idea of the Trinity that entered Christianity were recognized in the Fourth Century. **What is the position of those Christians who were unaware of the Gospels and the Trinity before then?**

I The idea of the Holy Spirit as divine emerged much later. **Were the Church and all other Christians who did not regard the Holy Spirit as divine before that all in a state of sin?**

I The Church regards the authors of the canonical Gospels, Matthew, Mark, Luke and John as people who received revelation. Were these people prophets? **How can anyone – even the disciples – who is not a prophet receive Divine revelation?** So could the disciples in question not **have attained the status of prophets?**

I **How can a majority vote by the Church decide whether someone received revelation or not?**

I **How is it possible for it to be agreed in a vote that someone received Divine revelation and to rule that what he wrote is "unalterable and unchanging" after a great many amendments have been made to it?**

I If the four Gospels are unalterable, **how can the Church have made additions to them over many years, rearranging some parts and removing others?**

I No earlier Christian could have adhered to those parts of the Gospels that were added on later. **So what is the position of the Christians in question up to that time?**

I How can a Christian arrange his life and faith, not on the basis of trustworthy verses from the Gospel and his own conscience and reason, but **on the basis of a form of belief set out by the Church and that altered over the course of time?**

I Why is it only in Christianity that **there are such differences of opinion** on the subject of the existence and oneness of God, the basis of all the true faiths and that is also explicitly set out in all other religions?

I Which one of the different Christian sects that all recognize different books **is on the true path? Which sect's books are unchanging and indisputably true?**

I How is it that the number of books can gradually rise from 23 to 27 in a single sect? Which should be regarded as true?

No Christian who supports the Trinity can give a truly logical, rational, comprehensible, convincing, clear and concrete answer to the above questions. This extraordinary confusion under the name of the Trinity is completely inexplicable.

The above questions refer to just some of the discrepancies on the subject of the four canonical Gospels on the basis of historical facts. The real issue is the profound logical collapse that belief in the Trinity brings with it. It is this profound and deep-rooted logical collapse that must cause sincere Christians to doubt their belief in the Trinity. This will be discussed in the pages that follow.

The Gospel Sent Down to Confirm the Torah Should Also Confirm Monotheistic Faith

A Christian who espouses the Trinity may at first reject the above statements based on historical documentation and interpretations of these. This does not alter the fact, however, that the present four canonical Gospels were chosen from a total of 27.

A council decree declared that these four Gospels represent the true scripture of Christianity. The discrepancies and inconsistencies among these Gospels are too great to be ignored or denied. Therefore, a sincere Christian should set aside the dogmatic decisions of the Church and think with reason and good conscience and reflect a little on whether these can be regarded as books "not one single letter of which has ever changed." The books in question, not one letter of which has ever supposedly been changed, **were in fact changed time and time again by the Church itself. This is established by Christian historical documents.** The footnotes regarding statements in old copies of

41

the Gospel in present-day editions by themselves make this perfectly clear.

Another important matter which must be mentioned here is the situation of Christians who lived during the three centuries after Jesus and the disciples up until the recognition of the four canonical Gospels containing belief in the Trinity. Even if these people believed in Jesus and the Gospel with all their hearts, they were still in a position, in the eyes of the dogma imposed by the Church, of having abandoned the faith. How can that be possible? Who could possibly maintain that people lived in ignorance of the truth for so long when there was a true faith and its holy book present as a warning? God would never permit such a thing.

What therefore calls for skepticism is not the period before the Fourth Century, when the original of the Gospel was around in handwritten manuscripts, when Aramaic, the original language of the Gospel was still in use, and when at the very least there were no errors of reproduction and translation, but the period that followed. The period immediately after the disciples was in all probability a time when genuine copies of the Gospel that Jesus caused to be written down [Jesus in all likelihood had the revelation that came to him written down in his own day] were present and applied. The monotheistic belief that was a continuation of Judaism survived in that period. Indeed, as also stated in the Koran, the Gospel was sent down to confirm the Torah. Therefore, the monotheistic belief that represents the basis of Judaism would also be confirmed in the genuine Gospel. As our Lord reveals in the Koran:

> **And We sent Jesus son of Mary following in their footsteps, <u>confirming the Torah</u> that came before him. We gave him the Gospel containing guidance and light, <u>confirming the Torah</u> that came before it, and as guidance and admonition for those who have piety. (Koran, 5:46)**

Some Christians maintain that the disciples spread the idea of the Trinity after Jesus, and that they even died for its sake. Yet this is false. The disciples who were at Jesus' side never espoused belief in Trinity, and never could have. (The only person known to have propagated belief in the Trinity is Paul, and as many Christian theologians and sources confirm, Paul never met Jesus and even opposed him in his time.) Like all the other first Christians, Jesus and the disciples were devout Jews and members of the People of Israel. There was no belief in the Trinity among these first Christians. The books they were sent to confirm the Torah confirmed the monotheistic faith set out in the Torah. It is very odd that in our day Christians do not consider them as Christians, referring to them as "Jewish Christians," as if Jesus were not a Jew before revelation came to him and also one of the Children of Israel.

Therefore, the period up to the Fourth Century was a continuation of Judaic monotheism, and in all probability one when a monotheistic faith predominated with the original of the Gospel. The period following the Fourth Century should be regarded as a time when the Roman Empire ruled, when paganism and the pagan belief in the Trinity spread across the world with that empire, when Aramaic, the original language of the Gospel was forgotten and Koine Greek began being used, and when political disorder, civil conflicts and religious wars prevailed. The historical information provided above therefore needs to be well considered in that light.

God Is Certainly Powerful Enough to Preserve the True Book He Revealed

It is of course understandable why some Christians are unwilling to admit the possibility of the Gospel, sent down by God as a source of light, changing over the course of time and being misinterpreted. They may be uneasy at the idea of obeying a true book that has been corrupted. But sincere Christians need to bear this in mind: **The present-day Gospel is to a large extent true.**

43

The original Gospel sent down to Jesus (pbuh) is revelation from God consisting of very profound and wise words and is praised in the Koran. Just like Christians, Muslims also have a duty to abide by those words.

In addition, **all the original, uncorrupted Gospel has been preserved.** It is waiting where it has been concealed for the time of its discovery. By God's leave, **the original of the Gospel** will be discovered in the time when we see the coming of Jesus and Hazrat Mahdi (pbuh). **There is therefore a Gospel that has not been altered in any way, as Christians maintain.** Our criticisms here are directed toward those parts of the four Gospels, which are currently regarded as true but that harbor numerous discrepancies, that have been distorted and misinterpreted. The existence of such sections is so evident as to be easily apparent to any honest Christian. The contents of this book call on our Christian brothers to reflect with reason, logic and good conscience.

Almighty God is of course powerful enough to preserve the true books He sends down as guides for people. Some Christians point to this sublime attribute of our Lord in order to repudiate statements about the Gospel having been corrupted. However, there is secret wisdom here that needs to be properly understood:

To reiterate, of course God is powerful enough to preserve His book. Almighty God is also powerful enough to create everything in the universe quite flawlessly. It is God Who also creates flaws and defects in the universe. There is particular wisdom behind God's creating flaws. Through these, we always remember that this world is a place of temporary testing, that we are weak before God and that our true abode is in the hereafter, not this world. One cannot grow proud in the face of deficiencies and one will always be aware of one's weakness before and need of God.

The corruption of the Holy Gospel, the evidence for which is perfectly clear, is something that happened by God's leave and will. It was created with wisdom as part of a very special test by God. If God creates it in this way and shows the evidence on the subject so clearly, then we must see and grasp the wisdom behind it, rather than being stubborn about it.

The Christian world is obviously being tested by this. They are being invited to heed their consciences.

This state of affairs is clearly required in order for people to seek the coming of Jesus and the true Gospel.

With this test, false beliefs may perhaps enfold the world, people may be encouraged toward conflict, disorder and bloodshed in the name of religion and the signs of the coming of Jesus and Hazrat Mahdi revealed in the Torah, Gospel, Koran and hadiths will come about. Therefore, the real task befalling sincere Christians is to seek and apply the true provisions of the Gospel.

At the same time, Christians must be aware of the reality that all the genuine provisions of the true Gospel are present and reported in the Koran. The true provisions of the Gospel are also contained in the Koran, for which reason Muslims also have an obligation to live by the true Gospel.

The Koran is a true book that confirms the Gospel. Therefore, in the same way that Muslims are followers of the Prophet Muhammad, they are also followers of Jesus who apply the true Gospel and followers of Moses who apply the true Torah. Therefore, if a sincere Christian wishes to abide by the truth of the Gospel and to arrange his life in the light of the true Gospel, he will find all the relevant provisions in the Koran. The true Gospel is one of our holy books that Almighty God praises in the Koran. God reveals in the Koran that the Gospel was a guide for the people at the time it was sent down:

> **He has sent down the Book to you with truth, confirming what was there before it. And He sent down the Torah and the Gospel, previously, as guidance for mankind ... (Koran, 3:3-4)**

> **And We sent Jesus son of Mary following in their footsteps, confirming the Torah that came before him. We gave him the Gospel containing guidance and light,**

45

confirming the Torah that came before it, and as guidance and admonition for those who have piety. (Koran, 5:46)

Then We sent Our messengers following in their footsteps and sent Jesus son of Mary after them, giving him the Gospel. We put compassion and mercy in the hearts of those who followed him. They invented monasticism – We did not prescribe it for them – purely out of desire to gain the pleasure of God, but even so they did not observe it as it should have been observed. To those of them who had faith We gave their reward but many of them are deviators. **(Koran, 57:27)**

In conclusion, our Christian brothers must read the Koran from that perspective before rejecting it out of prejudice. It must not be forgotten that everyone who seeks the understanding with which to differentiate truth from falsehood can attain this great blessing from God.

CHAPTER 2
THE ERROR OF THE TRINITY

God Is Unfettered by Natural Causes and Has No Children

The error of the Trinity will be considered in three sections in this book:

The first chapter concentrates on the way that the Church ultimately decided in 1870 that the Trinity "is not a matter for reason and logic, but a mystery not requiring reflection." It explains how the confused issue of the Trinity gradually became a dogma "not requiring reflection" and invites sincere Christians to reflect deeply on God's attributes.

The second section provides evidence from the Gospel and the Torah showing how the claims about the Trinity made by some Christians depart from the path of religion and logic, and suggests various ideas for Christians to reflect on.

The third and final section provides Christians with very important information about the nature of matter. This information about the true nature of matter definitely repudiates all the claims on which the error of the Trinity is based. It sets out a new understanding which will change our Christian brothers' lives and allow them to completely review their perspectives to date.

SECTION 1
There is certainly a Sign in that for people who reflect. (Koran, 16:11)

Everything, our hands, our cells, structures such as DNA, protein and enzymes, all the diversely created different life forms, the way that birds fly, fish swim and leaves make photosynthesis, the sky, the stars, the plants, the Sun and Moon, the way trees blossom in the spring and animals hibernate in winter, the way the day has 24 hours, rain, snow; in short everything we see and know, hear or are aware of, has a purpose. It is easy to live without reflecting on these and seeing the wisdom behind their existence, just to pass by without seeing them. The most profound difference that distinguishes some people from others is that they think deeply on everything that has been created, rather than taking the easy path. God reveals in the Koran that deep reflection is a property unique to believers.

If someone does not reflect then he cannot grasp the purpose behind the creation of his life. If he does not reflect, he will spend his life pointlessly and purposelessly, not knowing where he came from or what his responsibilities are. In contrast to other living things, however, human beings possess reason, conscience and the ability to think and make judgments. They therefore have an important responsibility. They have an obligation to think about how and why they were created, to understand the Creator and fulfill their responsibilities to Him. One can also ignore that responsibility. That is people's own choice. It is this choice that distinguishes people from one another. The greatest difference between believers who reason and will come off best in the hereafter and other people is that the former reflect on the signs

48

and evidence of Creation and are able to properly understand our Creator.

The importance of reflection is also noted in the Torah and the Gospel:

*... **Do you still not see or understand?** Are your hearts hardened? (Mark, 8:17)*

Reflect on what I am saying, for the Lord will give you insight into all this. (2nd Letter to Timothy, 2:7)

Brothers and sisters, think of what you were when you were called.... (1 Corinthians, 1:26)

... set your hearts on things above, where Christ is, seated at the right hand of God. Set your minds on things above, not on earthly things.... (Colossians, 3:1-2)

Great are the works of the Lord; they are pondered by all who delight in them. (Psalms, 111:2)

For all this I laid to my heart, even to make clear all this: that the righteous, and the wise, and their works, are in the hand of God; ... (Book of Ecclesiastes, 9:1)

... I am terrified before Him; when I think of all this, I fear Him. (Job, 23:15)

On my bed I remember You; I think of You through the watches of the night. (Psalms, 63:6)

but whose delight is in the law of the Lord, and who meditates on His law day and night. (Psalms, 1:2)

I will remember the deeds of the Lord; yes, I will remember Your miracles of long ago. I will consider all Your works and meditate on all Your mighty deeds. (Psalms, 77:11-12)

Though rulers sit together and slander me, Your servant will meditate on your decrees. Your statutes are my delight;

they are my counselors. (Psalms, 119:23-24)

Oh, how I love Your law! I meditate on it all day long. Your commands are always with me and make me wiser than my enemies. I have more insight than all my teachers, for I meditate on Your statutes. (Psalms, 119:97-99)

Consider the work of God; for who can make that straight, which He hath made crooked? (Book of Ecclesiastes, 7:13-14)

Listen to this, Job; stop and consider God's wonders. (Job, 37:14)

This book of the law shall not depart out of your mouth, but you shall meditate therein day and night, that you may observe to do according to all that is written therein. (Joshua, 1:8)

I meditate on all Your works and consider what Your hands have done.

I spread out my hands to You; I thirst for You like a parched land. (Psalms, 143:5-6)

But be sure to fear the Lord and serve Him faithfully with all your heart; consider what great things He has done for you. (1. Samuel, 12:24)

for I delight in Your commands because I love them. I reach out for Your commands, which I love, that I may meditate on Your decrees. (Psalms, 119:47-48)

*One generation commends Your works to another; they tell of Your mighty acts. They speak of the glorious splendor of Your majesty— and **I will meditate on Your wonderful works.** (Psalms, 145:4-5)*

Almighty God also reveals in the Koran that believers who turn to Him are people who reflect on the evidence of Creation and are thus properly able to appreciate His sublime might:

...those who remember God, standing, sitting and lying on their sides, <u>and reflect on the creation of the heavens and the Earth:</u> "Our Lord, You have not created this

50

for nothing. Glory be to You! So safeguard us from the punishment of the Fire." (Koran, 3:191)

Deep reflection is important in order to be able to be a true believer. True faith is impossible without reflection. Deep reflection is a condition of faith on which Muslims, Jews and Christians must all focus. Only when people think deeply can they realize the greatness and might of God and decipher the surface and hidden meanings of the profound words in the holy books. Religion is not a way of life that is merely to be taught and memorized.

The Ruling of the Vatican Council: "The Subject of the Trinity Is a Mystery Far Removed from Reason and Logic, and There Is no Need for You to Think about It"

There is a special reason for our telling our Christian brothers of the need to reflect deeply on the existence of God. That is to be able to show them how false the doctrine of "not thinking" that the Church recommends to Christians truly is.

To reiterate, the subject of the Trinity that was raised and attempted to be resolved in an endless series of councils from the Fourth Century onward was finally resolved at the First Vatican Council held in 1868-1870 in order to bring the unending debates to a halt. It concluded, "The Trinity is not a matter for reason and logic, and must therefore remain a mystery."

Another dogma set out by the Church was thus added to Christianity as an article of faith some 1,900 years after Jesus was sent to Earth as a prophet. Christians who go along with this decision by the Church have no qualms about regarding the Trinity as a mystery of faith not calling for any reflection, and even explicitly advocate that view.

The sole reason for the Church commanding people not to think about it is that it is a great error. God certainly creates all fabrications and superstitions with illogicalities, inconsistencies, discrepancies and defects: it is the same with the Trinity. Aware of these inconsistencies, the Church continued its dogmatic tradition because ever since the beginning of Christianity, Christians who have used their minds and logic a little have been aware of these discrepancies and illogicalities and thus been condemned as heretics by the authorities. They then either totally rejected the Trinity or else conceived of it in some other form and altered it. The Church is therefore aware of the huge crowds that will go against the doctrine of the Trinity it imposes when people start thinking and using their minds.

Today there are many Christians who believe that the Trinity is not something that should be thought about, but a mystery to be adhered to without understanding it. They imagine they have a religion that discourages them from reflecting on it and that they can survive without understanding God. They generally never state this explicitly, but they see nothing wrong in saying that the "incomprehensibility" here is normal, that we are not able to understand everything, and that there is therefore no need to think and try to achieve that.

Of course we have not been created with the ability to understand everything. However, God reveals that He clearly exhibits His might and that this can be understood by reflecting with faith. We have a responsibility to understand the Sublime Might that created us. How can someone have any conception of religion without knowing the God Who made him and without knowing Whom to worship and pray to and how? How can he discover the secrets in creation and the nature of the hereafter? How can he grasp that God sees and hears him at every moment? It is essential to reflect, understand God and appreciate His might if one is to be a devout believer. This is one of the most important elements of growing in faith.

Whichever Christian who believes in the Trinity you may meet, he will inevitably give highly inconsistent, incomprehensible and confused answers when asked about it. Moreover, every Christian will describe the Trinity in a different way because they themselves are generally unsure of what they are saying when it comes to the Trinity. Christians who try to describe the Trinity in a rational and logical way somehow go beyond what they are describing as the Trinity. Some try to understand it, but they also fail. Some of them try to use logic and to explain it in terms of formulae. A great many more just give up. They prefer "not to think about it," as the Church encourages, and say that the subject is a mystery on which we have no responsibility to reflect.

Everything is easy, of course, if one does not think. Responsibilities then superficially appear to vanish. Someone who feels no need to think will also feel no need to wonder about how an incomprehensible God (surely God is beyond that) created him, how He rules all His creations, his responsibilities or how he will account to himself to God. Life then becomes very simple indeed. A great many Christians today are living in just that way. This also applies to some Muslims and Jews of course but since Christians are conditioned not to think deeply about God and His creations, and especially about the Trinity, this situation is even more dangerous for them. Many of them think that they can attain God's mercy and paradise by going to church on Sundays only and by believing that Jesus (pbuh) is the son of God. And this leads a great many Christians to live in a state of ascribing equals to God, even though they are unaware of it, to live for this world, not to be scrupulous about the concepts of lawful and unlawful, to do nothing to earn God's approval apart from praying and going to church, not to strive against ideologies and movements produced in opposition to belief in God, such as Darwinism, communism, materialism and atheism, to distance themselves from attacks on believers and the oppressed all over the world and to close their eyes to the world, living in their own little worlds in their own homes. Of course, there are exceptions; however, it is undeniable that this is the situation of a great many Christians. Any Christian will know that this is the basis of the lifestyle of the average

Christian across the world. That is the kind of religious devotion that comes from living without reflection. The Christians in question must see the dangers of this conception of religion.

The Deception of Saying "A Three-in-One God"

One of the worst deceptions on the subject of the Trinity, and perhaps the very worst, is the way that some Christians claim that the Trinity actually refers to One God. Some Christians, uneasy at the Trinity being compared to a pagan belief, maintain that the three components refer to a single god. They themselves do not generally understand this very well, and they are basically describing a belief in three gods.

Some Trinitarians claim that the three elements unite in a single body, that the three elements are therefore God. Some say that the Father is the greatest and that the others come from Him. Others speak of a division of labor between the three gods, while still others say that the Son came from the Father and the Holy Spirit from the Son. There are many other such ideas regarding the Trinity. However, they all claim that the doctrine of the Trinity that they describe so confusingly actually refers to One God. If they really believe in the One God, that is of course an excellent thing, but the descriptions in question are totally wrong.

The entire Gospel tells Christians of the Oneness of God. This is very important. The Gospel contains many passages that speak of the Oneness of God and commanding people to serve the One God and all these passages are quite explicit. Similarly, in the same way that the term Trinity appears nowhere in the Gospel, it also contains no passages that could be used to support such an idea. The passages proposed as evidence are all interpreted in a forced manner, passages to which the "son of God" and the "Holy Spirit" have been added in parentheses or passages deliberately distorted so as to bear an entirely different meaning, such as the

Trinity. **The One God is explicitly present in the Gospel, while a tripartite deity appears nowhere in it.**

Supporters of the Trinity say that the three components they have fabricated, the Father, Son and Holy Spirit, are both three separate entities and also the same entity. But they have never been able to explain how the three can be both three and one. They have always been aware of this inconsistency. In the same way, they have never been able to explain how the tripartite god assumes different functions, how if creation supposedly belongs to the Father whether the other two also possess this property, or how a single Divine entity, that was not born and is unfettered by time and space, turned into different entities in time and space. And it is impossible for them ever to explain it.

If, according to Trinitarians' claims, the three deities are equal in all regards – an idea that most Christians who believe in the concept of the Trinity espouse – then in their eyes it should be enough to worship just one of them in their rituals. But Trinitarians believe the three have to be worshiped at once. This shows that the Trinity is essentially no different to pagan religions with three deities.

The idea of the oneness of three deities is extraordinarily illogical. How can God, He Who has the power to do all things, the Lord of all, He Who creates them all from nothing, need to manifest Himself as three separate entities? (Surely God is beyond that.) Moreover, the proponents of the Trinity who claim to believe in a single deity do not fully comprehend the "absolute Oneness of God" that represents the basis of the monotheistic faith of Muslims and Jew. **In monotheistic belief, God is absolutely One alone, and He has no equal or equivalent. Nothing can be His equal and nothing is like Him. That is the Oneness of God. The Trinity is therefore absolutely not a monotheistic belief. Those who claim to believe in both the Trinity and the One God are either mistaken, or lying.**

The real question, however, is why there is the need for such confusion. Why, in the face of the peace of mind, ease, comfort and happiness that come from believing in the One God, do some people feel the need for totally inconsistent and contradictory accounts? Believing directly in the One and Only God and turning to Him alone is far better than believing in all this confusion. The existence of One God Who sees and knows all is a great blessing. The existence of our Almighty Lord Who is with us at every moment, Who hears our prayers, Who knows and responds to even our most secret thoughts and Who keeps all things under His control is a huge blessing. Those of our Christian brothers who are swamped in the confusion of the Trinity need to be aware of the beauty of this monotheistic faith. If they knew the beauty of being so close to God, they would realize that with the Trinity they have turned away from their Creator. Knowing the omnipotence of God, believing in Him as the One and Only and properly appreciating His might is the greatest of all happiness.

> **Say: "I am only a warner. There is no god except God, the One, the All-Conquering, Lord of the heavens and the Earth and everything between them, the Almighty, the Endlessly Forgiving." (Koran, 38:65-66)**

There Is No Confusion in the True Faith, and If Confusion Is Present, Then the Presence of Superstition Must Be Suspected

Every true faith created by God is very easy. The commandments of the faith are not matters that are hard to reflect on or difficult to understand or that need to remain a mystery. The existence of our Almighty Lord is obvious. The existence of God, His creative artistry and His closeness to and dominion over the entities He creates are all matters that are easy to understand. Confusion never has any place in true faith. Anyone looking with reason and good conscience will perfectly grasp the fact that the Almighty Creator is the Lord and Sole Ruler of all, that His omnipotence means He has no need for a son, that He is the closest to all beings and that there is no other power than Him. This means that the proponents of the Trinity and their followers are mistaken.

If the presence of confusion of the kind that the proponents of the Trinity describe is alleged, then this is grounds for suspicion. The true faith must have given way to superstition there. If it has become so difficult to understand and describe the nature of Almighty God, Who clearly exhibits His sublime works in the tiniest speck of dust, in the giant void of the universe or in the depths of a single atom, then the trickery of the devil must be suspected.

There is one single Creator, and everything in the universe points to the artistry of this sublime Creator. God, the Creator of all, is certainly mighty enough to keep them all under His control and supervision at every moment. There is no need for intermediaries to reach our Lord. There is no need for other deities (surely God is beyond that). God is He Who knows us better than we know ourselves and who observes us at every moment. Therefore, sincere Christians must be aware that they are in a state of confusion and must open their hearts to the clear, comprehensible and delightful monotheistic conception of the true faith. God reveals in the Koran that any other way is "schism":

> If their faith is the same as yours then they are guided. But if they turn away, they are in schism. God will be enough for you against them. He is the All-Hearing, the All-Knowing. (Koran, 2:137)

Belief in the Trinity Is a Major Obstacle to Appreciating God

One of the greatest problems facing Christians who regard belief in the Trinity as an immutable Church doctrine is that they are unable to appreciate God properly. Almighty God created the entire universe, from giant voids to exceedingly minute worlds,

from nothing. There is no doubt that God, Who created a glorious universe from nothing, Who created everything within in it in a balance and order, Who flawlessly created man and all other living things inside this glorious system, and Who bestowed a destiny on human beings, has the power to watch over and protect every being He creates. Our Lord is omniscient. He sees and hears all. Nothing is secret from Him. Not a single living thing can take a single breath without His knowledge, not a leaf can move and not an electron can change location. God has the power, if He so wills, to destroy them all and then create them again from nothing with a beauty that has never been seen before. This is certainly an easy matter for God. Everything happens just by our Lord telling it to "Be!" God sees what all eyes see, and hears all sounds. It is also He Who creates what every eye will see and what every ear will hear. Some Christians, who fail to fully understand the Islam shown by God in the Koran, try, in their own eyes, to justify the dogma of the Trinity by claiming that God is far distant from human beings in Islam. Yet God is not distant from us. He is with us at every moment. God is everywhere, and Islam tells us so in the verses of the Koran. It is the idea of the Trinity, not Islam, that regards God as being at a distance. For that reason, the idea that God can only reach His servants through Jesus (pbuh) prevails. That idea stems from a failure to properly understand and appreciate God.

There are some Muslims, of course, who regard God as being far removed from them. But they base their ideas, not on the Koran, but on nonsense of their own fabrication. The knowledge of the thing they espouse therefore does not exist in Islam. In fact, those Muslims who think that God is far away from them and the Christians who believe in the Trinity and think that God can only access them through intermediaries share the same false perspective. As our Almighty Lord says in the Koran:

We created man and We know what his own self whispers to him. We are nearer to him than his jugular vein. (Koran, 50:16)

So wait steadfastly for the judgment of your Lord – you are certainly before Our eyes. (Koran, 52:48)

... He knows everything in the land and sea. No leaf falls without His knowing it. There is no seed in the darkness of the Earth, and nothing moist or dry which is not in a Clear Book. (Koran, 6:59)

... He knows what they keep secret and what they make public. He knows what their hearts contain. (Koran, 11:5)

... Nothing is hidden from God either on the Earth or in heaven. (Koran, 14:38)

As revealed in many other verses in addition to the above, **He is the closest** to everyone. Nobody, no other entity, is closer to one than God. God sees through every eye and hears through every ear. God is not only in the heavens, as some Muslims and Christians think, **but everywhere.** Even if nobody else sees a leaf fall, God sees it and knows. Even if the atoms, electrons and quarks in the depths of the universe, the seeds deep beneath the ground and the ever-present actions of our cells, a totally invisible world, are unknown to us, God knows each one at every moment and sees it at every moment.

Trinitarians who maintain the existence of three separate deities with different attributes are unaware of the sublimity, might and power of God described in these pages. Were they aware of it, they would immediately understand the falsity of the idea that God reaches them through various intermediaries. God has no need of intermediaries. God is He Who knows His creations before their creation and what is hidden in their hearts.

In order to understand this better, they need to know and understand the concept of "manifestation," and therefore the truth about matter. In that event, Christians will better realize that what is described here is not a metaphysical belief, and that this reality explicitly revealed by God has been scientifically proven. This subject is discussed in detail in the third section.

SECTION 2
Almighty God Has No Children

Almighty God is the Lord of all entities and all creation. God is unfettered by any natural causes, because He is the Creator of all that happens and the natural causes behind them. Everything in the universe takes place in association with specific causes. But our Lord has no need of these causes. Our Lord also created situations associated with human life such as parenthood, childhood and having children. Those who say that "God has a child" (surely God is beyond that) therefore fail to grasp the sublimity and attributes of God. Our Almighty Lord just decides on something and wills it to be to create it. Nothing is distant from Him. He is the One Who best knows His creations and predestines everything before their creation.

Those who attribute a son to God are people who do not know or cannot grasp these attributes of God as is due. As has already been mentioned, God reveals the effrontery of those who are unable to appreciate our Lord in these verses from the Koran:

> They say, "The All-Merciful has a son."
>
> They have devised a monstrous thing.
>
> The heavens are all but rent apart and <u>the Earth split open and the mountains brought crashing down,</u>
>
> at their ascription of a son to the All-Merciful!
>
> It is not fitting for the All-Merciful to have a son.
>
> There is no one in the heavens and Earth who will not come to the All-Merciful as a servant. (Koran, 19:88-93)

As these verses clearly show, attributing a child to God is a grave offense, severe enough to bring the whole universe crashing down, and deserving the wrath of our Lord. Several verses of the Koran emphasize the fact that our Lord has no children. Verses explicitly state that our Lord is unfettered by having children, that "He has not given birth and was not born," and that nothing can be His equivalent:

> **Say: "He is God, Absolute Oneness, God, the Everlasting Sustainer of all. He has not given birth and was not born. And no one is comparable to Him." (Koran, 112:1-4)**

> **No indeed, it is one of their blatant lies to say, "God has given birth." They are truly liars. (Koran, 37:151-152)**

> **They say, "God has a son." Glory be to Him! He is the Rich Beyond Need. Everything in the heavens and everything on the Earth belongs to Him. Have you authority to say this or are you saying about God what you do not know? (Koran, 10:68)**

> **If God had desired to have a son He would have chosen whatever He wished from what He has created. Glory be to Him! He is God, the One, the All-Conquering. (Koran, 39:4)**

Our Lord is the absolute Ruler of the entire universe. Our Lord has no need of any partner or helper (surely God is beyond that). When He wishes a thing He tells it to "Be," and it is. As God reveals in verses:

> **He to Whom the Kingdom of the heavens and the Earth belongs. He does not have a son and He has no partner in the Kingdom. He created everything and determined it most exactly. (Koran, 25:2)**

> **And say: "Praise be to God Who has had no son and Who has no partner in His Kingdom and Who needs no one to protect Him from abasement." And proclaim His Greatness repeatedly! (Koran, 17:111)**

61

It is not fitting for God to have a son. Glory be to Him! When He decides on something, He just says to it, "Be!" and it is. (Koran, 19:35)

Almighty God reveals that He is warning those who say, "God has a son" through the Koran. This means that the Koran will show the true path to those Christians who have fallen into error regarding the Trinity. God prevents them from committing this major error by means of the Koran:

[This Koran is] to warn those who say "God has a son." They have no knowledge of this, neither they nor their fathers. It is a monstrous utterance which has issued from their mouths. What they say is nothing but a lie. (Koran, 18:4-5)

The above verses also set out how neither those who claim that God had a son nor those who went before them had any information on the subject, in other words, that this is a complete deception. God describes the danger posed by this ignorantly fabricated claim in the words, **"It is a monstrous utterance which has issued from their mouths."**

One verse in which our Lord says He has no son also states that there is no other deity than God:

God has no son and there is no other god accompanying Him, for then each god would have gone off with what he created and one of them would have been exalted above the other. Glory be to God above what they describe. (Koran, 23:91)

This verse totally discredits both claims made by those Christians who believe in the Trinity – that Jesus (pbuh) is the son of God and that he has divine status.

In the Koran, Almighty God revealed to our Prophet Muhammad (pbuh) that he should respond as follows to those who make such claims:

Say: "If the All-Merciful had a son, I would be the first to worship him." (Koran, 43:81)

"Failing to properly appreciate God" means not comprehending the sublime attributes of God set out in verses. If someone goes along with belief in the Trinity, then he cannot have understood that God rules all things, that He has no need of instruments or helpers in order to create, that God could have a child if He wished but that He is unfettered by this, that He just says to it "Be" when He desires a thing and that all things in the earth and sky have submitted to His command. God has no need of creating any other deities from His essence. God knows what will be born before it is born, what will be said before it is spoken, what will be seen before people look and what is hidden in their hearts. In short, He knows everything from the beginning of time to the end. Our Lord reveals in one verse:

> **God, there is no deity but Him, the Living, the Self-Sustaining. He is not subject to drowsiness or sleep. Everything in the heavens and the Earth belongs to Him. Who can intercede with Him except by His permission? He knows what is before them and what is behind them but they cannot grasp any of His knowledge save what He wills. His Footstool encompasses the heavens and the Earth and their preservation does not tire Him. He is the Most High, the Magnificent. (Koran, 2:255)**

God's infinite might and power appears as follows in passages from the Gospel:

... Who is God over-all, forever praised. (Romans, 9:5)

... Great and marvelous are Your deeds, Lord God Almighty.... (Revelations, 15:3)

For no word from God will ever fail. (Luke, 1:37)

... for there is no authority except that which God has established. The authorities that exist have been established by God. (Romans, 13:1)

For from Him and through Him and for Him are all things. To Him be the glory forever! Amen. (Romans, 11:36)

Everything is submitted to Him. Nothing is left to its own devices. It is incumbent upon every entity to obey our Lord. God possesses a devastating, great and sublime might:

... when everything in the heavens and Earth, willingly or unwillingly, submits to Him ... (Koran, 3:83)

Jesus (pbuh) Is a Servant Who Lives by a Profound Love of God

Our Lord says in the Gospel:

When God raised up His servant, He sent him [Jesus] first to you to bless you by turning each of you from your wicked ways. (Acts of the Apostles, 3:26)

In a verse from the Koran God says:

The Messiah would never disdain to be a servant to God nor would the angels near to Him. If any do disdain to worship Him, and grow arrogant, He will in any case gather them all to Him. (Koran, 4:172)

As passages from the Gospel and verses of the Koran make clear, Jesus is a servant of God and as explicitly stated in this verse from the Koran, he is a lovely human being who delights in being a servant of God, who has submitted to Him and who is devoted to Him with a deep passion. The duty of serving God, which he undertakes with a profound love of Him, is unacceptable for some Christians. They misinterpret and deny the duty of service to God that he discharges with love and great delight.

The great majority of those who deny, despite the passages from the Gospel that we shall be examining in detail, that Jesus was created merely as a servant have probably fallen into that error out of ignorance. They imagine, out of their love for Jesus, that if they were to admit that he was a "servant" he would in some way

64

become less valuable and they would be lacking in the appropriate respect for him. Yet the duty of service that Jesus discharged with love and enthusiasm, as an act of worship, was actually a great blessing for him and takes nothing away from his worth. On the contrary, service to God with such a great love made Jesus many times more valuable, raised his station in paradise and made him the beloved of masses of people. Being a servant and prophet who seeks to please God, being someone with a profound intelligence who praised and believed in God unconditionally throughout his life is the greatest of blessings for Jesus.

The fact that Jesus was created solely as a servant of God is also confirmed in other verses:

He [Jesus] said, "I am the servant of God, He has given me the Book and made me a Prophet." (Koran, 19:30)

It is revealed in another verse that Jesus is mortal and that, like all human beings, he will be resurrected in the hereafter:

"Peace be upon me the day I was born, and the day I die and the day I am raised up again alive." (Koran, 19:33)

When the time appointed by God comes, our beloved Prophet Jesus will be sent back down to Earth and will complete his work as messenger, together with Hazrat Mahdi (pbuh), in the manner commanded by God. (This will be discussed in later sections of this book). Once Jesus (pbuh) has completed his duty in this world he will pass on, just like every other mortal human being, and his soul will be taken to paradise. Just as with everyone else, it is God Who creates his whole destiny, everything that will happen to him throughout his life. It is also God Who creates all the miracles he worked. Jesus performed these, not through himself, but through God's mercy on him. Throughout his life of this world, he expressed a powerful faith in God and called people to His straight path. It is a fact explicitly set out in the Gospel that Jesus called on people to believe in and serve God:

Jesus answered, "It is written: 'Worship the Lord your God and serve Him only.'" (Luke, 4: 8)

65

This is how the Koran reveals that Jesus called on people to believe in God:

God is my Lord and your Lord so worship Him. This is a straight path. (Koran, 19:36)

Christians Must See the Importance of Esoteric Interpretations

The greatest error into which some sincere Christians fall in interpreting the references to the "son" in the Torah is to evaluate these references in the literal sense and not to look at the hidden meaning. They make the same mistake in evaluating the words of the Gospel. The fact is, however, that esoteric interpretation is an important secret to understanding the word of God and a requirement for deep reflection.

God's words are explicit, accessible, pithy and wise. However, our Almighty Lord sometimes employs explicit terms and at other times esoteric ones (equivocal wording or statements requiring interpretation at different levels). In order to be able to see the deep meanings and secrets in these wise words, we need to be able to look at them through the eyes of faith; that is esoteric interpretation.

Our Almighty Lord sometimes imparts these deep meanings through metaphor and simile. For example, in one verse of the Koran God says, **"Hold fast to the rope of God all together, and do not separate..."** (Koran, 3:103), and in another verse He says, **"As for those who deny Our signs and are arrogant regarding them, the Gates of Heaven will not be opened for them, and they will not enter the Garden until a camel goes through a needle's eye..."** (Koran, 7:40)

The verses in question may be interpreted in their literal senses by some people. In fact, however, the metaphors in both are

66

exceedingly wise and contain meanings that grow deeper the more one reflects on them. Our Lord's reference to "the rope of God" advises people to cling tightly to Him and the path He shows, and to exhibit determination on the subject. Our Lord's reference to a camel passing through the eye of a needle neatly describes how the people in question will be unable to enter paradise - unless God so wishes. This is an extremely fine and profound description. But in order to understand it properly, we also need to perform an esoteric interpretation.

This applies to the Gospel and the Torah, as well as to the Koran. One wise passage from the Gospel requiring esoteric interpretation is this:

This is why I speak to them in parables:

"Though seeing, they do not see; though hearing, they do not hear or understand. In them is fulfilled the prophecy of Isaiah:"

'You will be ever hearing but never understanding; you will be ever seeing but never perceiving. For this people's heart has become calloused; they hardly hear with their ears, and they have closed their eyes. Otherwise they might see with their eyes, hear with their ears, understand with their hearts and turn, and I would heal them.' (Matthew 13:13-15)

We can cite other examples from the Torah:

Hear, you deaf, and look, you blind, that you may see… Seeing many things, you observe not; opening the ears, he hears not. (Isaiah, 42:18, 20)

The word of the Lord came to me: "Son of man, you are living among a rebellious people. They have eyes to see but do not see and ears to hear but do not hear, for they are a rebellious people." (Ezekiel, 12:1-2)

A similar passage appears in the Koran:

Can you make the dead hear or guide the blind and those who are patently misguided? (Koran, 43:40)

Deaf, dumb, blind. They will not return. (Koran, 2:18)

These passages from the Gospel, the Koran and the Torah do not, of course, refer to a physical blindness or deafness. What is being emphasized here is a spiritual blindness, deafness and dumbness. The people being referred to here are those who are still unable to see the existence of God even though all the evidence is there and constantly being laid out before their eyes, people who are unable to properly appreciate God. God curses these people with their spiritual blindness and deafness.

If this is taken in the classic sense of blindness and deafness, that will of course lead to very incorrect interpretations. It is very important to be able to perform esoteric interpretation in order to avoid these false analyses because through these profound meanings, God is giving us very great and important messages, and secrets that will lead people to the true path.

The term "son" in the Gospel must be evaluated through esoteric interpretation

It needs to be made clear that a lack of esoteric interpretation appears in various forms in Islam, Christianity and Judaism. Therefore, we should not regard this as a deficiency peculiar to Christians alone. However, given the subject matter, we shall be discussing only that part that involves our Christian brothers here.

Being able to perform esoteric interpretation is of paramount importance in terms of the errors in which some of our Christian brothers find themselves. The superstitious belief that Jesus (pbuh) is the son of God, which has persisted for hundreds of years (surely God is beyond that) is a very significant and major error that stems from a lack of esoteric interpretation. The term "the son of God," which appears in the Gospel and, as discussed above, in the Torah, has been considered in the literal sense alone and interpreted without proper consideration of its deeper meanings.

As we have already seen, however, the term "son" here refers to spiritual proximity to God, love, friendship and being chosen. It is a rather profound reference to being a beloved and chosen servant of God.

Christians must understand that the term "the son of God" has no physical meaning, but rather emphasizes a servant's closeness to God. When they look at the matter using esoteric interpretation they will better understand that a very different and profound message is being imparted through this form of address.

Evidence from the Gospel That Jesus (pbuh) Is Not the Son of God

Some Christians may think that only the Koran reveals that Jesus was merely a servant of God. The fact is, however, that Christians' own book, the Gospel, explicitly states, and in various ways, that Jesus was a human being who was tested, prayed, ate, slept when tired and served God. No matter how strongly Christians who believe in the Trinity resist the evidence Muslims bring against the Trinity, Christians' own book, the Gospel, says that Jesus is not the son of God. Every mind and conscience that is free from conditioning and prejudice will immediately understand these explicit and clear words of the Koran.

Evidence from the Gospel that Jesus is not the son of God, merely a human being who serves Him, is as follows:

The birth, lineage and family of Jesus (pbuh)

Historical information shows that Jesus is descended from the Prophet David (pbuh). Jesus is known to the people. The people know who he is descended from and where he was born and grew up. The people are also well acquainted with Jesus' family. Therefore he, like all other human beings, is someone with a specific lineage and birth:

He has raised up a horn of salvation for us in the house of His servant David (as He said through His holy prophets of long ago), salvation from our enemies and from the hand of all who hate us— (Luke 1: 69-71)

This is the genealogy of Jesus the Messiah the son of David, the son of Abraham: (Matthew 1: 1)

The crowds that went ahead of him and those that followed shouted, "Hosanna to the Son of David! Blessed is he who comes in the name of the Lord! Hosanna in the highest heaven!" When Jesus entered Jerusalem, the whole city was stirred and asked, "Who is this?" The crowds answered, "This is Jesus, the prophet from Nazareth in Galilee." (Matthew 21: 9-11)

"Isn't this the carpenter? Isn't this Mary's son and the brother of James, Joseph, Judas and Simon? Aren't his sisters here with us?"... (Mark 6: 3)

The human characteristics of Jesus (pbuh)

The fact that Jesus is a human being is a crucial matter that utterly discredits the idea of the Trinity. No matter how much the proponents of the three-in-one suggest the superficial logic that Jesus is a material entity in this world, that he assumed human form in other words, this does not eliminate the fact that Jesus

70

having human characteristics like everyone else totally invalidates the idea of the Trinity: Angels can also assume human form, yet as a manifestation of their superior creation they have no need to eat or rest. That being the case, it is a terrible thing to maintain, may God forbid, that a god could appear on Earth with such human needs (surely God is beyond that).

The information provided about Jesus in the Gospel makes it clear that this worthy person is "a blessed messenger of God, not His son." He lived just like everyone else. Like other human beings, he was born and went through infancy, childhood and adolescence. When he felt the need to eat, he gave thanks to God and ate, together with the disciples. Like everyone else, he became tired at the end of a long day and felt the urge to sleep. In addition, the Gospel says that Jesus had physical needs such as washing and keeping himself clean. Such human attributes totally invalidate the idea of the Trinity. Since Jesus was a servant and a prophet, and since he was tested like everyone else, he was created with human characteristics and needs. The place where needs and deficiencies no longer apply is, of course, paradise.

Some passages from the Gospel regarding the human features of Jesus and that disprove his supposed divine status are as follows:

> And Jesus grew in wisdom and stature, and in favor with God and man. (Luke 2: 52)

> When he [Jesus] was at the table with them, he took bread, gave thanks, broke it and began to give it to them. (Luke 24:30)

> And while they still did not believe it because of joy and amazement, he asked them, "Do you have anything here to eat?" They gave him a piece of broiled fish, and he took it and ate it in their presence. (Luke 24: 41-43)

> On the first day of the Festival of Unleavened Bread, the disciples came to Jesus and asked, "Where do you want us to make preparations for you to eat the Passover?" (Matthew 26: 17)

While Jesus was having dinner at Levi's house,... (Mark 2: 15)

Then Jesus entered a house, and again a crowd gathered, so that he and his disciples were not even able to eat. (Mark 3: 20)

While they were reclining at the table eating, he said, "Truly I tell you, one of you will betray me—one who is eating with me." (Mark 14: 18)

When one of the Pharisees invited Jesus to have dinner with him, he went to the Pharisee's house and reclined at the table. (Luke 7: 36)

... Jesus, tired as he was from the journey, sat down by the well. It was about noon. When a Samaritan woman came to draw water, Jesus said to her, "Will you give me a drink?" (John 4: 6-7)

Jesus was in the stern, sleeping on a cushion... (Mark 4: 38)

Then, because so many people were coming and going that they did not even have a chance to eat, he [Jesus] said to them, "Come with me by yourselves to a quiet place and get some rest." (Mark 6: 31)

...Tired of the voyage he made, Jesus sat near the well.... (John, 4: 4)

How Jesus (pbuh) was tested and how satan tried to tempt him

The Gospel explicitly describes how Jesus was a human being tested by God. It is absolutely out of the question for a human being who is tested by God to also be God (surely God is beyond that). It is impossible for someone who satan tried to lead away from the true path to possess such a characteristic. God reveals in the Gospel how Jesus was a human being who was tested by and served Him:

> *[Jesus:] "You are those who have stood by me in my trials." (Luke 22: 28)*

> *The devil led him up to a high place and showed him in an instant all the kingdoms of the world. And he said to him, "I will give you all their authority and splendor; it has been given to me, and I can give it to anyone I want to. If you worship me, it will all be yours." Jesus answered, "It is written: 'Worship the Lord your God and serve Him only.'" (Luke 4: 5-8)*

> *When the devil had finished all this tempting, he left him until an opportune time. (Luke 4: 13)*

The fact that Jesus (pbuh) was born without a father is no evidence for the Trinity; the Prophet Adam (pbuh) was also born with no mother or father

Trinitarian Christians point to the miraculous birth of Jesus without a father as supposed evidence for their claims. The fact is, however, that they never think, while regarding this as very powerful evidence, that the Prophet Adam was born without either a mother or a father. The Prophet Adam was created in paradise with no natural cause or intermediary, simply by God commanding him to "Be!" Such an act of creation is surely even more miraculous, yet no Christian has ever attributed divinity to the Prophet Adam. This way of thinking that some Christians propose as evidence for the Trinity is thus completely invalid. It can never, ever prove the so-called divine status they seek to bestow on Jesus.

The creation of Adam is described as follows in the Gospel and the Torah:

> *For Adam was formed first, then Eve; (1 Timothy 2: 13)*

73

Then the Lord God formed a man from the dust of the ground and breathed into his nostrils the breath of life, and the man became a living being. (Genesis 2: 7)

None of the references to "son" in the Gospel are understood in the literal sense. The idea of being a real son is only attributed to Jesus (pbuh)

The terms "the son of God" or "the sons of God" are employed in many places throughout the Gospel. As we shall be seeing in detail, the words "son of God" are an expression of love. They express the idea that someone is a blessed, trustworthy, loyal and beloved servant of God. They therefore quite definitely do not mean "son" in any physical or literal sense. This term is used in many places in the Gospel and is addressed to very different people, but nowhere it is used in the physical or literal sense. As in the expression *"Blessed are the peacemakers, for they will be called children of God"* (Matthew 5: 9), those who bring about peace will be the beloved and valued servants of God. No Christian can interpret this to mean a literal son or attribute any other meaning to it.

The term "son of God" in the Gospel has been interpreted in the physical and literal sense only with regard to Jesus. Although the same term appears, with absolutely no difference in the wording, only Jesus has ever been considered as being a real son. This shows how the term "son of God" has been distorted from its true meaning and how it is deliberately used with a meaning unique to Jesus. Various passages from the Gospel referring to a son or children of God read as follows:

> *[Jesus:] "But love your enemies, do good to them, and lend to them without expecting to get anything back. Then your reward will be great, and you will be children of the Most High, because He is kind to the ungrateful and wicked." (Luke 6: 35)*

And, I will be a Father to you, and you will be My sons and daughters, says the Lord Almighty. (2 Corinthians 6: 18)

Jesus is referred to as the "Son of Man" 80 times in holy scriptures. While Christians who support the Trinity try to explain this away in various ways, the term "son of man," *barnasha* in Aramaic, the mother tongue of Jesus, is a special one meaning "human." Therefore, the term "son of man" is the equivalent of saying "human" in that language. *(Prof. Dr. Mehmet Bayrakdar, The Birth of a Christian Dogma, the Trinity, Ankara School Press, September 2007, p. 168)*

The term of address "Father" in the Gospel is also metaphorical and calls on all mankind

As well as the word "son," the term "Father" also appears in the Gospel. The reference to "Father" here expresses protection, love and affection. It refers to people who bear the spirit of God, who are told of paradise and who are spiritually close to Him. It is not used in the literal sense, of course. Yet people who believe in the Trinity adopt the literal meaning of a word whose true sense is so clear in the Gospel and suggest that it means the biological father of Jesus in those passages referring to the prophet. This is blatantly misleading and a total distortion of a subject whose meaning is actually so very clear.

Some of the passages in the Gospel in which the term "Father" is used and whose metaphorical meaning is perfectly clear read as follows:

Then your Father, Who sees what is done in secret, will reward you... Do not be like them, for your Father knows what you need before you ask Him. (Matthew 6: 4, 8)

75

Be careful not to practice your righteousness in front of others to be seen by them. If you do, you will have no reward from your Father in heaven. (Matthew 6: 1)

But when you pray, go into your room, close the door and pray to your Father, Who is unseen. Then your Father, Who sees what is done in secret, will reward you. (Matthew 6: 6)

The term "children of God" in the Gospel is also a metaphorical one

The term "children of God," which appears in many passages in the Gospel, refers to believers and refers to a spiritual and metaphorical closeness. It emphasizes that these people are blessed and valued in the Sight of God, and who may hope to have earned His approval. There is no question of any divine status here. Anyone looking at the terms "Father," "son" and "children of God" in the Gospel from an unbiased perspective can easily see that these are metaphorical terms and are used in order to express God's closeness, love, affection and protectiveness. It is baffling why these words, so frequently employed in the Gospel, are interpreted differently when it comes to Jesus. The meaning does not change. The significance is the same metaphorical one, but Trinitarians deliberately distort it.

Some passages in the Gospel that refer to the "children of God" read as follows:

Yet to all who did receive Him, to those who believed in His name, He gave the right to become <u>children of God</u>. (John, 1:12)

Beloved, now are we <u>the sons of God</u>, and it does not yet appear what we shall be: but we know that, when he shall appear, we shall be like him; for we shall see him as he is. (1 John, 3:2)

76

This is how we know that we love the children of God: by loving God and carrying out His commands. (1 John, 5:2)

One example of the term "Father" having a metaphorical meaning is its use for the Prophet Abraham (pbuh)

In the Gospel, the Prophet Abraham is described as the "father" of the faithful. The word "father" is obviously being used metaphorically here; the use of that term emphasizes the Prophet Abraham's leadership, protectiveness and guidance to his followers.

Therefore, the promise comes by faith, so that it may be by grace and may be guaranteed to all Abraham's offspring— not only to those who are of the law but also to those who have the faith of Abraham. He is the father of us all. (Romans, 4:16)

"Abraham is our father," they answered. "If you were Abraham's children," said Jesus, "then you would do what Abraham did." (John, 8:39)

Serving the created instead of the Creator, a mortal human being instead of God, is condemned in the Gospel

The passages from the Gospel on this subject are highly significant. They report that people of the time worshiped a created entity, a mortal human being in other words, instead of the Creator, and adopted him as their deity. This is the current situation of Christians who believe in the Trinity. They have adopted a human being as their god and have declared that, in their eyes, a created entity is actually the Creator. God warns them as follows in the Gospel:

For although they knew God, they neither glorified Him as God nor gave thanks to Him, but their thinking became futile and their foolish hearts were darkened. Although they claimed to be wise, they became fools and <u>exchanged the glory of the immortal God for images made to look like a mortal human being</u> and birds and animals and reptiles. Therefore God gave them over in the sinful desires of their hearts to sexual impurity for the degrading of their bodies with one another. <u>They exchanged the truth about God for a lie, and worshiped and served created things rather than the Creator</u>—Who is forever praised. Amen. (Romans, 1:21-25)

How Jesus (pbuh) said "God is One"

God is One. Jesus explicitly said so. It is expressly stated in several passages in the Gospel that God is the One and Only, that only He must be served and that people must believe in Him without ascribing equals to Him. (You can find all the passages from the Gospel concerning the Oneness of God in the pages that follow.) Nowhere in these passages are there any illogical references to a three-in-one, nor to three separate deities meaning one deity or to three separate entities being essentially one. All the Gospel says is that "God is One." The fact set out in the Gospel is that there is no other god than Him. It is so easy to see this that it is astonishing how, despite these many explicit passages in the Christian Gospel, they could ever have developed the doctrine of the Trinity.

One of the teachers of the law came and heard them debating. Noticing that Jesus had given them a good answer, he asked him, "Of all the commandments, which is the most important?" "The most important one," answered Jesus, "is this: 'Hear, O Israel: <u>The Lord our God, the Lord is One. Love the Lord your God with all your heart</u>

*and with all your soul and with all your mind and with all
your strength.' The second is this: 'Love your neighbor as
yourself.' There is no commandment greater than these."
"Well said, teacher," the man replied. "You are right in
saying that God is One and there is no other but Him."
(Mark, 12:28-32)*

*To the only wise God our Savior, be glory and majesty...
(Jude, 1: 24)*

*You believe that there is One God; you do well: the devils
also believe, and tremble! (James, 2: 19)*

How Jesus (pbuh) commanded fear of God

According to the Gospel, Jesus commanded people to fear, not
him, but God alone. Some Christians may claim that the subject is
the three-in-one, for which reason Jesus is thus referring to
himself. This confusion is of course something that only
proponents of the Trinity can use to deceive people. Nobody with a
strong conscience must be taken in by this deception, however.
The meaning of the passage is clear and explicit. Jesus is not
calling on anyone to worship him. On the contrary, he calls on
them to turn to God, the One and Only, alone.

*[Jesus:] Do not be afraid of those who kill the body but
cannot kill the soul. Rather, be afraid of the One Who can
destroy both soul and body in hell. (Matthew, 10:28)*

How Jesus (pbuh) commanded people to love God

In the Gospel, Jesus also constantly desires people to turn to
and love God.

*"The most important one," answered Jesus, "is this: 'Hear,
O Israel: The Lord our God, the Lord is One. Love the*

79

*Lord your God with all your heart and with all your soul
and with all your mind and with all your strength.'" (Mark,
12:29-30)*

How Jesus (pbuh) commanded people to beseech God

Under the error of the Trinity, the person to whom prayers
should be addressed is Jesus. And present-day proponents of the
Trinity do indeed pray to Jesus. In the Gospel, however, Jesus
personally says that prayer should be addressed to God. There is no
doubt about that command. Nowhere in the Gospel does Jesus tell
people that they need to turn to him into order to pray to God. He
advises them to pray directly to God. Confused and misleading
ideas such as the need for intermediaries in order to pray and that
prayers can reach God only through Jesus are fabrications by
Trinitarians. The passages from the Gospel are clear to anyone
looking with the eyes of the heart and of logic.

> *Then he [Jesus] said to his disciples, "The harvest is
> plentiful but the workers are few. <u>Ask the Lord of the
> harvest</u>, therefore, to send out workers into His harvest
> field." (Matthew, 9:37-38)*

How Jesus (pbuh) said that God alone should be served

In the Gospel, Jesus calls on people to serve God, not him.
Those who seek to misinterpret these statements by Jesus to the
effect that he is referring to himself are those people who seek to
include the Trinity in the Gospel. The passage is explicit; like the
Prophets Abraham, Moses and Muhammad, Jesus (peace be upon
them all) preaches the message sent to him as a beloved prophet of
God and calls on people to serve God.

Jesus answered, "It is written: 'Worship the Lord your God and serve Him only." (Luke, 4:8, Matthew, 4:10)

How Jesus (pbuh) commanded people to believe in God

In the Gospel, Jesus performs the duty of prophethood bestowed on him and calls on people to believe in God.

"Have faith in God," Jesus answered. (Mark 11:22)

How Jesus (pbuh) recommended that everything be done for God's approval

In the Gospel, Jesus advises people to act for God's approval, not for his. This means it is Almighty God's approval that people must seek, not that of Jesus.

So whether you eat or drink or whatever you do, do it all for the glory of God. (1 Corinthians 10:31)

He who regards one day as special, does so to the Lord. He who eats meat, eats to the Lord, for he gives thanks to God; and he who abstains, does so to the Lord and gives thanks to God. For none of us lives to himself alone and none of us dies to himself alone. So, whether we live or die, we belong to the Lord. (Romans 14:6-8)

Whatever you do, work at it with all your heart, as working for the Lord, not for men, since you know that you will receive an inheritance from the Lord as a reward... (Colossians 3:23-24)

81

How Jesus (pbuh) encouraged people to praise and laud God alone

Jesus always told those around him that only our Lord God was to be praised and lauded, and encouraged them to praise and laud Him. Jesus does not refer to himself in these passages from the Gospel. Such an interpretation appears nowhere in these passages. Jesus says that the knowledge he possesses belongs, not to himself but to God, and he encourages people to turn directly to our Lord God.

> *The Jews there were amazed and asked, "How did this man get such learning without having been taught?"Jesus answered, "My teaching is not my own. It comes from the One Who sent me. Anyone who chooses to do the will of God will find out whether my teaching comes from God or whether I speak on my own. Whoever speaks on their own does so to gain personal glory, but he who seeks the glory of the One Who sent him is a man of truth; there is nothing false about him." (John, 7:15-18)*

> *As Jesus started on his way, a man ran up to him and fell on his knees before him. "Good teacher," he asked, "what must I do to inherit eternal life?" ... Jesus answered. "No one is good—except God alone." (Mark, 10:17-18)*

How Jesus (pbuh) obeyed God

Jesus says in the Gospel that he is a servant of God, that he was sent as a prophet and that, as required by his being a prophet, he has a responsibility to obey God's commands. He says that he does nothing of himself and that he fulfills the tasks given to him by Almighty God.

An omnipotent God rules His creations as described in the verse from the Koran **"When He decides on something, He just says to it, 'Be!' and it is."** (Koran, 2:117). Jesus is a servant who knows this and who obeys God.

82

Jesus praises the greatness of God, the Creator, in just about everything he says and states that he is obeying His commands. There is therefore nothing in Jesus' words in the Gospel on this subject to support the idea of the Trinity.

> *[Jesus:] "... For I have come down from heaven not to do my will but to do the will of Him Who sent me." (John, 6:38)*

> *[Jesus:] "By myself I can do nothing; I judge only as I hear, and my judgment is just, for I seek not to please myself but Him Who sent me." (John, 5:30)*

How Jesus (pbuh) said that he worked miracles by God's leave

God is of course the sole Ruler. And God, the Lord of All, is also the Lord of Jesus whom He sent as a prophet. Jesus of course knows that everything he does, he does by our Lord's leave. A great many passages in the Gospel show that Jesus spoke in the awareness of that, that he praised God and called people to Him.

> *... And the power of the Lord was with Jesus to heal the sick. (Luke, 5:17)*

> *Jesus knew that the Father had put all things under His power, and that he had come from God and was returning to God; (John, 13:3)*

Some Christians may interpret these statements from the Gospel as follows: "Jesus had both divine and human characteristics. It is therefore normal for him to have exhibited human ones." This interpretation perfectly illustrates the logical collapse at the root of the belief in the Trinity. How can an entity with human characteristics, created with the weaknesses demanded by the life of this world be divine? How can such an idea be acceptable to people who claim to love God? God is Almighty, He Who creates the deficiencies in this world as a test, although He Himself is unfettered by any deficiencies. As we have stressed many times and will be looking at in later sections of this book, the problem is one of a failure to understand the might of God and to properly appreciate Him.

All statements based on the Gospel clearly show that Jesus is a loyal and obedient servant of God and a human being. These statements cited in the Gospel have gradually been filtered through the illogicality of the Trinity, and attempts have been made to make the words of the Gospel compatible with Trinitarian doctrine through confusing interpretations. The fact is, however, that when someone who has not been exposed to this deceptive indoctrination looks at the Gospel he can easily see that Jesus is a servant and a human being. Such a person can easily see what a forced interpretation the idea of the Trinity is. He will be astonished at the way such a concept as the Trinity could have emerged from such explicit statements. Therefore, looked at with a clear mind and an unbiased perspective, every Christian will see that the Gospel contains nothing about the Trinity in any form and that, on the contrary, as shown by the passages quoted above, it is in fact full of statements that explicitly refute the idea of the Trinity.

Evidence from the Koran That Jesus (pbuh) Was a Human Being

God states in the Koran that Jesus and his mother Hazrat Mary (pbuh) were envoys with human characteristics. The words "Both of them ate food" in the following verse are deliberately employed to emphasize this important truth:

> **The Messiah, the son of Mary, was only a messenger,** **before whom other messengers came and went. His mother was a woman of truth. Both of them ate food. See how We make the signs clear to them! Then see how they are perverted! (Koran, 5:75)**

84

Almighty God also states that Jesus was born, that he had a childhood and that he worked his miracles by God's leave:

> Remember when God said, "Jesus, son of Mary, remember My blessing to you and to your mother when I reinforced you with the Purest Spirit so that you could speak to people in the cradle and when you were fully grown; and when I taught you the Book and Wisdom, and the Torah and the Gospel and when you created a bird-shape out of clay by My permission, and then breathed into it and it became a bird by My permission; and healed the blind and the leper by My permission; and when you brought forth the dead by My permission; and when I held back the tribe of Israel from you, when you brought them the clear signs and those of them who were unbelievers said, 'This is nothing but downright magic.'" (Koran, 5:110)

In another verse, Almighty God reminds the proponents of the Trinity that, like all other human beings, Jesus had no power to do anything unless God so willed it.

> Those who say, "God is the Messiah, son of Mary," are unbelievers. Say: "Who possesses any power at all over God if He desires to destroy the Messiah, son of Mary, and his mother, and everyone else on Earth?" The kingdom of the heavens and the Earth and everything between them belongs to God. He creates whatever He wills. God has power over all things. (Koran, 5:17)

Of course Jesus is a human being much beloved of God, who is honored and selected by Him; he is His prophet. But ultimately he is a servant. In the Koran, Jesus calls on the children of Israel to worship the One God, against those who would deify him:

> Those who say that the Messiah, son of Mary, is God are unbelievers. The Messiah said, "Tribe of Israel! Worship God, my Lord and your Lord. If anyone associates anything with God, God has forbidden him the Garden and his refuge will be the Fire." The

wrongdoers will have no helpers. <u>Those who say that God is the third of three are unbelievers. There is no god but One God.</u> If they do not stop saying what they say, a painful punishment will afflict those among them who are unbelievers. Why do they not turn to God and ask for His forgiveness? God is Ever-Forgiving, Most Merciful. (Koran, 5:72-74)

In other verses of the Koran, Jesus preaches as follows to the people of Israel:

"I come confirming the Torah I find already there, and to make lawful for you some of what was previously forbidden to you. I have brought you a sign from your Lord. So have fear of God and obey me. <u>God is my Lord and your Lord so worship Him. That is a straight path.</u>" (Koran, 3:50-51)

Jesus preached the fact that Almighty God is both his Lord and that of all created things. The few disciples who heeded this message of Jesus spoke of him as a "messenger":

... The disciples said, "We are God's helpers. We believe in God. Bear witness that we are Muslims. Our Lord, we have faith in what You have sent down and <u>have followed the messenger</u>, so write us down among the witnesses." (Koran, 3:52-53)

Almighty God says that He has sent messengers to Earth and makes it clear in a verse that it is impossible for them to say, "Abandon God and worship me:"

It is not right for any human being that God should give him the Book and Judgment and Prophethood, and then that he should say to people, <u>"Be worshipers of me rather than God."</u> Rather he will say, "Be people of the Lord because of your knowledge of the Book and because you study." (Koran, 3:79)

As shown by the evidence in these and many other verses, Jesus is a blessed and holy messenger created by God. He is a human being who is a friend of God, a prophet and a servant of God. But in no way is he the son of God; he never claimed to be divine, but sought shelter in God against that. When preaching his message he always reminded people that he was a servant of God and called on them to believe in Him.

Our Lord described those who, despite the evidence provided in the Koran and the Gospel, say that "God is the third of the three" as having "fallen into unbelief." The error of the Trinity is strongly opposed in the Koran, and is a grave and profound danger against which our Lord warns in several verses. Many of our Christian brothers today are going along with what they have been taught and are in all likelihood unaware of the scale of this profound error. The Christians in question must become aware of the magnitude of this danger.

The Koran is the last book. It was sent down to confirm the Gospel, and our Christian brothers therefore have a responsibility to pay heed to the truths revealed in the Koran. They must be open to the guidance of the Koran. This will be a blessing and a mercy for them.

(For more detail on the subject see *Jesus (pbuh) Is Not the Son of God, But the Prophet of God,* by Harun Yahya, www.harunyahya.com, www.bookglobal.net)

Those Christians Who Claim That the Trinity Originates from the Torah Are Mistaken

The term "Son of God" and the term "We," which God uses for His own person, appear in many places in the Torah. Some Christians regard these terms as the source of belief in the Trinity. However, they make a grave mistake.

1. One of the names of God in Hebrew is "Elohim." In Hebrew, the suffix *-im* is generally used to express the plural (such

as with *bayit*; home, *batim*; homes). Due to this suffix in the noun Elohim, some Christians have thought that the name of God here is a plural form and they have claimed that, according to the Torah, the Israelites also believed in the Trinity. However, there are several words in Hebrew that end with the suffix *-im* but still express a singular form: these include *Panim*; face, *Shamayim*; sky or skies, *Rahamim*; mercy or compassion, *Mayim*; water and, *Pnim*; interior, and many others. The idea that the Torah therefore contains the concept of the Trinity is based on ignorance.

In any case, in Hebrew the verb changes according to whether the subject is singular or plural. It is therefore easy to tell if a sentence refers to a single person or more than one by looking at the verb. If the word Elohim were plural, as some Christians maintain, then the Hebrew should read "Vayomru Elohim" (the gods said). But on every occasion the Torah reads "Vayomer Elohim" (God said).

2. The same thing applies to another name of God in the Hebrew Gospel. Some Christians mispronounce the word *"Adonai."* What it really means is "My Lords." But this is not the correct pronunciation in Hebrew. The word is read *"Adonoy"* and very definitely **is not a plural form.**

3. Christians try to use these words that appear in the Book of Genesis as evidence for the idea of the three-in-one:

> *Then God said, "Let Us make mankind in Our image, in Our likeness, so that they may rule over the fish in the sea and the birds in the sky, over the livestock and all the wild animals, and over all the creatures that move along the ground." So God created mankind in His own image, in the image of God He created them; male and female He created them. (Genesis, 1: 26-27)*

Christians seek to use this passage in which God refers to Himself in the plural saying, *"Let Us make mankind in Our image, in Our likeness,"* and then in the next passage His referring to Himself in the singular as major evidence for the Trinity. This is an exceedingly forced interpretation, however. Anybody, even a child, who has not been indoctrinated with the idea of the Trinity will immediately realize that the plural forms here are specially used to emphasize the might and greatness of God. The word "We" which our Lord uses for His own person appears in many verses of the Koran, which condemns the idea of the Trinity or the three-in-one:

> **We have decreed death for you and We will not be forestalled. (Koran, 56:60)**

4. Christians also interpret the following passage of the Torah according to their own mindset:

> *Come near me and listen to this: "From the first announcement I have not spoken in secret; at the time it happens, I am there." And <u>now the Sovereign Lord has sent me, endowed with His Spirit.</u> (Isaiah, 48:16)*

Christians also misinterpret this passage from the Torah and try to use it as evidence for the Trinity with some compulsory explanations made in parenthesis. They say that the three elements of the Trinity appear in it. However, the term "son of God" does not appear in it at all, while the section interpreted as the Holy Spirit actually refers to the spirit of God that He breathed into man. God also reveals in the Koran that He breathed His Own Spirit into man:

> **He Who has created all things in the best possible way. He commenced the creation of man from clay; then produced his seed from an extract of base fluid; then formed him and <u>breathed His Spirit into him</u> and gave you hearing, sight and hearts. What little thanks you show! (Koran, 32:7-9)**

God's breathing of His Own Spirit shows that every human being bears His Spirit and that nothing is separate from God. It is inconceivable how Christians interpret this to mean the Holy Spirit and manage to glean the idea of the son of God from this.

5. The following passage from the Zabur (the Book of Psalms in the Torah) is also misinterpreted by some Christians:

89

I will proclaim the Lord's decree: He said to me, "You are
My son; today I have become your father. Ask me, and I
will make the nations your inheritance, the ends of the
Earth your possession." (Psalms 2:7-8)

As also appears in other passages from the Torah, the concept being described as "son" here refers to Israel. The reference here is to how God will protect the devout people of Israel. This passage describes how God will protect His beloved servants as a father protects his sons.

6. Efforts have also been made to equate the reference to "son" of man" in the following passage from the Book of Daniel 7:13-14 to the misinterpretations of the Gospel and to claim that this refers to the divine nature ascribed to Jesus. This is a totally false interpretation, however:

"In my vision at night I looked, and there before me was
one like a son of man, coming with the clouds of heaven.
He approached the Ancient of Days and was led into His
Presence. He was given authority, glory and sovereign
power; all nations and peoples of every language
worshiped him. His dominion is an everlasting dominion
that will not pass away, and his kingdom is one that will
never be destroyed." (Daniel, 7:13-14)

The reference here is to a mortal human being, and Torah scholars are unanimously agreed that the "King" refers to the King Messiah, the Mahdi, who will come in the End Times. The King Messiah will reign over all nations, and all peoples and nations will be content with him.

It needs to be stated that the Jews never regarded the passages from the Torah in question in terms of the Trinity, neither in the time of the Prophet Moses (pbuh) nor afterward. These concepts were never understood in the sense of the Trinity when the Torah was first revealed. The Jews are perfectly well aware of the true and profound meanings of these terms in the Torah and seek shelter with God from interpreting them as involving the Trinity. They understand the sense of these terms and realize that they stress the love, protectiveness and closeness of God to His servant. Indeed, Jews also oppose the false impressions that some Christians seek to give through their literal interpretation of passages from the Torah.

The Christians who interpret these passages in terms of the Trinity also seek to produce evidence for their claims from the Koran. Yet the belief that appears in all these passages from the Torah and the Psalms is a monotheistic faith. The Gospel, which confirms the Torah, also praises this monotheistic faith. Our Christian brothers really must see this reality in the Gospel.

The Idea That God Appeared in Human Form Must Also Be Repellent to Christians

Devout Christians need to behave honestly on this subject and see that the attribution of divinity to a human being contravenes the Christianity brought by Jesus (pbuh) and the words of the Torah and the Gospel; they also need to see that it flies in the face of all reason and logic. They need to admit the possibility that such a belief, added to the true Gospel only many centuries later, can pose a major spiritual danger and to reflect deeply on the subject. What sense or meaning could there possibly be to ascribing the sublime attributes of God to a human being and regarding and portraying a person created to be weak as divine? Almighty God has no need of that (Surely God is beyond that). As we have recalled many times, such an attribution **means a failure to properly appreciate the might and greatness of God.**

Above and beyond this, Christians themselves must reject the idea of Almighty God appearing on Earth in the form of a human being. This is not only disrespect for the glory of Almighty God, this is the most flagrant paganism, as such tales of the gods such as Zeus, Apollo, Poseidon and others taking human form and interacting with people are numerous and well-known in the ancient Greco-Roman pagan religions. God's might, greatness, glory, might and infinite power are a blessing for Christians; **is it better to believe in an All-Powerful God** or to take as one's god a human being who sleeps, eats and has needs? All Christians will of course at once see the answer to this.

God has no need to appear as a mortal and needy entity in order to reveal His sublime Presence to human beings. (Surely God is beyond that.) Our Christian brothers must consider the Gospel and the Torah rationally and evaluate all these things in a manner compatible with the glory of God.

The fact that Jesus (pbuh) has human characteristics is not, of course, a state of affairs that will in any way reduce his value as a prophet. Jesus is a greatly valued and most holy prophet of our Almighty Lord. Like all other prophets, he occupies the loftiest and holiest position in God's Sight. He is God's beloved friend, a great messenger. Therefore, the fact he was created as a human being detracts nothing whatsoever from his worth, importance and lofty status as a prophet.

What is important is to believe in God – our One and Only Creator. God wants people to believe in and serve Him, without engaging in idolatry. There is no need for God to appear on Earth in human form for people to be able to serve Him. If our Christian brothers wish to approach this subject from a genuinely honest perspective they should ask themselves this question:

What would God lose from any of His attributes by not manifesting His Presence in Jesus? (Surely God is beyond that)

God not manifesting His Presence in a human being would take nothing away from His attributes, sublimity and beauty. Indeed, this will increase His beauty and make His sublime qualities better and more properly appreciated. How could it be possible to appreciate the sublime qualities of God by imagining that He manifested His Presence in a mortal, weak and needy human being who sleeps and eats? Of course, this is not possible.

The Gospel Rejects Belief in the Trinity Passages from the Gospel That Refer to the Oneness of God and Advise to Avoid Ascribing Equals to Him

*One of the teachers of the law came and heard them debating. Noticing that Jesus had given them a good answer, he asked him, "Of all the commandments, which is the most important?" "The most important one," answered Jesus, "is this: 'Hear, O Israel, **the Lord our God, the Lord is One.**" "Well said, teacher," the man replied. "You are right in saying that God is One and there is no other but Him." (Mark 12:28-32)*

*... **But God is One.** (Galatians 3:20)*

The Lord is One. There are different kinds of working, but the same God works all of them in all men. (1 Corinthians 12:6)

For there is one God... (1 Timothy 2:5)

*Jesus said to him, "... **Worship the Lord your God, and serve Him only.**" (Matthew 4:10)*

to the only God our Savior be glory... (Jude 1:25)

You believe that there is One God. Good! Even the demons believe that—and shudder. (James 2:19)

*Now to the King eternal, immortal, invisible, **the only God**, be honor and glory for ever and ever. (1 Timothy 1:17)*

*How can you believe if you accept praise from one another, yet make no effort to obtain the praise that comes from **the only God**? (John 5:44)*

As Jesus started on his way, a man ran up to him and fell on his knees before him. "Good teacher," he asked, "What *must I do to inherit eternal life?" Jesus answered, ".. **No one is good—except God alone.**" (Mark 10:17-18)*

*... We know that an idol is nothing at all in the world and that **there is no god but One... for us there is but one God,** the God, from Whom all things came and for Whom we live... (1 Corinthians 8:4-6)*

*... **You have one Lord**... (Matthew 23:9)*

*"Why do you ask me about what is good?" Jesus replied. **"There is only One Who is good. If you want to enter life [paradise], obey the commandments of [God]."** (Matthew 19:17)*

*For even if there are so-called gods [surely God is beyond that], whether in heaven or on Earth yet **for us there is one God,** the God, for Whom all things came and for Whom we live. (1 Corinthians 8:5-6)*

*... **One Lord**, one faith... **one God of all,** Who is over all and through all and in all. (Ephesians 4:5-6)*

*For every house is built by someone, but **God is the builder of everything.** (Hebrews 3:4)*

SECTION 3
EVERYTHING THAT EXISTS IS A MANIFESTATION OF GOD

An important Secret: We Can Have No Experience of Anything Apart from the Image Inside Our Brains

A great many people live unaware of a most important secret. This secret, which will change people's entire lives and their conception of the hereafter and this world, **is that we live entirely within our brains.** To put it another way, nobody can ever step outside the world shown to his soul inside his brain and therefore can never experience the original of matter on the outside.

This can be clarified as follows: The information reaching us as an image from the outside world is merely a quantity of light. If we can see the image of an apple, smell it, taste it and hold it in our hands, then all this comes about through a handful of light. In other words, nothing apart from this quantity of light reaches us from the apple on the outside. **We can never experience the apple itself.** For example, photons reaching our eyes from the apple are converted in the eye into an electric current and this electrical current received in the brain is interpreted as an image of an apple. To put it another way again, an image totally independent of the original on the outside forms in our brains and we only experience this apple inside our brains. **There is no direct connection between the apple on the outside and the one in our brains.**

This applies to everything we see, taste, touch, smell and hear. **None of the images that form in our brains are the originals of their counterparts on the outside. <u>Matter does exist on the outside,</u>** but the original of that matter is in its entirety <u>transparent and dark.</u> It is impossible for us to have any kind of direct contact with this dark and transparent matter on the outside. This is a scientific fact that scientists have identified and are unanimously agreed on. (It has been established that 99.9999% of the atom is empty space, and quantum physics has shown that atomic particles exhibit particle properties and also wave properties, thus establishing the true nature of matter and that there is no light and color on the outside. For greater detail on the subject see, *Darwin's Dilemma: The Soul*, by Harun Yahya)

The following point needs to be stressed here: The fact that we can never experience the original of matter **is an indisputable and scientifically proven fact**; it is not a question of personal belief. Science has proved that **all our life is created, in perfect detail and clarity, inside our brains, that we can never experience the world on the outside and that the matter on the outside is entirely transparent.**

Even if they are aware of this truth intellectually, a great many people still never escape the feeling that they do directly experience the outside world. The incessant sharpness and quality of the image keep them away from thinking about this fact. The reason for that is that the image created in our brains and consisting solely of electrical signals is extraordinarily vivid, colorful, active and flawless. This is of course a very easy matter for Almighty God, the Creator of all the worlds, Who creates the most astonishing worlds within the atoms and in the voids of space, Who is exalted in power to bring all things into being with perfect order and extraordinary artistry, the Owner of all beauty and He is Rich Beyond Need, Praiseworthy. Our Almighty Lord has created a world in every person's mind, unique to him or her alone, and equipped with the greatest detail and perfection.

What this means is this: All the planets, the Milky Way, the stars, the Sun, everyone on Earth, millions of living species, their lives, things underground, cells, proteins, atoms and all the worlds inside the atom **are all created by God's leave in a spot inside our brains no larger than a lentil bean.** This tiny space where the image is created is itself also an image. It is the soul that sees these images within the brain and perceives these sensations. And God causes our souls to experience what we call "our life" or "the outside world."

The soul has no brain or ears, but you still hear the signals reaching your brain without these, in the form of pleasant music, noise from the street outside or a friend's voice. The soul also has no eyes, but it still sees the signals reaching brain in the form of an electric current as a delightful view or familiar face. The world and the universe are therefore metaphysical. Whether or not people want to think about this, or pretend not to understand it, they only experience a world that God shows to their souls and – unless God wishes otherwise – they can never step outside that world and can never experience the matter whose original exists on the outside.

The Whole World inside Our Brains, Without Exception, Is A Manifestation of God

The fact that everything is created as an image inside our brains means we can better grasp the concept of manifestation. Since everything is just an image, and since the matter on the outside is dark and transparent, all the bright, active and colorful images created in our minds are exactly the same by nature. To put it another way, everything in the world we experience **is an illusion forming in our minds.** We watch all these illusory images on a screen in our brains. This is a law created by God. And under God's law, **matter does exist on the outside, but we can never go beyond this to experience the original of matter, and it is impossible to step outside the images inside our brains.**

Therefore, **"everything"; all the things that we see and experience in our brains is a manifestation of God.** All mothers and fathers are manifestations of God. And all children are manifestations of God. All butterflies, birds, trees, roses and fruits are manifestations of God. Planets, suns, stars and the vast universe are manifestations of God. When God called to the Prophet Moses (pbuh) from the bush, He was manifested in the bush. There are no exceptions because everything is a part of an image of matter on the outside created inside our brains. These images include attractive people, our families, fine houses, buildings and majestic mountains, as well as shanty homes, dirty

97

side streets, war, slaughter, conflict, ugliness and disease. Pleasant and unpleasant things are all part of the same image. They are all created as an illusion in our brains in order to produce the life of this world, and are therefore images created by God and manifestations of Him.

Some Christians are unaware or fail to understand that matter is just an image in the brain, and thus misinterpret references to "manifestations of God in this world." By saying that only Jesus is a manifestation of God, these Christians are ascribing divine status to him (may God forbid), while maintaining that everything else is independent of Him – surely God is beyond this.

Of course Jesus bears the spirit of God, and surely God manifests Himself in him in the most merciful way. But nothing in this world is independent of God; all things are the work of and manifestations of God. Everything, attractive or ugly, good or bad, exists through God's creation and by His leave. But these Christians in question are making a grave error by misinterpreting being a manifestation of God as meaning His Own Person. They maintain that only Jesus is a manifestation of God, and that nothing else on Earth, and especially evils and ugliness, can never be regarded as manifestations of Him.

A manifestation of God does not necessarily mean the Person of God. People can never see Almighty God, but they are in constant contact with His manifestations. Everything we see is an image of matter existing on the outside, and that image is a whole on one single screen. For us, the whole world consists of these images, because we can never have direct experience of the matter on the outside. **These copy images inside our brains are not independent of our Lord (surely God is beyond that), and it is impossible for them to be so.** Therefore, Jesus and all other entities are parts of the same image, and are all manifestations of God.

The subject of the reality of matter, scientifically described above, totally does away with these erroneous Christian beliefs regarding Jesus. Honest Christians must therefore consider the

98

matter in depth. As we have already said, this fact is not a personal interpretation or belief. **It is a proven, scientific fact,** and not a single scientist in today's 21st Century will deny it. To renounce it would be like maintaining an unscientific claim such as that the Earth is flat. Therefore, those who seek to ascribe divinity to Jesus by bringing up the existence of the material world have been deceived by materialism and thus discredited right at the very outset.

With his excellent fear and love of God, his superior morals and exemplary behavior, as well as the miracles bestowed on him by our Lord, Jesus (pbuh) is of course a very special manifestation of God. He is a beloved servant of God and a holy prophet who represents an intense manifestation of the Most-Merciful name of God. Some Christians may imagine that if they regard Jesus, a holy and blessed prophet and servant of God, as another manifestation of Him they will be betraying him and that this will damage the love they feel for him. The fact is, however, that **to deify God's blessed prophet [may God forbid] very definitely cannot be an expression of love.** On the contrary, it is a serious error stemming from failing to understand love of God. One must seek shelter in God from any such conception. Love is to be directed toward God, the Creator and the Lord of all worlds. That is why the most blessed manifestations of our Lord are very much loved. Our love for Jesus stems from our love of God. The more we love God, the more our love for Jesus will grow and be strengthened.

The fact that Jesus is a manifestation of God like all other things, **does not, of course, reduce his worth.** He is a virtuous and pure servant of God, a blessed and lovely prophet chosen by our Lord. Loving him for these fine qualities and for God's sake is far more valuable and excellent. And that is the form of love that God will find pleasing and that needs to be shown.

God Is Everywhere

We created humanity and We know what his own self whispers to him. **We are nearer to him than his jugular vein.** (Koran, 50:16)

Some Muslims and Christians interpret the passage **"We are nearer to him than his jugular vein"** to mean a kind of spiritual closeness, rather than a physical one, and thus try to deny the fact that God is everywhere. Under their own false beliefs, the Christians in question claim that a belief in a "remote God" prevails in Islam and that God is inaccessible in it (this is far from the truth). They imagine in this way they can build a foundation for the concept of "the son of God," and that instead of the supposed belief in the "remote" God (surely God is beyond this) they imagine to prevail in Islam, they claim that in Christianity God makes contact with His servants through Jesus (pbuh). This is a most serious error and stems from an inability to fully grasp the difference between the Person of God and His manifestation.

The term **"We are nearer to him than his jugular vein"** in the verse refers to a physical proximity as well as a spiritual one. As we have already explained, since everything is part of an illusion in our brains and our whole lives are the total of these images forming in our brains, then our bodies, cells and everything we possess and experience are images and, like all these copy images of matter, they are also manifestations of God. Therefore, **God is closer to us even than the person we imagine to be closest to us.** This is a completely physical closeness, because God enfolds people from all directions, inside and out.

The Person of God is of course different. But **the manifestations of God are everywhere.** If a person says that God is not there when he enters a room, then he has abandoned the faith. If he says, "Everything is a manifestation of God, except for this small box," then he has again abandoned the faith. By saying that, he is placing boundaries on the infinite greatness of God and claiming that there are other entities independent of Him (surely God is beyond that). Even if the thing he regards as independent of

God is just a box then he is again, albeit unwittingly, denying the greatness of God, may He forbid. But it is God alone Who is eternal and absolute. Therefore, when a person enters a room, the manifestations of God are everywhere he sees or does not see, including the room itself. **Wherever a person turns, the manifestation of God is there.**

Several verses of the Koran reveal that God enfolds all space, and that wherever we look, He is there. The expressions in these verses are clear judgments. In Chapter 2, verse 255 of the Koran, for instance, God says, **"... His Footstool encompasses the heavens and the Earth..."** In Chapter 11, verse 92, **"... But my Lord encompasses everything that you do!"** it is revealed that God enfolds people and all they do.

God makes this truth quite explicit in the Gospel:

He [God] is before all things, and <u>in Him all things hold together.</u> (Colossians, 1:17)

<u>Nothing in all creation is hidden from God's Sight. Everything is uncovered and laid bare before the eyes of Him</u> to Whom we must give account. (Hebrews, 4:13)

Once people realize the truth described above, that we can never have a direct experience of the matter on the outside, only with illusions or copy images in our brains, they will also fully understand that God is everywhere and the only absolute entity. God is not only in the heavens; **God enfolds and surrounds all places.** This knowledge is imparted by means of the Koran. When we pray, **God hears us everywhere and at every moment.** God shows us manifestations of Himself everywhere. God loves us and is **the closest to us. Nobody is closer to us than God.** There is no distance between us and God. People who understand that they can never have direct experience of the original of matter on the outside will also fully comprehend that **God is everywhere at all times, that He sees and hears them at all moments, that He witnesses everything and is closer to them than their own jugular veins, that He answers every prayer, and that both**

spiritually and physically, it is our Almighty Lord God Who is closest to us of all.

Since we are bound by time and space, we may fail to properly appreciate that God enfolds the heavens and the Earth and all that exists. But the fact is that God's enfolding all space means He also enfolds everyone's very cells and the atoms thereof. Not one atom is independent of God. Each is a manifestation of God, and God knows them all. **Nowhere is without God.**

The Error of Maintaining That a Material World Necessitates a Material Deity

Some Christians, who are unaware of or fail to properly appreciate the real issue about matter described above, set out the reason why they attribute divine status to Jesus (pbuh) as follows: "Since we are all material entities and this world is a material one, there has to be a material entity if we and the world are to be saved." Such a claim is a most superficial one and stems from **an inability to properly understand that God is everywhere and the closest to us at all times, and that He can reach all His servants whenever He desires and however He desires, and also from an ignorance of the true nature of matter.** First of all, nothing we have direct experience of is matter. And that includes ourselves. The matter on the outside we can never have direct experience of does not have a material nature as we understand it: it is dark and transparent. We live in a world that we see only in our brains, made up of copy images or illusions of originals in the outside world we can never have direct experience of. We imagine we experience the outside world through our five senses. Yet everything consists solely of electrical signals. If all the electrical signals going to the brain were cut off, the realm we refer to as the material world would instantly cease to exist. To summarize, nothing in the world we see is a material entity. For us, everything that exists on the outside consists of copy images we experience within our brains. The idea that there has to be a material deity (may God forbid) in such a world is therefore totally illogical. There is nothing material about this world in our brains.

The idea, as the Christians in question maintain, that God has to be manifested in a single human being in order to reach us and show us His love and closeness is an unrealistic and fantastical belief. God has no need of this. Our Almighty Lord is beyond all imperfection. (As we mentioned earlier, the manifestation here definitely does not implicate the Person of God). **God is everywhere. He is with us at every moment. He is manifested in all things.**

The conception of God being at a distance from His servant is a contradiction of the logic and reason behind the belief in the Trinity. The Christians in question have abandoned belief in God, Who is manifested everywhere and in everything, Who enfolds all things and Who is the nearest to His servants and adopted a belief in a distant God. **According to this pagan belief, God is so far removed from them that He can only contact His servants through a human intermediary** (Surely God is beyond that). This effectively means they are claiming that other than the person sent by God as His manifestation, all entities exist outside God: And that is polytheism. To ascribe equals to God or attribute independent power to entities other than Him is the worst sin in His Sight, and a failure to properly know and appreciate Him.

God makes His proximity to His servants quite clear in the Gospel:

> Do not be like them, for _God knows what you need before you ask Him._ (Matthew, 6:8)
>
> _Nothing in all creation is hidden from God's Sight._ Everything is uncovered and laid bare before the eyes of Him to Whom we must give account. (Hebrews, 4:13)
>
> _For there is nothing hidden that will not be disclosed, and nothing concealed that will not be known_ or brought out into the open. (Luke, 8:17)

103

For by Him all things were created: things in heaven and on Earth, visible and invisible, whether thrones or powers or rulers or authorities; all things were created by Him and for Him. He is before all things, and in Him all things hold together. (Colossians, 1:16-17)

But when you pray, go into your room, close the door and pray to your Lord, Who is unseen. Then your God, Who sees what is done in secret, will reward you. (Matthew, 6:6)

Are not five sparrows sold for two pennies? Yet not one of them is forgotten by God. Indeed, the very hairs of your head are all numbered. (Luke, 12:6-7)

Almighty God reveals this in the Koran:

... I know what you make known and what you hide. (Koran, 2:33)

As is made clear in passages from the Gospel and verses of the Koran, it is sufficient to pray with sincerity to make contact with God. Wherever one may be, God will hear and see one and will answer that prayer as He sees fit.

Therefore, some Christians who prepare the ground for belief in the Trinity by maintaining that Islam believes in a remote God have fallen into a grave error. When these people realize that Almighty God is the One and Only Creator of all and that He enfolds all things, when they grasp the truth about the reality of matter, then they will realize just how close God is to them.

But because of their error in the Trinity they have a misjudgment of God and His greatness; if they properly appreciated God, they would not claim the existence of entities that are not manifestations of Him and would avoid ascribing equals to Him.

We have a Lord Who creates all things and rules all things and places. Christians must rationally evaluate these realities and adopt a religious conception befitting the infinite might of God. God is everywhere, in the heavens and the Earth, wherever people live, whether they see these places or not. The image created in our brains that we refer to as "our lives" belongs to God alone. That being the case, how can one maintain one needs an intermediary to be close to God? God hears our prayers the moment we think of them. All Christian brothers and sisters should be rejoicing that God is so close to us. Sincere Christians must understand the true nature of matter, properly appreciate the glory of God and realize that He will never permit such illogical and specious accounts.

Why is the creed of the Trinitydangerous?

The creed of the Trinity and Trinitarianism advocated by some Christians in our day is a very serious delusion. Apart from being a great slander against God and Jesus (pbuh), it is also a serious threat. It is of great importance for our Christian brothers to be aware of these dangers that the creed of Trinity leads to and may give rise to in the future. Some of these dangers are as follows:

1. The danger of ascribing partners to God:

According to both the Gospel and the Torah, ascribing partners to God is "polytheism." Consequently, with the creed of the Trinity, genuine Christians inadvertently fall into this great danger of ascribing partners to God by ascribing divine status to Jesus (surely God is beyond that). This danger of ascribing partners to God is not an issue that can be ignored. Almighty God says this in the Koran regarding this great danger: **"The heavens are all but rent apart and the Earth split open"** (Koran, 19:90). Ascribing partners to God is a great sin in God's Sight. In the Koran, God threatens those who commit this sin:

> **God does not forgive anything being associated with Him but He forgives whoever He wills for anything**

other than that. Anyone who associates something with God has committed a terrible crime. (Koran, 4:48)

In the Gospel, Christians are forbidden to ascribe partners to God:

And [they] exchanged the glory of the immortal God for images made to look like mortal man and birds and animals and reptiles [surely God is beyond that]... They exchanged the truth of God for a lie, and worshiped and served created things rather than the Creator [surely God is beyond that]—Who is forever praised. (Romans, 1:23-25)

Jesus answered, "It is written: 'Worship the Lord your God and serve Him only.'" (Luke, 4:8)

Christians who claim they in fact worship a single deity under the name of the Trinity (surely God is beyond that) and claim that He is manifested in three forms, as body, soul and consciousness must not regard this as anything but danger of polytheism. Living in such a state of disorder rather than believing in One God as the Creator of All, Who is with us at all times, means turning away from the true faith. It is a grave perversion to practice a form of religion reminiscent of the idols of the pagan faiths instead of being sincerely bound to One God. Those who say they believe in One God while sheltering behind such accounts should be very careful. A Christian who believes in the Trinity may want to believe in One God, and may regard himself as doing so, and that is a good thing; but belief in the Trinity can never be belief in the One God. By believing in the Trinity a Christian is, knowingly or otherwise, falsely ascribing divine status to other entities and thus engaging in polytheism.

In one verse of the Koran, our Lord issues the following warning to those Christians who go astray on the subject of the Trinity:

People of the Book! Do not go to excess in your religion. Say nothing but the truth about God. The Messiah, Jesus son of Mary, was only the Messenger of God and

His Word, which He cast into Mary, and a Spirit from Him. So believe in God and His Messengers. <u>Do not say, "Three." It is better that you stop. God is only One God. He is too Glorious to have a son!</u> Everything in the heavens and in the Earth belongs to Him. God suffices as a Guardian. (Koran, 4:171)

2. The danger of all endeavors coming to naught

Another great danger our genuine Christian brothers will face because of the error of the Trinity is the **possibility of all the efforts they claim to make in the name of God coming to nothing.** This is a great danger for Christians who, disregarding reminders and warnings, continue to ascribe partners to God solely because of this delusion, and do not heed their consciences but assume they are on the true path. Such a danger should not be underestimated. In the Koran, God warns, **"some faces on that Day will be downcast, laboring, weary"** (Koran, 88:2-3). In another verse of the Koran, we are informed of people, **"People whose efforts in the life of the world are misguided while they suppose that they are doing good."** (Koran, 18:104) In the Torah, on the other hand, the prayers of those who sincerely believe are cited as follows:

> *May the favor of the Lord our God rest upon us; establish the work of our hands for us—yes, establish the work of our hands. (Psalms 90:17)*

Consequently there will be people whose endeavors will come to nothing in the hereafter. A devout believer should not regard himself as immune from this danger and should heed his conscience. Right now, God is calling our Christian brothers who have been indoctrinated with the creed of the Trinity for years to search their hearts in the light of these reminders and warnings.

3. The danger of hidden unbelief, hypocrisy and atheism

Another danger posed by the creed of the Trinity is that it causes hidden unbelief or that it causes people to drift into atheism. It is not difficult for any person who is well acquainted with the Gospel to grasp the irrationality of the creed of the Trinity. In fact, almost all Christians are aware of this fact. But they nonetheless make themselves believe in it, citing various pretexts, or else many of them remain silent under the threat that otherwise "they will have abandoned the faith."

Some of them, on the other hand, **drift into unbelief because consciously and logically they cannot accept this creed and they do not in fact believe it.** This is a great threat. There are **secret unbelievers in Christianity who are compelled to appear devout** although they are aware of the invalidity of the Trinity. The hidden unbelievers who lose their religion due to this superstitious creed constitute the danger of hypocrisy in Christianity. Hypocrites, on the other hand, are the main reason for conflict and division in Christianity, just as is the case in Islam and Judaism. They are the members of a dangerous group and the source of false beliefs developed to make Christians weak and prevent them from worshipping.

Apart from this, a growing number of Christians are straying from the true path and becoming atheists because of the idea of the Trinity which opposes sound logic and reason. As the reason for their irreligiousness, the atheists in question raise the discrepancies and forced logic in Christianity. Christians who espouse the Trinity are, no doubt, aware of this situation.

Of course, the possibility of these people drifting into secret disbelief, hypocrisy or atheism simply because they cannot be convinced about the truth of the Trinity is definitely a danger. If a person is truly sincere, he is obliged to turn to God in his heart, strive to see and understand the truth, and to abide by what his conscience guides him towards. However, this danger must in no way be ignored.

The history of Christianity also reveals the great ideological conflicts caused by the idea of the Trinity, which have come down to our own day. It is impossible for a righteous creed to be the source of such great conflicts and tribulations. It is possible that to date, some Christians have not properly assessed the dimensions of this danger. It is likely that they are simply trying to uphold a false belief inherited from their forefathers, assuming that it is commanded in the Gospel. However, this is a belief definitely contrary to God's command. When they consider the Gospel in a rational way and refer to their conscience, and see the tribulations caused by a superstitious belief, they will understand this better. Consequently, we call on genuine Christians to take refuge in God, to think without indoctrination rooted in Christianity and to make their decision with their purest of conscience.

Passages from the Gospel Regarding Serving God without Ascribing Equals to Him

Jesus answered, *"It is written: 'Worship the Lord your God and serve Him only.'"* (Luke, 4:8)

Jesus said to him, *"... Worship the Lord your God, and serve Him only."* (Matthew, 4:10)

... My dear friends, flee from idolatry. (1 Corinthians, 10:14)

For they themselves report what kind of reception you gave us. They tell how you turned to God from idols to *serve the living and true God...* (1 Thessalonians, 1:9-10)

[Jesus:] "No servant can serve two masters... *You cannot serve both God and money."* [May God forbid] (Luke, 16:13)

... If then the light within you is darkness, how great is that darkness! *No one can serve two masters.* Either he will

109

hate the one and love the other, or he will be devoted to the one and despise the other. You cannot serve both God and money. (Matthew, 6:23-24)

*... **Some people are still so accustomed to idols that when they eat such food they think of it as having been sacrificed to an idol,** and since their conscience is weak, it is defiled. But food does not bring us near to God; we are no worse if we do not eat, and no better if we do. (1 Corinthians, 8:7-8)*

*No, but the **sacrifices of pagans are offered to demons, not to God**, and I do not want you to be participants with demons. You cannot drink the cup of the Lord and the cup of demons too; **you cannot have a part in both the Lord's table and the table of demons.** (1 Corinthians, 10:20-21)*

*So then, about eating food sacrificed to idols: We know that an idol is nothing at all in the world and that **there is no God but One.** (1 Corinthians, 8:4)*

*Dear children, **keep yourselves from idols.** (1 John, 5:21)*

*The rest of mankind that were not killed by these plagues still **did not repent of the work of their hands**; they did not stop worshiping demons, and idols of gold, silver, bronze, stone and wood—idols that cannot see or hear or walk. (Revelation, 9:20)*

CHAPTER 3
THE ERROR THAT THE PROPHET JESUS (PBUH) WAS CRUCIFIED

Various Contradictions in the Four Gospels about the Idea of Jesus' (pbuh) Supposed Crucifixion

After it was modified, Christian faith is now based on the belief that the Prophet Jesus (pbuh) was crucified and killed on the cross and that he was then resurrected. However this information does not reflect the truth. As revealed in the Koran in detail, Jesus was not crucified, and was therefore not killed. On the contrary, he was raised to the heavens while still alive and taken into the Sight of God to be sent back to Earth again in the End Times. The reason for the Christian community defending the belief that Jesus was crucified lies in some contradictory explanations written in some chapters in the Gospel. However, the statements written in the chapters in question are, as we have stated before, contradictory ones, which were added to the Gospel after Jesus (pbuh), in the 3rd Century.

The four Gospels contain differences regarding the supposed crucifixion of Jesus and what happened immediately before and after. Let us look at these contradictory accounts in the Gospels:

Contradictory statements in the Gospels about Jesus' (pbuh) supposed crucifixion

Who carried the cross?

There are statements in Mark 15:21, Matthew 27:32 and Luke 23:26 that the cross was carried by Simon of Cyrene:

> *As they were going out, they met a man from Cyrene, named Simon, and they forced him to carry the cross. (Matthew 27:32)*

The Gospel of John states that Jesus (pbuh) carried the cross himself:

> *Carrying his own cross, he went out to the place of the Skull (which in Aramaic is called Golgotha). (John 19:17)*

The crucified thieves:

Sections of Mark 15:27-28, Matthew 27:44 and Luke 23:39-42 say that Jesus was supposedly crucified along with two thieves. The inconsistency here is that the Romans never crucified thieves; historically, the punishment of crucifixion was reserved for those in rebellion to the Roman Empire.

> *They crucified two robbers with him, one on his right and one on his left. (Mark 15:27-28)*

> *In the same way the robbers who were crucified with him also heaped insults on him. (Matthew 27:44)*

Contradictory information about the time of Jesus' (pbuh) supposed crucifixion:

In the relevant passages from Mark 15:25, Matthew 27:45-46, Luke 23:44-46 and John 19:14-15 the time of Jesus' (pbuh) supposed crucifixion differs from one another.

> It was ***nine in the morning*** when they crucified him.(Mark 15:25)

> It was now ***about noon***, and darkness came over the whole land ***until three in the afternoon***, for the sun stopped shining. And the curtain of the temple was torn in two. Jesus called out with a loud voice, "My Lord, into Your hands I commit my spirit." When he had said this, he breathed his last. (Luke 23:44-46)

The so-called last words of Jesus (pbuh):

There is also contradictory information in the four Gospels about the last words of Jesus (pbuh) during his supposed crucifixion. Mark 15:34-37 and Matthew 27:46-50 say that Jesus (pbuh) called out:

> And at the ninth hour Jesus cried out in a loud voice, "Eloi, Eloi, lama sabachthani?"—which means, "My God, my God, why have You forsaken me? [God is beyond that.]" (Mark 15:34)

In the Gospel of Luke, the supposed last words of Jesus (pbuh) are cited differently:

> Jesus called out with a loud voice, "God, into Your hands I commit my spirit." When he had said this, he breathed his last. (Luke 23:46)

In the Gospel of John, the statements on this subject are completely different:

> *When he had received the drink, Jesus said, "It is finished." With that, he bowed his head and gave up his spirit. (John 19:30)*

The earthquake during the supposed burial of Jesus (pbuh):

This account comes from the Gospel of Matthew:

> *At that moment the curtain of the temple was torn in two from top to bottom. The Earth shook and the rocks split. The tombs broke open and the bodies of many holy people who had died were raised to life. They came out of the tombs, and after Jesus' resurrection they went into the holy city and appeared to many people. (Matthew 27:51-53)*

In the Gospels of Mark, Luke and John, there are several descriptions of the supposed burial of Jesus (pbuh). However, no mention is made of an earthquake, which is impossible to have been forgotten if such an earthquake had ever occurred.

Events that took place following the supposed burial of Jesus (pbuh):

Events alleged to have taken place following the supposed burial of Jesus (pbuh) are described differently in the four Gospels:

> *At that moment the curtain of the temple was torn in two from top to bottom. The Earth shook and the rocks split. The tombs broke open and the bodies of many holy people who had died were raised to life. They came out of the tombs, and after Jesus' resurrection they went into the holy city and appeared to many people. (Matthew 27:51-53)*

But when they looked up, they saw that the stone, which was very large, had been rolled away. As they entered the tomb, they saw a young man dressed in a white robe sitting on the right side, and they were alarmed. (Mark 16:4-5)

They found the stone rolled away from the tomb, but when they entered, they did not find the body of ... Jesus. While they were wondering about this, suddenly two men in clothes that gleamed like lightning stood beside them. (Luke 24:2-4)

So Peter and the other disciple started for the tomb. Both were running, but the other disciple outran Peter and reached the tomb first. He bent over and looked in at the strips of linen lying there but did not go in. Then Simon Peter, who was behind him, arrived and went into the tomb. He saw the strips of linen lying there, as well as the burial cloth that had been around Jesus' head. The cloth was folded up by itself, separate from the linen. (John 20:3-8)

The competent authorities to which Jesus (pbuh) was supposedly taken are described differently:

In the Gospels of Mark 14:53, Matthew 26:57 and Luke 22:54, the competent authority to which Jesus was taken is described as Caiaphas, the high priest. But in the Gospel of John it is Annas, the father-in-law of Caiaphas.

They took Jesus to the high priest...(Mark 14:53)

Those who had arrested Jesus took him to Caiaphas, the high priest... (Matthew 26:57)

Then seizing him, they led him away and took him into the house of the high priest. Peter followed at a distance. (Luke 22:54)

... and brought him first to Annas, who was the father-in-law of Caiaphas, the high priest that year. (John 18:13)

Jesus (pbuh) supposedly standing trial over accusations:

In the four Gospels, all of the descriptions of the supposed trial of Jesus contradict one another.

According to the Gospel of John, only the high priest interrogates Jesus:

> *Then the detachment of soldiers with its commander and the Jewish officials arrested Jesus. They bound him and brought him first to Annas, who was the father-in-law of Caiaphas, the high priest that year. Caiaphas was the one who had advised the Jews that it would be good if one man died for the people... Meanwhile, the high priest questioned Jesus about his disciples and his teaching. (John 18:12-14,19)*

According to the Gospels of Mark, Luke and Matthew, Jesus is tried by the whole of the High Council:

> *At daybreak the council of the elders of the people, both the chief priests and teachers of the law, met together, and Jesus was led before them. "If you are the Christ," they said, "tell us." (Luke 22:66-67)*

> *They took Jesus to the high priest, and all the chief priests, elders and teachers of the law came together... The chief priests and the whole Sanhedrin were looking for evidence against Jesus so that they could put him to death, but they did not find any. Many testified falsely against him, but their statements did not agree. (Mark 14:53-56)*

> *Those who had arrested Jesus took him to Caiaphas, the high priest, where the teachers of the law and the elders had assembled. But Peter followed him at a distance, right up to the courtyard of the high priest. He entered and sat*

116

down with the guards to see the outcome. The chief priests and the whole Sanhedrin were looking for false evidence against Jesus so that they could put him to death. (Matthew 26:57-59)

Jesus' (pbuh) so-called interrogation by Herod:

The Gospel of Luke says that Jesus was interrogated by Herod:

On hearing this, Pilate asked if the man was a Galilean. When he learned that Jesus was under Herod's jurisdiction, he sent him to Herod, who was also in Jerusalem at that time. When Herod saw Jesus, he was greatly pleased, because for a long time he had been wanting to see him. From what he had heard about him, he hoped to see him perform some miracle. He plied him with many questions, but Jesus gave him no answer. The chief priests and the teachers of the law were standing there, vehemently accusing him. Then Herod and his soldiers ridiculed and mocked him. Dressing him in an elegant robe, they sent him back to Pilate. That day Herod and Pilate became friends—before this they had been enemies. (Luke, 23:6-12)

In the Gospels of Matthew, Mark and John, the supposed interrogation of Jesus by Herod is not mentioned.

The contradictions in question are open evidences that those accounts told about the supposed crucifixion of Jesus are based on completely false information and the descriptions of that moment and environment contradict one another. If Christians point to the Gospels as evidence that Jesus was killed, then they need to see that they cannot arrive at definitive and clear information from the four different versions of the canonical gospels. In order to see the truth they need to look at the Koran, which God says that He sent to confirm the Gospel. **Almighty God reveals in the Koran that Jesus was not crucified, that he was definitely not killed, but**

117

that He created an environment that made unbelievers believe that it happened in that way. Our Lord reveals in the Koran that these claims about Jesus are invalid; the traps set by hypocrites and unbelievers for Jesus came to nothing, and **Jesus was taken up into God's Sight.** When the contradictions in the Gospel passages in question are analyzed in the light of the Koranic verses, the uncertainty between the four Gospels is immediately clarified: Jesus did not die, but a special image was shown to make people think he had been crucified.

Jesus (pbuh) did not die,but was raised into God's Sight

In the Koran God provides accurate information about the crucifixion of Jesus, which is described in the Gospel in a contradictory and doubtful manner. In the Koran, God makes it clear that **plots against Jesus were thwarted and that they certainly did not kill him:**

> ... and their saying, "We killed the Messiah, Jesus son of Mary, Messenger of God." <u>They did not kill him and they did not crucify him</u> but it was made to seem so to them. Those who argue about him are in doubt about it. They have no real knowledge of it, just conjecture. <u>But they certainly did not kill him.</u> **(Koran, 4: 157)**

In the Koran, the fact that Jesus was not killed is stressed twice in the same verse. It says that those who advocate the belief that Jesus was killed have **"no real knowledge of it, just conjecture."** This is a very clear statement and one that cannot possibly be interpreted in any other way.

Someone resembling Jesus (pbuh) was crucified:

In the same verse in the Koran God reveals, **"They did not kill him and they did not crucify him <u>but it was made to seem so to them</u>."** (Koran, 4:157), and informs us that the person who was crucified was another person who resembled Jesus.

The individual who was crucified instead of Jesus was **Judas Iscariot, who betrayed Jesus.** As a great miracle, God made Judas Iscariot resemble Jesus. When they came to take Jesus to crucify him, they took Judas Iscariot, who was present there, instead and crucified him. Besides, since Judas Iscariot's face was covered with blood, people did not realize that it was not Jesus who was crucified. In the latter part of the verse 157 of the 4th surah, God relates, **"They have no real knowledge of it, just conjecture."** Those who set the trap and those around just went along with their own misapprehensions, and as set out in the verse, they have no other knowledge of it.

Indeed, in the Gospel, the last words of Jesus are given as *"Elohi, Elohi, lama sabachthani?"* which means, *"My God, My God, why have You forsaken me?"* This is a continuation of the same delusion and the expression of weakness of faith in question belongs to Judas Iscariot, whose plot was thwarted and who was crucified instead of Jesus. Indeed, it is obvious that Jesus, who was a servant of God, who wholeheartedly submitted to God and loved Him and who knew that everything comes from Him, could not have spoken these words. But one would expect such rebellious statements to come from the mouth of a hypocrite such as Judas Iscariot.

The disappearance of Judas Iscariot according to the Gospels:

Parallel to what is revealed in the verses of the Koran and also supported by various sources, there are passages in the Gospels that may provide evidence that Judas Iscariot, who betrayed Jesus (pbuh), was crucified instead of him. According to these passages we need to notice that just after the crucifixion, Judas Iscariot disappeared. The authors of the Gospels tried to explain this away in various ways and contradicted one another because they did not know that Judas Iscariot had been crucified instead of Jesus. The contradictory explanations regarding the disappearance of Iscariot in the Gospels read as follows:

> *Early in the morning, all the chief priests and the elders of the people came to the decision to put Jesus to death. They bound him, led him away and handed him over to Pilate, the governor. When Judas, who had betrayed him, saw that Jesus was condemned, he was seized with remorse and returned the thirty silver coins to the chief priests and the elders. "I have sinned," he said, "for I have betrayed innocent blood." "What is that to us?" they replied. "That's your responsibility."* **So Judas threw the money into the temple and left. Then he went away and hanged himself.** *(Matthew 27: 1-5)*

> *In those days Peter stood up among the believers and said, "Brothers, the Scripture had to be fulfilled ... through the mouth of David concerning Judas, who served as guide for those who arrested Jesus—he was one of our number and shared in this ministry." With the reward he got for his wickedness, Judas bought a field;* **there he fell headlong, his body burst open and all his intestines spilled out.** *(Acts 1: 5-18)*

Despite the fact that some descriptions in the Gospel contradict one another, there is consensus on **the certain disappearance** of Judas Iscariot just after the crucifixion. Judas Iscariot disappeared, because the person who was crucified and killed was Judas Iscariot. Judas Iscariot, who normally looked like Jesus in the physical sense, was made to appear even more like Jesus as a miracle of God. The soldiers were duly mistaken and took him to the crucifix instead of Jesus. Just before this incident, **by God's command, Jesus was taken up to the heavens by angels, into**

120

the Sight of God. For that reason, the officials who came to the room at the crucifixion of Jesus found only Judas Iscariot there.

In the Koran, God says that the plot against Jesus (pbuh) was "thwarted"

It is a known fact that under the leadership of Judas Iscariot, a hypocrite, unbelievers plotted against Jesus. **The purpose of this plot was to kill Jesus.** However, in the Koran **God informs us that the plot against Jesus was thwarted.** If Jesus had, in one way, died, this would mean the unbelievers' plot had worked, and this is impossible, because the promise of God is always fulfilled. **That plot to kill Jesus was thwarted. Jesus did not die and was not murdered.** God informs us of this as follows in the Koran:

> **When Jesus sensed unbelief on their part, he said, "Who will be my helpers to God?" The disciples said, "We are God's helpers. We believe in God. Bear witness that we are Muslims. Our Lord, we have faith in what You have sent down and have followed the Messenger, so write us down among the witnesses." They plotted and God plotted. But God is the best of plotters.** (Koran, 3: 52-54)

If the plots of the unbelievers had succeeded, this would surely be related in the Koran. On the contrary, we know from the Koran that the plots against Jesus came to nothing and that he was raised into the Sight of God.

It is a great blessing for sincere believers that the sly plot against Jesus (pbuh) was thwarted:

Despite very clear evidence, those who insist on the claim that Jesus was killed should think wisely and re-read the Koran with an open mind and keep their minds free of any prejudices. Jesus did

121

not die; he was honorably raised to the heavens. For a sincere Christian, it is pointless to insist on the claim that he was killed. **For a Christian, it is a blessing to know and believe that Jesus did not die, that he was saved from the plots of unbelievers and that he is in our Lord's Sight.** Christians who maintain this are unwilling to forego one of the basic beliefs of Christianity, that Jesus died to redeem Christians' sins. Yet there are various errors on this subject. This will be examined shortly.

Some Christians claim that Muslims object to the belief that Jesus died because they think it is unbecoming for a prophet to suffer. But the reason why Muslims believe as they do is simply because it is so stated in the Koran. The key point that deserves mention here is the following:

Surely God has tested prophets with various afflictions, hardships and trials. As required by the test in this world, He sometimes granted a temporary triumph to unbelievers. But He never let His prophets appear weak in the eyes of unbelievers. This also holds true for Jesus. Believing that Jesus did not die is also good for Christians. Indeed, in the End Times **when he will be sent back to Earth, Christians will see that he has no scars on his palms or feet.** In this age in which we are living, Jesus will come back to Earth with the clothes and belongings he had on 2,000 years ago, and money dating back 2,000 years. These great evidences will make Christians better convinced, by God's leave.

The Christian belief that their sins can be redeemed through the blood of Jesus (pbuh) is a huge error

The belief that Jesus died in order to expiate the sins of all Christians and that death lies at the remission of sins is a grossly mistaken one. In order to see the error in this belief, our Christian brothers need to reconsider God's justice and the purpose behind creation by using their minds and consciences, and to bear in mind the following points:

* The idea that people are born in a state of sin is a violation of God's infinite justice:

Everyone comes to this world to be tested. A person has a responsibility to spend every rational second serving God and living for His approval in the very limited amount of time bestowed on him. God says in one verse of the Koran:

> **He Who created death and life to test which of you is best in action. He is the Almighty, the Ever-Forgiving. (Koran, 67: 2)**

Therefore, a person whom God created from nothing is tested from the moment he enters this world and will be held to account for all he does in it. People's sin or merit is based on the actions they perform in this world. It is impossible, under the law of God, for a baby, unaware even of its own existence, who has not begun to be tested and who has only just opened his eyes on the world, to be in a state of sin.

* It is a violation of the infinite justice of God for a person to assume the sins of another and to suffer for them:

It is impossible in the system of testing created by God for anyone to redeem the sins of anyone else, even if that person is Jesus. Everyone who exists or has ever existed in the world **is responsible only for himself.** Neither his parents nor his relatives nor the Prophet **can assume** responsibility for his sins. **Nobody will be held responsible** for the deeds of anyone else. **Nobody can redeem anyone else.** When the moment of death comes, every individual, Christians included, **will give account, all alone** and in the Presence of God for what they did in this world. God has revealed this to us in the Koran:

> There is no one in the heavens and Earth who will not come to the All-Merciful as a servant. He has counted them and numbered them precisely. Each of them will come to Him on the Day of Rising all alone. (Koran, 19: 93-95)

Almighty God has also revealed in the Koran that nobody will be able to assume the sins of another:

> Say: "Am I to desire other than God as Lord when He is the Lord of all things?" What each self earns is for itself alone. No burden-bearer can bear another's burden. Then you will return to your Lord, and He will inform you regarding the things about which you differed. (Koran, 3: 164)

> ... That no burden-bearer can bear another's burden; that man will have nothing but what he strives for; that his striving will most certainly be seen; that he will then receive repayment of the fullest kind... (Koran, 62: 38-41)

Jesus is God's beloved servant and prophet. Just as there are sincere individuals in all societies and faiths, there are sincere Christians, and there are also ill-intentioned ones. Therefore, it is a terrible violation of good conscience to maintain that God took the soul of a holy servant beloved of Him because of the irresponsible behavior, sins and excesses of some of those who came after him; it is a failure to properly appreciate God. It is a matter of great urgency for our sincere Christian brothers to realize the major error here.

Jesus (pbuh) did not die

Another important point that completely rebuffs the idea in question, as we have seen in detail above, is the fact that Jesus did not die. Jesus was raised into the Presence of God. **He is alive in body and spirit and was protected and taken into the heavens in a state of sleep.** By itself this fact totally rebuffs the claim that "Jesus died as a redeemer of sins."

Those who fail to properly avoid sin by incorrectly imagining that Jesus' death will redeem their sins, who are flexible when it comes to what God has made unlawful, or who do not regard abiding by the obligations imposed by the religion of which they are a member as a matter of importance are making a grave error. Like everyone else, their every deed is written down. And everything they do will be held before them in the hereafter.

Sins are cleansed by repentance and regret, not by death

It is Almighty God Who creates people in this world, determines a destiny for them and also creates the environment of the test. Of course, God is He Who best knows His servants. He has created events and instruments by which they will be tested in this world.

Human beings, on the other hand, are created weak and ignorant. They can easily fall into error, make mistakes, forget the truth despite knowing it very well or unwittingly make a mistake despite having a great fear of God because people are tested in this world. Learning from their mistakes, seeing their weaknesses, repenting of their sins and intending never to repeat them are means whereby a person of good conscience draws closer to God.

This is part of the environment of the test our Lord creates in this world. In creating such a system in the world, Almighty God tells His servants that He is the "Ever-Pardoning, Ever-Forgiving" and opens the doors of repentance to them. God is the most merciful of the merciful. When a person makes a mistake, deliberately or otherwise, when he commits a sin, great or small, he has the privilege of repenting to God and begging His forgiveness.

To claim that death is the repayment for all sins is to fail to grasp and appreciate God's attribute of being very compassionate, merciful and accepting repentance. This claim is in total conflict with the purpose of human beings' existence in this world. Such a claim is also a violation of God's justice and nature of the test. If death were the reward for everyone's sins, and if Almighty God did not forgive people out of His own goodness, then God reveals that the whole world would be devastated:

> **If God were to punish people for their wrong actions, not a single creature would be left upon the Earth, but He defers them till a predetermined time. When their specified time arrives, they cannot delay it for a single hour nor can they bring it forward. (Koran, 16: 61)**

God also reveals in the Koran that human beings have been given great favor because of His sublime mercy and acceptance of repentance:

> **Were it not for God's favor to you and His mercy . . . and that God is Ever-Returning, All-Wise. (Koran, 24: 10)**

The fact that God accepts repentance and forgives sinners is also revealed in the Gospel. It is of the greatest importance for our Christian brothers to consider these true and accurate statements in the Gospel:

> *... **In Whom we have the forgiveness of sins, according to the riches of His grace.** (Ephesians, 1:7-8)*

> *When they heard this, they had no further objections and praised God, saying, **"So then, God has granted even the Gentiles repentance unto life."** (Acts, 11:18)*

> *For He [God] has rescued us from the dominion of darkness... we have redemption, **the forgiveness of sins.** (Colossians, 1:13-14)*

> *If we confess our sins, **He is faithful and just and will forgive us our sins and purify us from all unrighteousness.** (1 John, 1:9)*

126

*And the prayer offered in faith will make the sick person well; the Lord will raise him up. **If he has sinned, he will be forgiven.** (James, 5:15)*

Forgive us our debts, as we also have forgiven our debtors. *And lead us not into temptation, but deliver us from the evil one. For if you forgive men when they sin against you, God will also forgive you. **But if you do not forgive men their sins, your Lord will not forgive your sins.** (Matthew, 6:12-15)*

*He [Jesus] said to them, "When you pray, say: 'God, hallowed be Your name... **Forgive us our sins,** for we also forgive everyone who sins against us. And lead us not into temptation.'" (Luke, 11:2-4)*

*Do not judge, and you will not be judged. Do not condemn, and you will not be condemned. **Forgive, and you will be forgiven.** Give, and it will be given to you. A good measure, pressed down, shaken together and running over, will be poured into your lap. For with the measure you use, it will be measured to you. (Luke, 6:37-38)*

Repent, then, and turn to God, so that your sins may be wiped out, that times of refreshing may come from the Lord... (Acts, 3:19-20)

*... **pray to the Lord. Perhaps He will forgive you for having such a thought in your heart.** (Acts, 8:22)*

To claim that death is the reward for all sins, and that this is His law, when God bestows the blessing of forgiveness on us, opens the doors of repentance and reveals that He is forgiving, loving and accepts repentance may turn out to be a most grave responsibility. In addition, this completely violates God's title of the Forgiver, He Who accepts repentance, in the Gospel. It is very important for genuine Christians to reflect on why this belief has been added on to Christianity and to make the appropriate decision by the use of their conscience.

It Is a Major Inconsistency for Christianity to Claim To Be a Religion of Love and Also to Espouse the Idea That Sin Is Cleansed with Death

All Christians maintain that Christianity is a religion of love and act in the name of love. It is of course true that Christianity is a true religion sent down by God, and that applies to all the other Divine faiths. Almighty God wants love from His servants, and true love is only possible through genuinely loving God – scrupulously abiding by all our Lord's commandments and prohibitions.

But this fact conflicts with the mistaken belief held by some Christians that death redeems sins. God is He Who loves His servants and wants to forgive them. God reveals in the Koran that:

> He is the Ever-Forgiving, the All-Loving, (Koran, 85: 14)

> God desires to turn towards you, but those who pursue their lower appetites desire to make you deviate completely. (Koran, 4: 27)

The fact that our Lord is loving and forgiving is revealed as follows in the Gospel:

> ... *The Lord is full of compassion and mercy. (James, 5:11)*

> *But because of His great love for us, God, Who is rich in mercy, made us alive—it is by grace you have been saved. (Ephesians, 2:4-5)*

> *And we know that in all things God works for the good of those who love Him, who have been called according to His purpose. (Romans, 8:28)*

> *But when the kindness and love of God appeared, He saved us, not because of righteous things we had done, but because of His mercy. (Titus, 3:4-5)*

*Dear friends, **since God so loved us,** we also ought to love one another. (1 John, 4:11)*

It is very important that our Christian brothers should fully understand these sublime attributes of Almighty God, Who loves His servants, protects and watches over them, feels affection for them and forgives and pardons them. That is because only people who can properly comprehend the titles of God can see what a grave danger the error in question poses.

Christians Are Responsible for Their Every Deed, at Every Moment of Their Lives, and They Will All Be Called to Account in the Presence of God

Like everyone who has ever lived, is living now or will ever live in the future, Christians will also be called to account for their actions. **None of their sins have been redeemed.** Just like everyone else, all Christians are responsible individually for their actions and will be repaid for all their sins and good deeds on the Day of Reckoning. Nobody will be able to say, in the Presence of God, "My sins have been paid for already, and have been cleansed by the blood of Jesus (pbuh)." Nobody in the Presence of God will be able to claim he is free of sin, and nobody will attain salvation only by saying, "I had faith." On the Day of Reckoning, a book in which all his deeds are written will be placed before every individual, and all he did will be laid open.

No matter how much some Christians think that their sins have already been expiated, and no matter how much they seek to avoid their responsibilities before God, they will be unable to avoid the Day of Reckoning. The false belief they espouse in this world is invalid in the Sight of God. It is therefore of the greatest importance for devout Christians to be warned on this subject and see the truth. This is essential for their happiness and positions in the hereafter.

Indications from the Koran that Bestow a Special Status on Jesus (pbuh)

We must not forget that information or statements about Jesus in the Koran are **not revealed** in the context of the other prophets.

• The word **tawaffa** (taking away of the soul) is not used for the death of any other prophet.

• No other prophet is described as **having been taught the books of the three revealed faiths as set out in the words "... I taught you the Book and Wisdom, and the Torah and the Gospel..."** (Koran, 5:110).

• No prophet is described as **"He is a Sign of the Hour."** (Koran, 43: 61)

• No prophet is described as having ascended in the way that Jesus ascended into the skies.

• Of no other prophet are we told that **"I will place the people who follow you above those who are unbelievers until the Day of Resurrection."** (Koran, 3: 55)

• Of no prophet is it revealed that **"There is not one of the People of the Book who will not believe in him before he dies."** (Koran, 4:159)

These are all evidence that God **appointed Jesus a special destiny,** in line with which **Jesus is alive in the Presence of God and will return to Earth again.**

The Prophet Jesus (pbuh) did not die. He is at this moment in the Presence of God. It is revealed that this blessed prophet will return to Earth in these times, the End Times, and **he has been sent. He is living on Earth now and awaiting the time to appear.** The time when all believers will embrace Jesus with love is close at hand. All these explanatory statements are directed toward our Christian brothers so they can prepare for this excellent time. Those Christian brothers and sisters who read this book must bear this very important fact in mind.

CHAPTER 4
CHRISTIAN ERRORS ON THE SUBJECT OF FEAR AND LOVE OF GOD

In Genuine Faith, Love of God Is Experienced together with Fear of God

The basis of all righteous religions is love. In time, some people who appear in the name of God, and strive to manipulate religion, sometimes promote terror, war, massacre and lovelessness in the name of religion. Albeit they claim to advocate religion, these people are definitely ignorant and imposters, because God does not desire any wrongdoing or strife; rather He desires love, friendship, and peace for His servants.

The purpose of the information here is this: some Christians depict their faith as a religion of love while they consider Judaism, and especially Islam, as religions based on fear. However, this is a serious error. All true religions, especially Islam, preach love, friendship, and call people to peace and brotherhood, for these are what God demands from us. Those who propose any other conception are lying in the name of true religion. The essence and basis of religion is love. (You can find statements of ours on the subject of Islam being a religion of love in the pages that follow.)

Surely, our Christian brothers are right in believing in the purity of love. However, some of them interpret the concept of love in a desperate and erroneous way. It is a great danger for these people to eliminate fear of God from their lives on the basis of the idea that fear has no place in love.

The actual meaning of fear of God

Before explaining the kinds of danger that may result from misconceptions on this subject, it is of great importance to understand what the "fear of God" really is. The majority of people misunderstand the meaning of the fear of God, and also claim that fear results in involuntary faith, which would render that faith invalid. However, this is not what fear of God means.

The fear of God is to submit to God with awe, with a fear that is derived from deep and abiding respect. Meanwhile, one should avoid any attitude or thought with which God will not be pleased solely due to one's deep love of God. It is a fear of losing the love of God. **For a believer, to lose the friendship of God is an even worse pain than the sufferings of hell.**

Love of God and fear of God are part of a single whole. Fear and love of God become one when a person who loves God very deeply fears committing an act that will offend God. This is actually the "fear of God" that a person who loves God experiences. A person who truly loves God remains loyal to Him with passion, affection, and loves no matter what conditions he may be under or how much hardship he may undergo. No conditions, occurrences or hardships can overshadow it or hinder it. Fear of losing the love of God constantly motivates a person who experiences the love of God: It gives him joy. It is impossible for such a person to be careless in performing his acts of worship, to intentionally have any flaws in his role as servant or to recklessly engage in unlawful deeds. Throughout his life, a person of such sincere faith will do his best to please God.

The necessity of God's wrath on unbelievers

The Avenger, one of the names of God, is misinterpreted or intentionally distorted by some people. The wrath of God is only upon cruel people, hypocrites, those who commit fraud in the name of God and furious unbelievers. To believers, on the other hand, God gives a sense of full security and ease. In one verse of the Koran, God gives the news that there will be no fear for those who believe, including Christians:

> **Those who have faith and those who are Jews and the Sabaeans and the Christians, all who have faith in God and the Last Day and act rightly will feel no fear and will know no sorrow. (Koran, 5:69)**

A person remains immune from God's wrath as long as he serves God and strives to earn His good pleasure. God takes revenge only on those who are cruel. This is the law of God. A human is in deep fear of God's wrath only when he acts wrongly. However, when he engages in good deeds and strives to earn God's good pleasure, he trusts in God and his conscience remains at ease.

The attribute of God described in the title *the Avenger* is a great blessing for believers. For instance, seeing that a person who mistreats a little girl and then murders her is punished in the hereafter and thus seeing the manifestation of God's justice is a great blessing for a believer. This repayment a cruel person receives in the hereafter is also a great blessing for the child who was mistreated. That is why, in the same way that paradise is a blessing for believers, so hell is where cruel people are punished. Both paradise and hell are the places where God's infinite justice is manifested in the hereafter. Those who strive to oppress prophets,

134

those who betrayed Jesus (pbuh), or murdered innocent children and others have been - and will be - repaid by our Lord as a requisite of His beautiful name, the Avenger. The opportunity to repent is surely available to each one of them in this world. However, repayment of those who are arrogant and do not repent is a relief for those who are exposed to cruelty and those who see such things happening. Consequently, the Avenger title of God brings joy to a person of faith who has a conscience.

Mercy is a subject that must be very well evaluated. It is God Who teaches us mercy. If God so willed, nobody on Earth might know of such a feeling. All people would live bereft of the feeling of mercy. It is therefore the height of ignorance and a crime to seek to produce as evidence against God something that He has created and teaches, or to have the effrontery to seek to teach mercy to Him [may God forbid]. God is infinitely merciful. **It is Almighty God Who best knows** how people's natures are created, and **who deserves mercy and who merits punishment.** Nobody will suffer the slightest injustice in the hereafter. God is infinitely just, and everyone will be justly judged in the hereafter. Some passages from the Gospel that refer to our Lord's infinite justice are as follows:

> *When they hurled their insults at him, he did not retaliate; when he suffered, he made no threats. Instead, he entrusted himself to Him Who judges justly. (1 Peter 2: 23)*

> *Anyone who does wrong will be repaid for his wrong, and there is no favoritism. (Colossians, 3:25)*

> *There will be trouble and distress for every human being who does evil... but glory, honor and peace for everyone who does good... For God does not show favoritism. (Romans, 2: 9-11)*

> *God "will repay each person according to what he has done." To those who by persistence in doing good seek glory, honor and immortality, He will give eternal life. But for those who are self-seeking and who reject the truth and follow evil, there will be wrath and anger. (Romans, 2:6-8)*

135

God is not unjust [God is surely beyond that]; He will not forget your work and the love you have shown Him as you have helped His people and continue to help them. (Hebrews, 6:10)

God reveals thus in the Koran:

We will set up the Just Balance on the Day of Resurrection, and <u>no self will be wronged in any way.</u> Even if it is no more than the weight of a grain of mustard-seed, We will produce it. We are sufficient as a Reckoner. (Koran, 21:47)

If every self that did wrong possessed everything on Earth, it would offer it as a ransom (as a provision for wrath). They will conceal remorse when they see the punishment. <u>Everything will be decided between them justly. They will not be wronged.</u> (Koran, 10:54)

Fear of God is essential in order to be a good servant of God and to deserve paradise

What is explained above are great facts that motivate a person of faith. The outlook of a person who really loves God and thus seriously fears of having any flaws in his role as a servant of God is totally different from of that other people. Such a person does not commit unlawful deeds and does not neglect acts of worship or remain heedless to the voice of his conscience. In brief, he remains extraordinarily meticulous in everything he does in order to earn God's good pleasure. Such a person is scrupulous, not egotistical, and until the end of his life, he remains self-sacrificing and compassionate. Such a person never does any harm to others, and greatly fears doing something for which he will not be able to account to God. He lives every moment of his life aware that he will account to God for his actions and that God watches him every moment. Aware that the real life is not in the life of this world but in the hereafter, he feels the joy and fervor of loving God. This fervor in no way abates until the end of his life. **Therefore, a person who has a fear of God lives in abundance and blessings.**

In the Gospel, fear of God is described in the following words and thus Christians are called to have fear of God:

> ... *live out your time as foreigners here* <u>*in reverent fear*</u> *[of God]. (1 Peter, 1:17)*

> *Since, then, we know what it is to* <u>*fear the Lord*</u>*, we try to persuade others. What we are is plain to God, and I hope it is also plain to your conscience. (2 Corinthians 5:11)*

> ... *Your wrath has come. The time has come for judging the dead, and* <u>*for rewarding Your servants*</u> *the prophets and Your people* <u>*who revere Your Name*</u>*, both great and small—and for destroying those who destroy the Earth. (Revelation 11:18)*

> ... <u>*let us be thankful, and so worship God acceptably with reverence and awe.*</u> *(Hebrews 12:28)*

If a person is not in awe of being a good servant to God, and he claims to have love of God but does little to nothing to earn God's good pleasure, yet still asserts that merely his love of God suffices for deliverance in the hereafter, then that person is making a grave error. Such an idea is not compatible with the sincerity God asks for. Fear of God is the most basic element that encourages man in being a better servant to God. Therefore, someone who regards fear of God as unnecessary (surely God is beyond that) and who thinks that love of God alone is sufficient will not live in a state of fear and hope. That will prevent that person from constantly striving to earn God's approval and mercy, and constantly lead him to sloth.

This is the position of some Christians who reject the importance of having fear of God, and simply maintain that love of God is sufficient. Consequently, these people need to reflect once again over the meaning of the fear of God in the manner as it is described above and to abide by the call of the Gospel, that is, "[to] worship God acceptably with reverence and awe."

CHAPTER 5
THE ERROR THAT THOSE WHO BELIEVE JESUS (PBUH) TO BE DIVINE WILL GO TO PARADISE

True Believers Are Tested by Difficulties

Many Christians who believe in the error of the Trinity also without any hesitation believe implicitly that they will go to paradise. According to that erroneous belief, it is enough to believe in the divinity of Jesus (God is beyond this) in order to go to paradise. This false idea certainly has no place in true Christianity and is one of those subsequently set out by the Church; but Christians think they have to go definitely along with this erroneous belief because of sanctions and pressure from the Church. Christians therefore believe that Jesus was crucified in redemption of all their sins and that popes or priests can forgive their sins. They fall into the error of believing that this belief will save them and they will definitely go to paradise. According to these Christians, if there is to be punishment in the hereafter, it is only for those who deny the divinity of Jesus (surely God is beyond that).

The statements that follow are directed toward those Christians who have fallen into this error:

We would like to ask those Christians who hold that belief the following questions:

- In that case, why is there a test? Why are people tested?

- Why are difficulties, disasters, atheism, communism, lovelessness, murder, war, earthquakes, hurricanes and death created?

- Why are some things lawful or unlawful?

- What is the basis of good and evil?

- Is the purpose of this world to sit, eat, drink and wait for death, saying that Jesus is divine?

- What about striving for God's approval, suffering troubles, restraining one's earthly desires and being patient in the face of difficulties, sickness and tribulations?

- Since it is so easy to attain paradise, what need is there to practice such virtues as loyalty, altruism, forgiveness, consideration, friendship and protectiveness?

- What place does the struggle against perils such as atheism, irreligion and communism occupy in this belief?

- Are religious obligations involved in this belief?

- Does one have to strive for God's approval under this belief?

Of course God would not create such a faith.

It is a law of God that there is a reason for the creation on Earth. Almighty God reveals this purpose in the Koran:

He Who created death and life <u>to test which of you is best in action.</u> He is the Almighty, the Ever-Forgiving. (Koran, 57:2)

140

The Gospel also reveals that Christians must be in a constant state of striving and hope:

We want each of you to show this same diligence to the very end, so that what you hope for may be fully realized. We do not want you to become lazy, but to imitate those who through faith and patience inherit what has been promised. (Hebrews, 6:11-12)

Therefore, my dear friends, ... continue to work out your salvation... (Philippians, 2:12)

For this very reason, make every effort to add to your faith goodness; and to goodness, knowledge; and to knowledge, self-control; and to self-control, perseverance; and to perseverance, godliness; and to godliness, mutual affection; and to mutual affection, love. (2 Peter 1:5-7)

"We must go through many hardships to enter the kingdom of God [paradise]," they said. (Acts, 14:22)

The purpose behind our creation is to be tested; this test distinguishes between those people who live for God and unbelievers. As it is stated in the verse, everyone will be tested in terms of behavior and good deeds, and those who pass the test will go to paradise.

The wisdom behind the difficulties in this world is revealed thus in the Gospel:

See what this Godly sorrow [the difficulties that you face as a test from God] has produced in you: what earnestness, what eagerness to clear yourselves.... (2 Corinthians, 7:11)

The test in this world is challenging. That is why the prophets were also confronted by difficulties. That is why they were **threatened with death, exiled from their homes or wrongfully imprisoned.** Everyone who preaches for God's approval, who describes the existence of God, who opposes all the irreligious trends currently prevailing across the world, will face similar problems. Everyone who believes in God, who speaks of His might

141

and greatness will undergo the difficulties of the test. In this way, they exhibit sincerity toward God. **Loving God and being determined to worship Him, regardless of the difficulties, makes a person truly devout.** This sincerity and love of God are proved by this determination and fortitude. Therefore, the determinant of faith is to face difficulties for God's sake, to make no concessions in worshiping Him, no matter what the prevailing conditions, and **to live for God, not for this world.**

Someone who lives for God is not looking for ease in this world. On the contrary, he knows he will face troubles. He knows he will be tested by trials and tribulations. He believes this is how he will display his sincerity toward God. This is an explicit truth that God sets out in the Koran:

> **Or did you suppose that you would enter the Garden without facing the same as those who came before you? <u>Poverty and illness afflicted them</u> and they were shaken to the point that the Messenger and those who believed with him said, "When is God's help coming?" Be assured that God's help is very near. (Koran, 2:214)**

Since Jesus (pbuh) is a prophet and one who preaches the word, he encountered difficulties because he called on people to believe in God. This is revealed in several passages from the Gospel:

> *At once the Spirit sent him [Jesus] out into the wilderness, and he was in the wilderness forty days, <u>enduring temptations from satan.</u> He was with the wild animals, and angels attended him. (Mark, 1:12-13)*

> *Instead he went out and began to talk freely, spreading the news. As a result, <u>Jesus could no longer enter a town openly but stayed outside in lonely places.</u> Yet the people still came to him from everywhere. (Mark, 1: 45)*

> *Then Jesus entered a house, and again a crowd gathered, so that he and his disciples were not even able to eat. When his family heard about this, they went to take charge of him, for they said, <u>"He is out of his mind." And the</u>*

teachers of the law who came down from Jerusalem said, "He is possessed by Beelzebub! By the prince of demons he is driving out demons." (Mark, 3: 20-22)

"Isn't this the carpenter? Isn't this Mary's son and the brother of James, Joseph, Judas and Simon? Aren't his sisters here with us?" And they took offense at him. Jesus said to them, "A prophet is not without honor except in his own town, among his relatives and in his own home." (Mark, 6: 3-4)

... "and the Son of Man will be delivered over to the chief priests and the teachers of the law. They will condemn him to death and will hand him over to the Gentiles, who will mock him ...." (Mark, 10: 33-34)

Now the Passover and the Festival of Unleavened Bread were only two days away, and the chief priests and the teachers of the law were scheming to arrest Jesus secretly and kill him. "But not during the festival," they said, "or the people may riot." (Mark, 14:1-2)

The chief priests and the whole Sanhedrin were looking for evidence against Jesus so that they could put him to death, but they did not find any. Many testified falsely against him, but their statements did not agree. (Mark, 14: 55-56)

But Jesus, knowing their evil intent, said, "You hypocrites, why are you trying to trap me?" (Matthew, 22:18)

Then the chief priests and the elders of the people assembled in the palace of the high priest, whose name was Caiaphas, and they schemed to arrest Jesus secretly and kill him. (Matthew, 26: 3-4)

The Gospel also describes the situation of the disciples who accepted all kinds of risks for the sake of God:

"I tell you the truth," Jesus replied, "no one who has left home or brothers or sisters or mother or father or children or fields for me [for the approval of God] and the Gospel [God's commandments] will fail to receive a hundred

143

times as much in this present age (homes, brothers, sisters, mothers, children and fields—and with them, persecutions) and in the age to come, eternal life. But many who are first will be last, and the last first." (Mark, 10:29-31)

[Jesus said:] And <u>everyone who has left houses or brothers or sisters or father or mother or wife or children or fields</u> for my sake [for the approval of God] will receive a hundred times as much and will inherit eternal life. But many who are first will be last, and many who are last will be first. (Matthew 19:30-31)

... <u>Those who suffer according to God's will</u> should commit themselves to their faithful Creator and continue to do good. (1 Peter, 4:19)

[Jesus:] "You must be on your guard. <u>You will be handed over to the local councils and flogged</u>... On account of me [because you obey me to gain God's good pleasure] <u>you will stand before governors and kings as witnesses to them.</u> And the Gospel [God's commandments] must first be preached to all nations. Whenever you are arrested and brought to trial, do not worry beforehand about what to say. Just say whatever is given you at the time, for it is not you speaking, but the Spirit of God. <u>Brother will betray brother to death, and a father his child. Children will rebel against their parents and have them put to death. All men will hate you</u> because of me [because you obey me to gain God's good pleasure], but he who stands firm to the end will be saved." (Mark, 13:9-13)

"But before all this, they will lay hands on you and persecute you. <u>They will deliver you to... prisons,</u> and you will be brought before kings and governors, and all on account of my name [because you obey me for the approval of God]... You will be betrayed even by parents, brothers, relatives and friends, and they will put some of you to death. Everyone will hate you because of me [because you obey me for the approval of God]. But not a

144

hair of your head will perish. Stand firm, and you will win life." (Luke, 21:12-19)

On that day a great persecution broke out against the church at Jerusalem... Saul <u>began to destroy the church. Going from house to house, he dragged off men and women and put them in prison.</u> Those who had been scattered preached the word wherever they went. (Acts, 8:1-4)

[Prophets] who through faith conquered kingdoms, administered justice, and gained what was promised; who shut the mouths of lions, quenched the fury of the flames, and escaped the edge of the sword; whose weakness was turned to strength; and who became powerful in battle and routed foreign armies... <u>Others were tortured and refused to be released, so that they might gain a better resurrection [in the hereafter]. Some faced jeers and flogging, while still others were chained and put in prison. They were stoned; they were sawed in two; they were put to death by the sword. They went about in sheepskins and goatskins, destitute, persecuted and mistreated—the world was not worthy of them. They wandered in deserts and mountains, and in caves and holes in the ground.</u> (Hebrews, 11:33-38)

[Jesus:] "All this I have told you so that you will not go astray... in fact, a time is coming when <u>anyone who kills you will think he is offering a service to God.</u> They will do such things because they have not known God or me. I have told you this, so that when the time comes you will remember that I warned you..." (John, 16:1-4)

(For other passages from the Gospel on the subject see *Pleasant Words from the Gospel, chapter 17, Harun Yahya*)

What the Gospel and the Koran tell us is this: since believers have faith, and preach and follow the path of God;

* They are killed

145

- They are exiled
- They hear harsh words
- They are put on trial
- They are often imprisoned
- They are beaten and tortured
- They are beaten with whips and chains
- They are accused by false witnesses
- They live in poverty
- They are accused of madness
- They are rejected and even killed by their families
- They live up in the mountains or in caves or underground
- They are hated
- And they suffer

These are attributes of believers according to the Gospel. Prophets and true believers have lived like that; they were tested and suffered. That all happened solely because they believed in God and made no concessions in their faith. This means that a believer is someone who undergoes hardships for God's sake and is harshly tested.

That is why we love all the prophets. We also love the disciples and companions for that reason. They showed the depth of their faith, their love of God and their desire to live for God's approval and that they desired the hereafter, not this world. And that is why they have been rewarded with the finest mansions of paradise.

That is true faith. It is a fact revealed by God in the three Divine books and proved in the lives of the prophets. True faith does not mean sitting at home saying how much one loves God. Those who claim to love God must know the content of faith.

The Idea That "If You Believe Jesus (pbuh) Is Divine You Will Go to Paradise" Is Very Dangerous

How evangelists and many other Christian churches that espouse belief in the Trinity conceive of the hereafter is very mistaken. Under such a belief, there is no need for an intellectual struggle for God's sake. There is no need to strive against such irreligious tendencies as atheism, Darwinism and communism. There is no need for worship. In that person's own eyes, he has already long since gained God's approval; all he needs to do is go to church once a week and indeed, some people see no need even to do that. There is no conception of facing difficulties for God's sake in such a belief. That person will not enter into places and subjects where difficulties are going to be encountered. There is nothing in such an environment that conflicts with a person's earthly desires, that requires sacrifices for God or that requires the exhibition of patience, loyalty, determination and steadfastness before God. The person lives for this world, in this world. He never encounters anything that will trouble his desires, family or life; even if he is cruel or sinful, he still thinks he will go to paradise because he believes Jesus (pbuh) is divine. And in such a religious conception, this is regarded as sufficient.

Of course, we need to exclude some Christians here. Certainly, not all Christians hold this belief. This is directed solely toward those Christians who espouse the idea of the Trinity and have an erroneous conception of paradise.

There is no system of justice in such an erroneous conception of religion. There is no distinction between wrongdoers and those who do good for God. The only distinction between people is based on whether they believe in the Trinity or not. Even if someone who has suffered for God all his life, who has done good and spent his life making sacrifices for Him, the moment he rejects the idea of the Trinity, then according to this belief he will go to hell.

Our call to our sincere Christian brothers is this:

Various additions and innovations have been made to all the true faiths over the course of time. Various groups have attempted to corrupt them all. Those who make such additions to Christianity are not true believers so to blindly follow these additions may end in terrible regret. Sincere Christians need to find the true path by becoming acquainted with God, obeying the true words of the Gospel and making resort to good conscience, faith and reason.

Being religious requires a fear of God. Religious observances can be performed with joy and without concessions through a fear of God based on love of Him. One can display fortitude in the face of troubles and spend every moment of one's life for God. **A devout believer's life will change.** True believers live with God. Their lives are thus different to those of the majority of people. Of course, devout people too enjoy the blessings of this world in the very finest way, but they have no worldly expectations. Trials and difficulties do not upset them; they know that, like all goodness, troubles also come from God. They give more thanks with difficulties, and are made stronger by them. This fact is revealed as follows in the Gospel:

> *<u>Consider it pure joy,</u> my brothers and sisters, <u>whenever you face trials of many kinds,</u> because you know that <u>the testing of your faith produces perseverance.</u> Let perseverance finish its work so that you may be mature and complete, not lacking anything. (James, 1:2-4)*

> *[You] who through faith are shielded by God's power until the coming of the salvation that is ready to be revealed in the last time. In all this <u>you greatly rejoice, though now for a little while you may have had to suffer grief in all kinds of trials.</u> These have come so that <u>the proven genuineness of your faith</u>—of greater worth than gold, which perishes even though refined by fire—<u>may result in praise, glory and honor</u>... Though you have not seen him*

148

[the Messiah], you love him [for the sake of God]; and even though you do not see him now, you believe in him [as a prophet of God] and are filled with an inexpressible and glorious joy, for you are receiving the end result of your faith, the salvation of your souls. (1 Peter, 1:5-9)

That is why those who love God are strong enough to do anything for Him at any moment. Love of God involves determination, persistence, perseverance and moral virtue. It requires self-sacrifice. Therefore, **paradise can only be attained through striving for it.** It is only possible by pleasing God, living for Him, persevering in the test and, when necessary, turning one's back on all worldly things, especially life and possessions, for His sake.

"Blessed are you when people insult you, persecute you and falsely say all kinds of evil against you because of me [obeying me to please God]. Rejoice and be glad, because great is your reward in heaven [hereafter], for in the same way they persecuted the prophets who were before you." (Matthew, 5:11-12)

Those who will not be disappointed in the hereafter, be they Christian, Jew or Muslims, **are those who believe in God the One and Only** and who do good works. This is revealed as follows in the Koran:

> **Those who believe, those who are Jews, and the Christians and Sabaeans, all who believe in God and the Last Day and act rightly, will have their reward with their Lord. They will feel no fear and will know no sorrow. (Koran, 2:62)**

> **Those who believe and those who are Jews and the Sabaeans and the Christians, all who believe in God and the Last Day and act rightly will feel no fear and will know no sorrow. (Koran, 5:69)**

If sincere Christians continue to believe, may God forbid, that thinking that Jesus (pbuh) is divine will cause the gates of paradise to open up for them, and to maintain a belief in the Trinity, then

149

this may lead them to suffering a regret in the hereafter they never imagined in their lives. For that reason, Christians who believe in the Trinity must heed the warnings given throughout this book, revise their life styles in the light of the conditions for faith set out by God that are pleasing to Him and seek to grasp what true faith really is. Of course, as we stated at the beginning of this book, the prerequisite for true faith is to believe in **God, the One and Only**.

A reminder is called for here; this reminder is intended solely for the good of our Christian brothers. Such a reminder is clearly not intended to benefit anyone else. Everyone is responsible for his own actions in the hereafter. But such a reminder is required as a religious obligation because Muslims are commanded in the Koran to "command what is good and forbid what is evil."

In this book, some of our Christian brothers may be reading facts they have never heard before. When Jesus appears again, that holy prophet will tell our Christian brothers of these terrible errors they have fallen into and the additions that have been included in Christianity at later dates. All these things are written in the Koran, which was sent to complete and confirm the Gospel and the Torah, and is therefore a holy scripture for Christians and Jews as well as Muslims. As we show with numerous examples in this book, many passages from the Gospel that are compatible with the Koran confirm these. Therefore, our Christian brothers must act in line with reason and good conscience. They must spend this valuable period by striving hard to replace the oppression, disorder, suffering and difficulties in the world with peace, brotherhood and love. They must not forget that only in this way can they enjoy a fine reward in the hereafter.

CHAPTER 6
SOME CHRISTIANS' ERROR REGARDING ARMAGEDDON

The End Times Is When the Corruption of the Antichrist Will Take Place

We are now living in the End Times. This important period is the last time before the Day of Judgment. This blessed age is described in detail in the hadiths of our Prophet (pbuh) and in passages from the Gospel and the Torah. This period before the Day of Judgment, the End Times, will be when the corruption of the antichrist, disasters, oppression, disorder and unhappiness, slaughter, war, degeneration, economic crises, material collapse, terror and violence will all reach the most intense levels and all people will seek a savior from them. A great many people will spread evil in this time, will tend to forget God and religious observances and will seek false solutions to problems through war, slaughter and evil, and will cause all manner of disorder and corruption.

With the spread of the corruption of the antichrist in the End Times, disasters being visited on societies and people begging God for a savior, our Lord will send us the holy individuals of the End

Times. These holy personages are Jesus (pbuh) and Hazrat Mahdi (pbuh). With their coming, peace will descend on the earth, the corruption of the antichrist will disappear and there will come a Golden Age, the like of which has never been seen before. Wars will come to an end in this time, not a drop of blood will be shed, there will be no use for guns and other weapons, and nobody will be oppressed any more. Hazrat Mahdi will bring an environment of peace to the world.

He will rule with justice and not so much as wake anyone who is asleep. This great and important truth is revealed thus in the hadiths of our Prophet (pbuh):

> People will seek refuge in Hazrat Mahdi as honeybees cluster around their sovereign. He will fill the world that was once full of cruelty with justice. His justice will be as such that he will not wake a sleeping person or even shed one drop of blood. The world almost turns to the time of the Age of Bliss. (Ibn Hajar al-Haythami, Al-Qawl al-Mukhtasar fi `Alamat al-Mahdi al-Muntadhar, pp. 29 and 48)

> In his [Hazrat Mahdi's] time no one will be woken up from their sleep or have a bleeding nose. (Ibn Hajar al-Haythami, Al-Qawl al-Mukhtasar fi `Alamat al-Mahdi al-Muntadhar, p. 44)

> Those swearing allegiance to him [Hazrat Mahdi] will swear allegiance between Rock and Pillar (around Ka'bah). They never wake a sleeping person, never shed blood. (Ibn Hajar al-Haythami, Al-Qawl al-Mukhtasar fi `Alamat al-Mahdi al-Muntadhar, p. 24)

There will be no war in the time of Hazrat Mahdi (pbuh):

> The (components of) battle will abandon its load (arms and equipment). (Sunan Ibn Majah, 10/334)

(The components of) war will abandon its load (namely, arms and the like). (Al-Sharani, Mukhtasar Tazkirah al-Qurtubi, p. 496)

He will do away with enmity and hatred... The world will be filled with peace as a bowl is filled with water. There will be unity of religion, and none other than God will thenceforth be worshiped. War will also relinquish its burden. (Sunan Ibn Majah, 10/334)

There will be no more enmity between anyone. And all enmity, conflict and envy will disappear. (Ash-Sharani, Mukhtasar Tazkirah al-Qurtubi, p. 496)

All evils will disappear and be replaced by goodness in the time of Hazrat Mahdi (pbuh):

Through Hazrat Mahdi's love, compassion, moral virtue and profound faith, his time will be one when "the goodness of good people increases, and even the wicked are treated well." (Al-Muttaqi al-Hindi, Al-Burhan fi Alamat al-Mahdi Akhir az-Zaman, p. 17)

Earth will be filled with peace just like water fills the pot. No hostility will remain and all hostilities, quarrels, envy will absolutely vanish. (Sahih Muslim, 1/136)

The Torah also reveals that wars will come to an end in the time of Hazrat Mahdi (pbuh):

.. In the last days... He [the Lord]... will settle disputes for many peoples... Nation will not take up sword against nation, nor will they train for war anymore. (Isaiah, 2:2-4; Micah, 4:1-3)

I will take away the chariots from Ephraim and the warhorses from Jerusalem, and the battle bow will be broken.... (Zechariah, 9:10)

In that Era [in the era of Hazrat Mahdi]... there will be no starvation or war, jealousy or enmity... (Maimonides, Mishnah Torah, Laws of Kings 12:5)

... Bow and sword and battle I will abolish from the land, so that all may lie down in safety. (Hosea, 2:18)

... I will grant peace in the land, and you will lie down and no one will make you afraid... and the sword will not pass through your country. (Leviticus, 26:5-6)

... "Burn them [the weapons] up—the small and large shields, the bows and arrows, the war clubs and spears... They will use them for fuel"... declares the Sovereign Lord. (Ezekiel, 39:9-10)

... They will beat their swords into plowshares and their spears into pruning hooks.... (Isaiah 2:4; Micah, 4:3)

There will therefore be no more bloodshed and no more wars in the time of Hazrat Mahdi (pbuh) and Jesus (pbuh). The corruption of the antichrist will have come to an end. Peace will come to the nations of the world. Nobody will seek war in that time; that is because the main reasons for war - superstitious ideas, the Darwinist-materialist mindset and the self-interest, selfishness and soullessness that this mindset brings with it - will have disappeared.

The radical faith and ideologies that turn people away from true devotion, and thus the mindset underlying violence and lovelessness, will also disappear. The Golden Age that will take place with the appearance of Jesus and the Mahdi will be the happiest, most comfortable, most peaceful and most plentiful period ever. The Mahdi is alive and Jesus has descended. We now await the appearance of these two blessed personages. Both are currently engaged in an intellectual struggle against the corruption of the antichrist secretly or openly. When they appear we will be

154

heading directly toward peace and comfort. Before that, however, we are told of a time when corruption and war afflict the whole world. The time we are living in is the time of corruption and conflict preceeding the appearance of the Mahdi and Jesus.

Some Evangelicals believe that a war known as Armageddon will take place in the future in the Middle East, and specifically in Mesopotamia. Their worst error lies in the fact that Armageddon has long since broken out in the Middle East, and is still continuing.

The sinister objectives behind the scenarios of Armageddon

Some Christians claim that blood reaching as high as horses' halters will be shed during Armageddon, which is reported in the Gospel to take place in the time of the coming of the Messiah (pbuh). They say that there will be a time of disaster lasting seven years, that during the war in question - which is expected to take place in the near future - three-quarters of the Jews and all Muslims will be slaughtered, that Israel and part of the Middle East will be totally devastated, and that all these things are portents of the coming of Jesus (pbuh).

According to these terrifying scenarios, as long as the Jews cannot win the war against Muslims known as Armageddon, Jesus will not return to Earth. For that reason, some Christians regard it as essential for there to be a major war - and for that war to be won by the Jews - in order for Jesus to return to Earth. Then when the war is over, all Jews apart from 144,000 who believe in Jesus are expected to be killed. They believe that as a result of these bloody wars, all Muslims and almost all Jews will be annihilated, and that only those Christians loyal to Jesus and those 144,000 elect Jews will be saved.

The Evangelical Christians in question completely misinterpret the battle of Armageddon that the Gospel foretells will take place in the End Times and describes in some detail. In their view, turmoil needs to be created in the same region in order for this great future war to happen, for the shaping of the Middle East and in order to accelerate the coming of this war and therefore of Jesus. They maintain that the constant bloodshed in the Middle East, brother fighting brother and unending tension are all essential for the coming of Jesus. They are making preparations for a savagery in the End Times in which blood will flow in rivers, that will involve the Southeast of Turkey, Iraq and Syria and extending as far as the Middle East and in which, according to their belief, Muslims and most Jews will be annihilated. For a great many Evangelical Christians, this expectation of bloodshed has become an indispensable aim and an objective that grows stronger by the day. That is because, under their superstitious belief, the region needs to be drowned in blood as a matter of urgency and Armageddon needs to take place if Jesus is to appear.

As a result of this dreadful expectation, rather than attempting to eliminate war, conflict and disagreements, some evangelical Christians **support policies that literally encourage bloodshed and even incite war.** They foolishly describe this savagery as birth pangs and believe that they need to support that savagery for the coming of Jesus.

Yet these Christians are making a very great error. Armageddon has already begun in the Middle East, and is still raging. The 2003 Iraq War was the beginning of this great war, known as Armageddon in the Bible, a sign of the End Times described with all the relevant portents in the hadiths and the Torah. Ever since that date the conflict in the Middle East has been unending and Muslim blood has constantly been shed, and is still being spilled today. The numbers of Muslims martyred can be put in the millions, and the great majority of Muslim countries are wracked by conflict, civil strife, turmoil and terror. The Armageddon anticipated by the Evangelicals has therefore been raging in the Middle East since 2003. This war has been taking place over a long period of time. There is therefore no great war that will occur in the future other than the one currently taking place in the Middle East. The expectation of an even greater war in the future is leading the Christians in question into a number of errors concerning the Middle East.

The ironic part is that some Christians who seek to portray Muslims as being in favor of war and slaughter and themselves as supporting peace and love actually harbor such an excited expectation of war. According to Islamic belief, however, **it is the Muslim Prophet Muhammad (pbuh) who foretells that there will be no wars in the time of the Mahdi (pbuh)**, who will appear immediately before the coming of Jesus (pbuh) in the End Times and who will bring about the global reign of Islamic moral values together with Jesus. In other words, in stark contrast to global Christian propaganda, it is Islam that pictures an End Times favoring peace, tranquility, justice, love and affection.

The way that some Christians suggest that the shedding of the blood of millions and the destruction of whole countries is essential for the coming of Jesus and who heedlessly describe the coming of the Mahdi, eagerly awaited by all Muslims, as the system of the antichrist is a very dangerous mentality.

In this scenario, the side that is mistaken are those Evangelical Christians who misinterpret certain passages in the Gospel, which has already been badly distorted, and excitedly expect to see blood as high as horses' bridles. Rivers of blood are already being spilled in the Middle East, and the horrifying scenario in question is already being played out. To believe in another war and another even more horrifying scenario in the future, to provoke the Middle East to that end and to advocate the reshaping of the Middle East, merely serves the purposes of the antichrist.

This is all a trick being played by forces that appear to be Christian and wish to take power by pointing to passages that were added to the Gospel at a later date or else that are misinterpreted as evidence. They are working this trick by pretending to be religious. The army of the antichrist has no compunctions about repeating this trick that it has successfully used so many times in the past. The aim is to prevent **devout Muslims, Christians and Jews**

157

being brothers and engaging **together** in an intellectual struggle against Darwinism, materialism and atheism.

As a result of this stratagem employed over such a long period of time, the devout have been weakened and the proponents of the system of the antichrist have been strengthened. In this way, it has been easy for them to propagate a Darwinist and materialist mindset that disregards spiritual values, that regards selfishness as the only legitimate value and that thinks of life as an unending struggle and an arena in which only the strong survive. Armageddon is currently the most savage of these forces' plans. People who are unaware of this stratagem may well have a totally mistaken idea of Islam, a religion of peace and love.

The Negative View of Islam Is a deliberately Planned Scenario

With this bloody scenario of the End Times they have developed, some circles affiliated with the antichrist that have led to an expectation of a great war by pointing to various passages from the Gospel as supposed evidence are, in fact, trying to establish a false impression of Islam. Through various publications that support scenarios of war, false reports, biased commentaries and provocative statements they are attempting to portray sincere Muslims as the supporters of the antichrist. That is the underlying reason for the hate-filled attitude toward Islam and biased perspectives on the part of some evangelical Christians. These people depict themselves as religious and claim to be basing their ideas about the End Times on the Gospel, and are seeking, in their own eyes, to attribute provisions favoring war and cruelty to Islam, a faith that actually describes a world in which all people will live in peace and security. The aim of these forces is to camouflage the people who are encouraging war and policies intended to lead to a major war in the Middle East by focusing people's attention toward Muslims instead. It is to prevent unity between the People of the

Book and Muslims, which if it were to happen, would represent a huge force against atheism, irreligion and materialism.

As a result of this ugly trickery, some sincerely devout Christians are falsely acquainted with Islam, misinterpret it and are unaware of the beauty of Islam and the fact it is a religion of peace and love. This stratagem is also leading to an artificial separation between Muslims and Christians. As a result of this pernicious plan, true believers in the same God are unable to unite: On the contrary, an artificial strife and hatred is being established between them. This state of affairs is producing the ideal basis for the system of the antichrist, which seeks to disseminate irreligion, Darwinism, anarchy, violence, war, murder and degeneracy, to cunningly continue with its activities. The global arena belongs to that system as members of the three great faiths, Muslims, Christians and Jews, squabble among themselves.

The weakening of believers means the strengthening of the supporters of the antichrist. That is why believers need to be weakened and divided among themselves if the supporters of the antichrist are to be able to spread atheism, materialism and moral degeneracy and to strengthen their own ideologies. That is why the supporters of the antichrist are striving so hard to thwart an alliance between sincere believers and to divide them in this way. As a result of this cunning stratagem, devout Christians become tools, albeit unaware and of course unwillingly, in these forces' policy of spreading irreligion.

It is a matter of the greatest urgency for all true believers to be on their guard against this foul trickery and to wage, in a spirit of unity, the essential intellectual struggle against those ideologies that oppose belief in God and seek to distract whole societies from religious moral values. It must never be forgotten that the greatest threat to people being able to live in peace, tranquility, justice and security is the system of the antichrist, which seeks to spread irreligion, and perverse ideologies such as Darwinism and materialism throughout the world.

159

The description of the antichrist in the Gospel is in complete agreement with the hadiths related by our Prophet Muhammad (pbuh). Therefore, the antichrist described in Islamic sources and expected for centuries by the Muslim world possesses the same characteristics as the antichrist expected by the Christian world, and will employ the same deceptive methods and wage a foul campaign to spread the same perverse ideologies. To put it another way, Christians must act together with Muslims against their common enemy, the antichrist.

Armageddon has long since begun and is still raging

As explained above, **the Armageddon that is said to take place in the future has in fact long since started and is still continuing. Armageddon has begun with the Iraq War that took place in recent years and is still continuing.** The portents in both Islamic and Christian sources completely confirm this. Those forces that support the antichrist that say, "There will be a great and bloody war" are in fact well aware of this, but they deliberately conceal it.

Iraq was invaded by troops from the USA, Great Britain, Australia, Spain, Denmark and Poland in 2003. During the invasion many people, military and civilian, Muslims, Christians and members of other faiths, were martyred or killed.

The invasion of Iraq in the End Times is described as follows in the Gospel:

> *The merchants of the earth will weep and mourn over her [Babylon *] because no one buys their cargoes anymore—cargoes of gold, silver, precious stones and pearls; fine linen, purple, silk and scarlet cloth; every sort of citron wood, and articles of every kind made of ivory,*

---

* Babylon: The name of an ancient city near Baghdad, the capital of modern-day Iraq

160

*costly wood, bronze, iron and marble; cargoes of cinnamon and spice, of incense, myrrh and frankincense, of ... olive oil, of fine flour and wheat; cattle and sheep; horses and carriages... They will say, "The fruit you longed for is gone from you. All your luxury and splendor have vanished..." The merchants who sold these things and gained their wealth from her will stand far off, **terrified at her torment**. They will weep and mourn and cry out: "Woe! Woe to you, great city, dressed in fine linen, purple and scarlet, and glittering with gold, precious stones and pearls! **In one hour such great wealth has been brought to ruin!**" Every sea captain, and all who travel by ship, the sailors, and all who earn their living from the sea, will stand far off. When they see the smoke of her burning, they will exclaim, **"Was there ever a city like this great city?"** They will throw dust on their heads, and with weeping and mourning cry out: "Woe! Woe to you, great city, where all who had ships on the sea became rich through her wealth! **In one hour she has been brought to ruin!"** ... **"With such violence the great city of Babylon will be thrown down...** Your merchants were the world's great men." (Revelations, 18:11-23)*

The invasion of Iraq by various countries, the slaughter that will result in Iraq, the fighting that will come to Sham, in other words Syria, and the Battle of Armageddon in the Middle East are described down to the finest detail in the hadiths:

*In the End Times **Baghdad will be destroyed by flames** ... (Risalat al-Khuruj al-Mahdi, Vol. 3, p. 177)*

Baghdad was one of the cities exposed to the most intense bombing from the day the invasion of Iraq began. This heavy bombing caused Baghdad to burn in flames, just as described in the hadith. Images of Baghdad in newspaper and television reports exactly matched the situation noted in the hadith.

The Messenger of God (pbuh) said: "... There will be such scourges and afflictions that nobody will have a place to

161

shelter. ***These scourges will prowl around Sham and*** ***settle on Iraq.*** *They will tie the hands and feet of the* *Arabian peninsula ... As people try to eliminate these* *scourges in one place, they will spring up in another." (Al-* *Muttaqi al-Hindi, Kanz al-Ummal, Qitab-al Qiyama qism* *al-Afal, vol. 5, pp. 38-39)*

The reference in the hadith to "... scourges prowling around Sham and settling on Iraq" emphasizes unending conflict in Syria and Iraq. Indeed, Syria and Iraq are today the scenes of the worst turmoil in the Middle East.

*... **Doomsday will not take place until Iraq is attacked.*** *And innocent people in Iraq will seek places of shelter* *toward Sham. Sham will be rebuilt, and Iraq will be* *rebuilt. (Al-Muttaqi al-Hindi, Kanz al-Ummal, Qitab al-* *Qiyama qism al-Afal, vol. 5, p. 254)*

The hadith notes that Iraq and Syria will be rebuilt. Indeed, Iraq, and also Syria since 2011, have both been largely destroyed by the ongoing conflict. Rebuilding became an inescapable necessity in both countries.

The people of Iraq will be divided into three groups. Some *will be looters. Some will abandon their families and flee.* ***Some will fight and die. When you see these things,*** ***prepare for the Reckoning.*** *(Yusuf al-Maqdisi, Fara Idu* *Fawaid al-Fiqr Fi al-Imam al-Mahdi al-Muntadhar)*

As reported in the hadith, one group of people will join the "looters" following the disorder in Iraq and the invasion of certain Iraqi regions. Indeed, during the clashes, some people engaged in widespread activities described as pillaging or "looting." The hadith goes on to say that some people will prefer to immediately flee because of all the oppression going on, and will even never think of their families they abandoned. It then goes on to say that some people will join in the fighting and be killed. There was indeed much conflict during the occupation of Iraq first by the USA and later by various radical groups, many people lost their lives and many others fled the region.

*Abu Nadre said; We were with Jabr, and he said: "The time is coming when neither a 'kafiz' (a measure) nor a 'dirham' (a measure of weight) will be sent to the people of Iraq." We said: "because of whom will that happen?" He said: **"The non-Arabs will not permit it."** He then said: "Neither a dinar nor a 'müdy' (a measure of weight) will be sent to the people of Iraq." "Who will that be because of?" we asked. **"Because of the Rum"** he said. (At-Tajj, Ali Nasif al-Hussaini)*

Iraq was invaded by non-Muslim foreign states, and beforehand, as described in the hadith, a long-term embargo was imposed on Iraq by those same foreign states.

*"**No measure or dirham will be given to Iraq.** No measure or dirham will be given to Sham, either. No measure or dinar will be given to Egypt. You will return to where you began," he said, and repeated this three times. Abu Hurairah's flesh and blood witnessed this. (Muslim, Fitan 33, (2896); Abu Dawud, Haraj 29, (3035))*

The Iraqis will have almost no more weighing devices and no money with which to buy anything. (Al-Muttaqi al-Hindi, Kanz al-Ummal, Qitab al-Qiyama qism al-Afal, vol. 5, p. 45)

It is significant that the hadiths refer to three countries. Iraq, Syria and Egypt are three major Middle Eastern countries where conflict is increasing for a number of reasons. As stated in the hadiths, the economies of all three countries have been seriously harmed by the fighting in question. The Iraqi dinar was also demonetarized in the wake of the invasion. The Egyptian economy has suffered grave harm following the internal conflict that broke out. In Syria, there is no longer any economy left to speak of.

As is clear from passages from the Gospel and the hadiths related from our Prophet (pbuh), the war that began in Iraq and then spread over a wide part of the Middle East completely matches with all the descriptions of Armageddon. Armageddon is one of the signs of the End Times that will take place before the coming of Jesus (pbuh) and Hazrat Mahdi (pbuh). All the plans dreamed up prospectively about Armageddon will be thwarted with the coming of the Mahdi and Jesus. The expectation of bloodshed and violence on the part of some Muslims and Christians who have become supporters of the forces of the antichrist will all be in vain. The appearance of Jesus will not herald war or bloodshed, but rather the end of war, and peace and prosperity for the Middle East and the world.

True Muslims, true Christians and true Jews will forge an alliance for peace and praise the name of God together. In contrast to all the scenarios of savagery, **the time of the coming of Hazrat Mahdi will be one of love, peace, security and tranquility.**

In the time of Hazrat Mahdi, **wars and slaughter will come to an end. There will be no crime and the prisons will be empty.** Tanks and guns and shells will all be melted down.

Not only will there be no war or disorder in the time of Hazrat Mahdi, not a single person's nose will even be made to bleed. With his affection, love, justice and fine moral virtues, Hazrat Mahdi (pbuh) will lead the whole world to brotherhood, peace and love. The world will enter a **Golden Age** in which peace and plenty prevail and people live in peace and blessings.

Almighty God praises love, peace and brotherhood in all three faiths. The fact that the perverse mindset that seeks to depict the time of Hazrat Mahdi, sent by God as a blessing on all believers, as a time of slaughter and terror is a stratagem of the antichrist. Every sincere Muslim and Christian must ponder on this rationally and be aware of this trickery.

CHAPTER 7
THE ERRORS IN THE ATTITUDES OF SOME CHRISTIANS TOWARD MUSLIMS

A fundamentalist is someone who appears to live by the requirements of a faith, but who actually lives by superstitions that have been added to it later, or even makes up superstitions for himself. There may be fundamentalists in all faiths. The most distinguishing feature of a fundamentalist is that he not only refuses to abide by the rules of the faith to which he claims to belong, but adopts his own concept of religion and attempts to impose that on society as a whole. Practices that are not actually part of a faith can easily be made part of it in the fundamentalist's eyes. Matters external to that faith can shamelessly be applied, and even murder can be committed in the name of religion, societies can be swamped in ignorance, people can be pressured and the true faiths that insist on love can be misrepresented as religions of hate. That is what makes fundamentalists so dangerous.

As we have just seen, fundamentalists can emerge from all religions. In the same way that there are Christian fundamentalists who totally misrepresent Christianity and portray that religion of love as one of hatred, so there are fundamentalists who also seek to misrepresent Islam. The mindset that is equated with anger, ignorance, hatred, suicide killings and slaughter under the name of Islam, that opposes science, art and all fine things, that takes no pleasure from blessings and that assumes an attitude that loathes

Christians and Jews, is the mindset of fundamentalists, not of true Muslims. Many people criticize this strange image that they wrongly equate with Islam and therefore oppose Islam itself. But what they should really be opposing is not Islam, but fundamentalism and the radical mindset.

Radicalism is the name of a loveless system diametrically opposed to the Koran

The dark and bloodthirsty system that some people ascribe to Islam is actually fundamentalism, not Islam at all. This means espousing radicalism under the guise of religion. **A fundamentalist - a radical in other words - is loveless, dark of soul, bigoted and lacking in understanding. He is opposed to all forms of beauty, aesthetics, art and science. He is opposed to life, and absolutely opposed to joy and happiness.**

Someone with a fundamentalist mindset will regard all objects of beauty with hatred. He will hate flowers, and children, cats and dogs and rabbits. His soul is empty; there is nothing about love in their souls. They do not value other people, nor any other living thing. The concepts of consideration, love and compassion are entirely foreign to them.

As a result of all this, a fundamentalist **will also hate women.** The hatred of women that some people seek to ascribe to Islam is in fact a characteristic of fundamentalist radicals, not of Islam, which actually attaches the greatest value to women, and which praises and exalts them. (This will later be discussed in greater detail.)

In the same way that someone with a fundamentalist mindset loves nobody, nobody loves him, either. Everyone is made uncomfortable by the presence, lifestyle and ideas of a fundamentalist. Fundamentalists even detest other fundamentalists. They are never at once in friendship and ease; this, of course, stems from their living at a great distance from the Koran.

It needs to be reiterated as a matter of great importance that a fundamentalist - a radical in other words - can be found in every faith or section of society. People who seek to turn people away from the essence of their faiths and to replace the joy and fervor resulting from faith in God with a dark and bloodthirsty spirit can be found in Christian and Jewish communities, as well as Muslim ones. However, the subject under discussion here is those fundamentalists who seek to insinuate themselves among Muslims.

No matter what section of society or faith he comes from, a fundamentalist always stands for the same polluted and sinister ideas. **As a result of this terrifying state of his soul, someone with a fundamentalist mindset will always seek <u>bloodshed</u>. He will seek bloodshed everywhere. Only bloodshed and wickedness will satisfy him.** He can only express the hatred inside him through bloodshed and wickedness. People who appear in the name of Islam and encourage hatred and enmity toward Christians and Jews, and even Muslims, are not **true Muslims** as described in the Koran, but **fundamentalists** under the influence of the system of the antichrist.

Therefore, it is very important for our Christian brothers to distinguish very carefully between fundamentalists and true Muslims, and between the fundamentalist mindset and true Islam. Only then will they be able to see that what they are against is not Islam, but radicalism.

But why is Islam misrepresented by fundamentalists, and why is this being allowed?

The System of the Antichrist that Incites Opposition to Islam and Its Links to Radicalism

Spreading opposition to Islam is one major aim of the system of the antichrist because Islam is the final true faith and the Koran has remained unchanged for 1,400 years. The verses of the Koran are under the protection of God and are sufficient for people to live by the true faith in an unsullied manner. The true Islam that comes from living by the Koran leads to a sound and powerful faith.

This powerful faith, people becoming increasingly devout, and solidarity between the three Divine faiths represent a major peril and threat to the antichrist. The material and spiritual strength that stems from unity and solidarity, which represent an important part of Islamic moral values, is powerful enough to eliminate all the satanic systems and ideologies developed by the antichrist over the years. The antichrist is very well aware that when Muslims are completely united and when they establish an alliance with Christians and Jews, this will result in a major force, and that this major force will inflict a huge intellectual defeat on his own philosophy.

Leading members of the system of the antichrist have for a long time been aware of the presence of this spiritual force standing in opposition to the satanic system they have constructed. That awareness explains the plans they have made for a bloody Armageddon through calculated policies and strategies. As a part of that plan, **various people who are actually Darwinists and atheists have been raised as terrorists under the guise of being "Muslims" and sent off to wreak slaughter, supposedly in the name of Islam.** These very same circles have depicted concepts totally opposed to the spirit of Islam, such as killing and murdering innocent people and suicide bombings, as if these were part of Islam. They have so widely disseminated ideas that stand in complete opposition to Islam that **even some people who portray themselves as Islamic scholars** have openly come to advocate this plan for a bloody war that will take place between the faiths and result in the deaths of millions. They have managed to influence hundreds of thousands of people into thinking that killing and murder are legitimate. In addition, they have convinced themselves and others that they are doing this in the name of God.

Like the expectations of Armageddon discussed earlier, the scenarios of war and slaughter that are being ascribed to Islam are part of the same mindset, that of the antichrist. The antichrist aims to use this technique in order to create division between the faiths,

168

to set them against one another, to weaken believers and thus to produce the means and climate through which to implement his own perverse plans.

We must always remember this; the antichrist has always used the name of God in his dealings with believers. He never shows his true face, and always **uses religion and people who appear to be devout** in order to lead believers astray from the true path. That is how the antichrist has managed to influence many devout people and easily been able to spread all kinds of superstitious and perverse ideas that can support and strengthen his own devilish systems.

The perverse claims that some people are seeking to attribute to Islam – including the idea that Muslims want to slaughter Christians and Jews, that they deny the right to life of non-Muslims and that they are devoid of love and affection - are complete fabrications.

People who are unaware of the true essence of Islam, a religion of peace and love, and of the brotherhood, justice, peace, compassion and love in the verses of the Koran, may fail to see the perverse aspects of these false claims. In order to see that this image that the forces of the antichrist are trying to ascribe to Islam is wrong and perverse, there needs to be people who **judge by the Koran, know the spirit of the Koran and conceive of - and live by - the Koran in the same way as our Prophet (pbuh) did**. If someone is a "fundamentalist," in other words, if he interprets Islam in the light of perverse superstitions, if he makes up rules and regulations that contravene all logic and reason – as well as conflicting with the Koran – if he portrays Islam, a religion of ease, as difficult, inaccessible, aggressive and loveless (Islam is surely beyond all that), then he can never understand the reality, unless God decides otherwise, of course. The important point is that fundamentalism is a major threat, not just to Islam, but also to Christianity and Judaism. Therefore, in order to be able to see the origins of the perverse ideas that are being ascribed to Islam, people need to realize how far removed fundamentalism is from the Koran and from all the true faiths in general.

Fundamentalists neither apply the Koran nor do they allow others to do so

Fundamentalism, or radicalism, **is the antichrist's greatest supporter against Islam.** Our Prophet (pbuh) reveals this in a hadith:

> *Seventy thousand turbaned scholars from my Community will follow the antichrist. (Ahmad ibn Hanbal, Musnad, p. 796)*

In describing the people who will follow the antichrist, our Prophet makes special reference to people who **will emerge from the Muslim community and portray themselves as "scholars."** He also says in a hadith that the group who will work on the side of the antichrist against all the friends of God and who will inflict the worst harm on the Islamic faith are **fundamentalists who depict themselves as Muslims.**

In another hadith our Prophet says:

> *There will be deviants in the End Times; their minds will not function. They will speak eloquently. **They will read the Koran, but their faith will not descend beyond their throats...** (Bukhari, Sahih 3611, 5057, 6930, Muslim, 1066, Abu Dawud 4767, Ahmad ibn Hanbal, Musnad 1, 81, 113, 131, 289; Tayalisi, al-Musnad, no. 1984.)*

As the hadith says, these people will use eloquent speech and read the Koran, "... but their faith will not descend beyond their throats." In other words, **they will not heed the Koran.** They will speak of the Koran, but they will not be devoted to it. They will rule not according to the Koran but according to the superstitions they fabricate in the name of the Koran. They will not regard the Koranic accounts as sufficient and they will act on a faith of their own invention under the name of Islam.

The aim of the fundamentalists is to stop people from applying the Koran. While adding elements that are not in the Koran onto

170

Islam, they also reject the commands and advice in the Koran that does not square with their own superstitious fabrications.

The fact that the Koran recommends love, affection, brotherhood, unity and peace, the fact that all beauty is praised in the Koran and art and science are encouraged cause them to feel an intense rage. The quality of the soul bestowed by living by the moral values of the Koran and the depth of a Muslim model that is rational, esthetic, modern and loving is entirely incompatible with their own fabricated religions. That is why the antichrist, in his own way, uses fundamentalism to try to strike at the real Islam in the Koran, with the foolish idea that he can thus eradicate it. However, it is important to state that a large part of the army of the antichrist is made up of fundamentalists who will emerge from every faith with the aim of harming their own religion and the world as a whole. Christian, Jewish and Muslim fundamentalists come together around the same bloody and violent scenario and are doing whatever they can to incite this war and spread the system of the antichrist across the entire world.

It needs to be made clear here that there may be people who sincerely love Almighty God and who only espouse ideas that are not part of Islam out of ignorance or because they have been misinformed: Such people make up a large part of today's radicals, and affectionate and meaningful educational activity needs to be directed toward such people. Once they are illuminated with the light of the Koran, these people will see and admit the truth. Almighty God shows the true path to His sincere servants.

Fundamentalism is also a threat to Christianity

As we have just seen, fundamentalists can emerge from any religion. Indeed, those who, in their own eyes, imagined they could harm Jesus (pbuh) were also fundamentalists of that time who appeared in the name of religion.

171

Jesus describes the fundamentalists in explicit terms as hypocrites, the blind and snakes in the Gospel:

"Woe to you, teachers of the law and Pharisees, you hypocrites! You shut the door of the kingdom of heaven in people's faces. You yourselves do not enter, nor will you let those enter who are trying to. Woe to you, teachers of the law and Pharisees, you hypocrites! You travel over land and sea to win a single convert, and when you have succeeded, you make them twice as much a child of hell as you are. ... Woe to you, teachers of the law and Pharisees, you hypocrites! You give a tenth of your spices—mint, dill and cumin. But you have neglected the more important matters of the law—justice, mercy and faithfulness. You should have practiced the latter, without neglecting the former. You blind guides! You strain out a gnat but swallow a camel. Woe to you, teachers of the law and Pharisees, you hypocrites! You clean the outside of the cup and dish, but inside they are full of greed and self-indulgence. Blind Pharisee! First clean the inside of the cup and dish, and then the outside also will be clean. Woe to you, teachers of the law and Pharisees, you hypocrites! You are like whitewashed tombs, which look beautiful on the outside but on the inside are full of the bones of the dead and everything unclean. In the same way, on the outside you appear to people as righteous but on the inside you are full of hypocrisy and wickedness. You snakes! You brood of vipers! How will you escape being condemned to hell? Therefore I am sending you prophets and sages and teachers. Some of them you will kill ...; others you will flog in your synagogues and pursue from town to town. And so upon you will come all the righteous blood that has been shed on earth, from the blood of righteous Abel to the blood of Zechariah, son of Berekiah, whom you murdered between the temple and the altar." (Matthew 23: 13-35)

172

Christians Must Not Confuse Fundamentalism with True Islam

A model of Islam that has no place in the Koran, that causes war in the name of Islam, that oppresses others, that organizes suicide attacks and that desires killing and bloodshed causes Christians and Jews to develop a false impression of Islam.

As we have already said, **those who espouse a bloody and wicked system have absolutely nothing to do with Islam, in other words, the moral values of the Koran.** They do this because it is what their superstitious faiths, filled with nonsense of their own making and superstitious beliefs, require. **There is absolutely no place in the Koran for such a loveless, ruthless and aggressive mindset.**

In the Koran, our Lord describes such people, no matter what their religion, who espouse fundamentalism, who seek to confuse religion with superstitions and make it impossible to live by and who seek to deceive people using the name of God as follows:

> **Among them is a group who distort the Book with their tongues so that you think it is from the Book when it is not from the Book. They say, "It is from God," but it is not from God. They tell a lie against God and they know it.** (Koran, 3:78)

Being a true Muslim means abiding by the moral values of Islam as revealed by God in the Koran and represented by our blessed Prophet (pbuh). In other words, Muslims have a responsibility **to live according to the Koran and the way of life of our Prophet,** not the superstitions and fabrications of fundamentalists. The criteria are the Koran and the way of life of the Prophet, not fabrications. True Islam is the Islam of the Age of Bliss, lived according to the Koran and the life of our Prophet. The loving, affectionate, protective and noble life of our Prophet, who valued art, beauty, cleanliness and kindness, is the perfect model for all Muslims. It is therefore **a major error for non-Muslims to evaluate Islam on the basis of the murky lives of various**

173

fundamentalists rather than on the true facts. *(For detailed information, see Harun Yahya's Bigotry: The Dark Danger)*

Our Christian brothers should read the following statements with great care:

SECTION 1
Equating Islam with Violence Stems from Being Unacquainted with the True Islam

Some people, who equate Islam with terrorist attacks, mass slaughter and suicide bombings, make the mistake of assuming that those who spread terror in the name of Islam are actually Muslims. They also imagine that such people are real Muslims who live by the Koran. But the truth is that these people have nothing to do with either Islam or our holy book, the Holy Koran.

Islam Curses Terrorist Attacks, Slaughter, Suicide Bombings and All Forms of Violence

The great majority of the infamous terrorist leaders who have inflicted great evil on their countries are generally intelligence agents specially trained to commit acts of provocation. **They are members of well-known intelligence agencies in America and Europe and receive their orders directly from them.** These people have all received a Darwinist and materialist education. They never reflect the true moral values of Islam commanded by God in any sphere of their lives, have nothing to do with the loving and affectionate, compassionate, forgiving and just values of our Prophet (pbuh) and **have been indoctrinated by Darwinism. According to the terrible error in which these people find themselves, the only way to survive and be strong is through fighting and conflict. This requires violence and cruelty, while virtues such as love, affection and compassion are regarded as weaknesses.**

Fulfilling a few religious obligations, being a citizen of an Islamic country or carrying ID documents that describe them as "Muslims" does not change the reality. These people have a completely Darwinist world view. They also look at those around them in terms of that Darwinist-materialist perspective.

According to this major error of theirs, "Human beings are just slightly more advanced animals; they have no souls and identities, they have no responsibilities toward anyone. Like all animals, human beings have to be selfish and think only of themselves in order to survive. The weak members of this community of animals must be eliminated and weeded out." Of course, someone under the influence of this perverse logic will lack the moral values and conscience to prevent them from carrying out mass slaughter.

The terrorist leaders in question have in fact been brought up to be "spoiled and arrogant," far removed from the moral values of Islam, in America and various countries of Europe. They spend all their time in night clubs and possess atheist mindsets that have signed up to all the negative and degenerate aspects of Western culture. It needs to be stated here that one may have any kind of lifestyle before beginning to live by religious moral values, and there is nothing to criticize in that; if a person sincerely repents and turns to belief in God, then it may be hoped that He will forgive their mistakes. But the situation is entirely different with the people in question.

When the time comes for these people to start work, they grow their beards and assume the appearance of Muslims. They receive their instructions from covert sections of various intelligence agencies and unhesitatingly carry them out. **They have nothing to**

do with Islam or being Muslim. Their religion is materialism and Darwinism, not Islam. It is impossible for genuine Muslims who fully abide by the Koran to support and be a part of such a wicked system that contradicts the Koran. **Those who perpetrate this wickedness are Darwinists, materialists and admirers of Stalin, Che, Lenin, Mussolini, Hitler and Mao.** They are people who, in their own way, seek to apply the perverse ideas of bloody materialists, communists and fascists in the name of Islam, and think in a way totally incompatible with religious moral values. This is how the evil system that some circles wrongly seek to attribute to Islam operates.

Some Muslims might claim that these atrocities committed in the name of Islam do not reflect the facts and might choose to deny them completely.

Yet the right thing to do is not to deny these actions, but to tell people that they are most probably carried out by various intelligence agents opposed to religion in order to supposedly neutralize Islam and prevent it growing any stronger. The right thing is to tell everyone that these things are unlawful actions in the eyes of Islam.

The Bomb Dropped on Hiroshima Was Not Blamed on Christians, and Terrorist Actions Cannot Be Laid at the Door of Genuine Muslims

In making these groundless claims against Muslims, Christians who think along the lines just described ignore one very important point. The United States of America once caused hundreds of thousands of innocent people to lose their lives by dropping atomic bombs on Hiroshima and Nagasaki. It is entirely possible there were Muslims, Christians and Jews among them. There were children and old people, and innocent men and women. Yet the Islamic world has never laid the blame for this action carried out by the U.S. government, the majority of whom were Christians, at the door of Christians.

It never concentrated on the faiths of those who dropped the bombs or claimed that these were "Christian attacks." In the same way, thousands of Muslims were savagely murdered during the Crusades, and even Christians belonging to different sects were tortured and killed during that dark era. Churches as well as mosques were destroyed. The blood so recently shed in Iraq, Afghanistan and other Islamic countries was Muslim blood but Muslims have never used this to suggest that those who abide by the Gospel are bloodthirsty by nature.

Any rational person can easily see that irreligion prevails wherever there is wickedness. Reasonable Muslims who abide by the Koran and have faith in God would never hold Christians responsible for the killings in question. This is not something that a person who sincerely believes in God could ever do.

The time has now come for those Christians who make such ugly allegations against Muslims to abandon these false ideas and habits. Ignorance generally plays a major role at the root of such claims. Christians should therefore read the Koran with an unbiased eye, examine the life of our Prophet (pbuh) and bear in mind the lifestyles, ideas and actions of sincere believers who live by true Islamic moral values.

Statements by Mr. Adnan Oktar regarding the hadith concerning the tree of Gharkad (the Boxthorn tree)

The Hadith about the Tree of Gharkad Foretells the Hidden Camera Systems in the End Times

ADNAN OKTAR: The hadith says, *"You must fight the Jews and kill them."* If someone who is a Jew is also opposed to religion and attacks Muslims, if he sheds blood and kills children and others, then you have a right to defend yourself. This hadith is speaking about legitimate self-defense. Otherwise, it is a sin to go and kill an innocent Jew.

"Such that even a stone will say, 'O Muslim, here is a Jew (hiding) behind me, come and kill him'." Now, say there is a child of three or four years old behind the stone, and someone hears a voice coming from that stone saying, "O Muslim, there is a Jew behind me, come and kill him." That means you must be hallucinating. Satan is speaking to you. Children, innocent people, women must not be killed. But you can legitimately defend yourself. Apart from that, killing is wrong. Therefore, if we see a Jewish child hiding behind a stone and hear a voice coming from a stone, then we should say, "I must be hallucinating" and refuse to heed it.

Imagine that someone kills ten Jewish children, may God forbid. If we ask him why he did that and he says, "A stone told me to do it, so I did," then we can be sure that he is crazy and a murderer. He has blatantly killed people and done evil, and the reward for that is hell.

We must understand this hadith correctly. Our Prophet (pbuh) is referring to communications in the End Times. Operations are carried out on the basis of information emanating from rocks or trees. Cameras are hidden in trees and secret information obtained from them. This is a reference to a defensive system that will emerge. Our Prophet is indicating the advanced technology of the time of Hazrat Mahdi (pbuh). Otherwise, killing innocent people is a grave sin.

No Jew was ever killed in that way in the time of our Prophet, nor any Christian. Our Prophet personally took his robe off and spread it on the ground for them, for the People of the Book to sit on. Our Prophet respected them. Muslims in the time of our Prophet sought shelter alongside Christians. They entrusted their own safety to them. They were brothers with them and went to eat with them and married Christian women.

ALTUĞ BERKER: Let me read a verse from the Koran about what you said; verse 5 of Surat al-Ma'ida: **"Today all good things have been made lawful for you. And the food of those given the Book is also lawful for you and your food is lawful for them. So are chaste women from among the believers and chaste women of those given the Book before you, once you have given them their dowries in marriage, not in fornication or taking them as lovers. But as for anyone who rejects faith, his actions will come to nothing and in the hereafter he will be among the losers."**

ADNAN OKTAR: One can marry Christian women and one can also marry Jewish women. What does marriage mean? It means the presence of love, friendship and brotherhood, doesn't it? She becomes the mother of one's children. You sleep in the same bed. You eat and drink together. This is made clear in the verse. *(Excerpt from Mr. Adnan Oktar's interview on November 21, 2010)*

Stones and Trees Will Give Muslims Information in the End Times

ADNAN OKTAR: ... Our Prophet (pbuh) says; *"The Day of reckoning will not come until Muslims war with Jews."* They already fought the Jews in Palestine. There was the Six-Day War. That was a major event. They fought Egypt and Syria and Jordan. This hadith came true. It has already happened.

In another hadith our Prophet says; *"Every stone and every tree will say, O Muslim, there is a Jew behind me, come and kill him."*

179

For one thing, a person must be punished according to his offense. If we come across an innocent Jewish child behind a rock and the rock tells us "Look, there is a Jewish child here behind me, come and kill him" then that voice comes from satan. We must not heed it because it is a hallucination inciting us to murder. What should we do? We can establish whether is there is anything behind us, using an electric device, for example.

We can locate someone's position using electronic communications but only to neutralize them, not to kill them. And only if the person is engaged in doing harm, is an irreligious, or atheist Jew, if he has no book, if he does not obey the Torah, if he does not obey the Koran because the Torah says nothing about wronging Muslims. According to the Torah, Jews must regard Muslims as the people of Noah (pbuh). What does the People of Noah mean? Muslims, believers. Since every Jew regards a Muslim as one of the people of Noah, as a believer, it is a sin to attack his life, property or honor. But it may be a Jew who acts wickedly, in which case stones, objects of all kinds, even furniture may give him away by means of micro-cameras and technical devices. Then we can locate and neutralize that person.

Killing here means neutralization in the ideological sense. That also applies to Hazrat Mahdi (pbuh). He will slay the antichrist. In other words, he will slay his ideas. It is an intellectual, mental killing, not a physical one. Therefore, stones and trees giving information to Muslims is already happening now in the End Times.

I said, "micro-cameras should be installed in the Southeast with our troops' permission and locate the whereabouts of the enemy." Where are cameras installed? If there is a covert campaign against the enemy, then they can be hidden in rocks. Or they should be placed in trees so they cannot be seen. Our Prophet refers, through revelation and in a most perfect manner, how a secret intelligence network will be set up with flawless technology.

This is only happening now, in the End Times. It does not apply to all Jews, but we must identify atheist Jews, Muslims or

Christians who do evil and inflict suffering, if they kill people. The Messenger of God describes one aspect of this but we can deduce the whole matter from that. Our Prophet describes it in its essence and very briefly. When the time comes to defend ourselves, it means that Muslims will obtain secret intelligence of this kind in the End Times. For example, our Prophet says, *"People will look at the palms of their hands and see Hazrat Mahdi."* They have done that now. There are iPods and telephones. One can see the other person just by looking in the palm of one's hand. This has happened. That is what it refers to. *(Excerpt from Mr. Adnan Oktar's interview on November 14, 2010)*

The Allegation of "Violence in Islam" Is a Fabrication by the Antichrist and His Fundamentalist Followers

According to the Koran, there is absolutely no place in Islam for violence, terror and suicide bombings. According to the Koran, war is only permissible for defensive purposes if life, property or honor are endangered. Even under such circumstances, however, Muslims must not overstep the line. They have a responsibility to treat any prisoners they take justly, to feed their prisoners even if they have to go hungry themselves, to establish peace as quickly as possible and to protect civilians and the innocent. An examination of the life of our Prophet (pbuh) reveals exactly how one should behave in this regard.

Muslims have always waged war for defensive purposes

Throughout the thirteen years they lived in Mecca, the Prophet and his companions were subjected to the most terrible torments, assaults and slanders by the Meccan pagans. They were forced from their homes and threatened with death. Yet they never resorted to violence despite all of this aggression and persecution.

When the persecution in Mecca became intolerable they migrated to Medina. Since they were subjected to the same attacks in Medina, and their lives were in danger during the Medina period, they had no option but to fight for purely defensive purposes. For example, the Battle of Badr took place because the pagans of Mecca gathered their armies and attacked with the aim of martyring the Muslims.

The Battle of the Trench was an entirely defensive one in which the Muslims dug a trench around the city for their own protection. To summarize, these past battles were always defensive ones stemming directly from aggression on the part of the pagans: Not one was a war of aggression. The commands regarding defense revealed to our Prophet during this time are verses that apply only to such exceptional conditions in war.

The Prophet Muhammad (pbuh) is a man of love and compassion like Jesus (pbuh)

Some Christians rather ignorantly presume to compare the two prophets, both of whom are very valuable to us. They make highly unbecoming assumptions, along the lines that Jesus was a man of love while the Prophet Muhammad favored war. This is a slander on the part of certain ignorant and prejudiced Christians who ignore the fact that both the Prophet Muhammad and Jesus were submitted to God and that they were blessed messengers who acted through His revelation.

Due to their being lovers and friends of God, both of these blessed people were of course full of love, affection and compassion. Nothing else is possible.

Our Prophet spent 23 years as a prophet. During those 23 years, which included very difficult times involving direct assaults by the pagans, our Prophet undertook various wars in order to protect believers against attacks intended to martyr Muslims, and that continued uninterrupted despite Muslims' peaceable attitudes.

And during all these wars he acted through God's revelation and took all his decisions in the light of that revelation. Had the responsibility regarding fighting intended to protect Muslims that came in the form of revelation from God also been imparted to Jesus, then he would have abided by that obligation in the same way that our Prophet did. But Jesus was not exposed to such attacks from pagans during the three years of his prophethood. There was therefore no need for these provisions about war and defense to be revealed to him.

A verse from the Koran reveals that war can be essential even though the Prophet and Muslims dislike it.

Fighting is prescribed for you even if it is hateful to you. It may be that you hate something when it is good for you and it may be that you love something when it is bad for you. God knows and you do not know. (Koran, 2:216)

Islam commands people to be forgiving in war and not to go to extremes

Someone capable of seeing the depth of faith that God reveals in the Koran can also easily grasp that the essential thing for a Muslim is forgiveness. For example, God tells us in the Koran that Muslims must not go to extremes in the event of war, and that if one side in a state of war puts an end to hostilities, Muslims must do so, too:

Fight in the way of God against those who fight you, but do not go beyond the limits. God does not love those who go beyond the limits. (Koran, 2:190)

But if they cease, God is Ever-Forgiving, Most Merciful. (Koran, 2:192)

In order for Muslims to be able to go to war, it is essential for the other side to have attacked first. War is a last resort for protection against the wickedness of a community that is

183

aggressive and refuses to listen to reason. Even then, Muslims have a responsibility not to go to extremes; they can still only defend themselves. As our Lord reveals in the above verse, if the aggressors call a halt to hostilities, then Muslims are advised to do so as well. In addition, it is also very important in Islam for care to be shown to women, children, the elderly and the disabled and for extraordinary pains to be taken to protect them and keep them from harm.

It is unlawful in Islam to deliberately and unjustly take a life

The Koran also explicitly states that it is unlawful to take life:

... if someone kills another person – unless it is in retaliation for someone else or for causing corruption in the Earth – it is as if he had murdered all mankind. And if anyone gives life to another person, it is as if he had given life to all mankind. Our Messengers came to them with clear signs but even after that many of them committed outrages in the Earth. (Koran, 2:32)

Those who do not call on any other god together with God and do not kill anyone God has made inviolate, except with the right to do so, and do not fornicate; anyone who does that will receive an evil punishment. (Koran, 2:68)

As these verses make clear, the Koran makes it unlawful for a Muslim to kill for no reason. In the Koran, God reveals that most people still overstep the bounds, despite the envoys He sends telling them that this is unlawful. In other words, the Koran speaks of a community that does not regard the Koran as sufficient and thus goes to excesses, killing and shedding blood. This community is various fundamentalists who appear to act in the name of Islam, but in fact are following the bidding of the antichrist.

184

The Koran also recommends that prisoners of war should be forgiven and released. God reveals in the Koran that even if murder is committed, it is better for the perpetrator to be forgiven by the victim's family. According to the Koran, the responsibility of Muslims is always to choose the best course for God's approval. Since God regards forgiveness as the best course, even in murder, that is what Muslims should abide by. Islam is a religion of affection, compassion, love, peace, justice and tranquility. Those who depict Islam differently from how it is described in the Koran need to abandon that behavior as a matter of urgency.

SECTION 2
Enmity toward Women Is a Characteristic of Darwinists and Fanatics, Not of Islam

Enmity toward women and the error of regarding them as second-class citizens is a shared characteristic of Darwinists, fascists, communists and fanatics. Fanatics attach no importance to women, and even hate them, because they live by the superstitions they invent, and Darwinists because they regard them as a supposedly less advanced species of animal. All these are, of course, inhuman ideas that emerge through encouragement by satan.

We have already discussed how fanaticism is as great a threat to Christians and Jews as it is in Muslim societies. There are a great many fanatics among Christians and Jews who also regard women as second-class citizens and make their hatred of them abundantly clear at every opportunity. However, in the same way that this false perspective of some Christians or some Jews cannot be laid at the door of all of Christianity or all of Judaism, so the same mistaken perspective of some Muslims cannot be attributed

185

to all of Islam. Men and women are equal in Islam. Indeed, women are made superior and protected in the Koran. God reveals in the Koran that piety is the only measure among human beings. Islam exalts and praises women. Those who claim that Islam contains a kind of language that despises women are therefore gravely mistaken.

The perverse idea that Islam supposedly regards women as second-class human beings is one of the most basic tactics employed by satanic forces in order to disseminate opposition to Islam. These circles make use of fanatics in order to spread this totally false and baseless idea across the world and install an incorrect perception of Islam.

These people are oblivious to the affectionate and compassionate attitude of our Prophet (pbuh) toward women, and from all the rights bestowed on them in the Koran and the attitude that should be adopted toward them. They seek to portray nonsense of their own invention, oppression of and injustice and lack of compassion towards women and even a refusal to regard them as people at all, as supposedly a commandment of the faith. The masses who have ignorantly followed them have persisted in maintaining these attitudes for centuries and this unpleasant belief has become rooted in some Muslim societies. The source on which these fanatics base their nonsensical ideas is false hadiths that espouse hostility to women.

The value that Islam places on women with examples from the hadiths of our Prophet (pbuh)

ADNAN OKTAR: Our Prophet says, *"Loving women is one of the moral values of the prophets."* That is in Quleyni, Qafi and several other places. Another hadith from the Messenger of God says, *"I do not think that anyone can increase his faith so long as he does not increase his love of women."* Love of women is correlated with faith.

Another hadith from the Messenger of God reads, *"It was decided the light of my eyes should be prayer and the source of my delight should be women."* By God, as a blessing. Another hadith from the Messenger of God: *"A person's faith grows in terms of virtue as his love of women increases."* *"Shall I tell you the most auspicious thing a person must hold onto? A pure woman,"* our Prophet says.

Umar ibn al-Khattab said, *"I swear that we attached no value to women in the time of ignorance."* It was the same in those days as it is with unbelievers now. *"We began to value and love women after God sent down verses about them and gave them various rights."* (Excerpt from Mr. Adnan Oktar's interview on October 7, 2012 on A9 TV)

How women should be valued in the End Times

ADNAN OKTAR: ... Love for women will be a feature of the End Times. Women will be loved and free in the time of the Mahdi (pbuh). Our Prophet (pbuh) recited special hadiths about that. For instance, our Prophet says that women will be able to travel long distances on their own or with their friends.

Women cannot go around now. There are very few women in the Parliament. This is very wrong. At least half of parliament and key positions should be occupied by women.

A woman could be Prime Minister or President, or Parliament Spokesperson. Women are very fine beings. Let us see their fine and warm features everywhere. Women are manifestations of God's names of the Compassionate and Merciful, of His Names of al-Latif [the Subtle One] and an-Nur [the Light]. ... *(Excerpt from Mr. Adnan Oktar's interview on Kocaeli TV and Aba TV on November 27, 2010)*

Women's rights are always to the fore in the Koran, and women are exalted in it

In order to properly understand the place of women in Islam, we need to look at the verses of the Koran and the policies of our Prophet (pbuh).

According to the Koran, women are holy and exalted beings. They were created by our Almighty Lord as a great blessing, an adornment to the heart. They are also an important part of Islam's intellectual struggle against materialism, Darwinism, communism and all other such irreligious movements. Look at verses of the Koran; women's rights are always held above those of men. Women are always protected in the verses of the Koran. Their rights are observed and they are supported by rights to ensure they suffer no material or other losses. That is the wisdom behind more onerous responsibilities being placed on men. God has created women as a fine manifestation, a symbol of chastity and purity, and as a source of love and affection. Women teach the world warmth, love and the finest friendship. God has created them as adornments, a fine blessing whom He praises and sustains.

A woman is regarded as a queen in Islam. That is the reason why various physical responsibilities are placed on men in Islam. Women are not obliged to work inside or outside the house or to earn money. Of course, they can work if they wish, but men have an obligation to take care of women and meet their needs so they are not left in want or difficulties. Thus, a man cannot force a woman to work in the fields, in a factory or anywhere else. On the contrary, the man is under a duty to watch over and protect her, to ensure her comfort and to make sure no harm comes to her.

People who presume to criticize Islam on the subject of male-female equality are unaware of this superior value the Koran attaches to women. They make a lot of fuss about gender equality and accuse Islam in various ways but since they possess a prejudiced mindset and are ignorant of the true moral values of Islam as described in the Koran **they do not realize that women are held much superior to men in the Koran.**

With the revelation of the Koran, the perverse perspective toward women in the time of ignorance was eliminated and women gained a respected place in society. Our Prophet (pbuh) always attached great value to women, and through the verses of the Koran, sent down to him as a mercy by our Lord, he never allowed women to be treated as second-class people. At the same time, our Prophet regarded women as a blessing and harbored a profound love, compassion, affection and respect for them. Our Prophet expresses these profound feelings for women in the following wise words:

I was made to love three things in this world; fine scent, pure women andprayer, the light of my eyes. (An-Nasai, Ishrata an-Nisa 1, [7, 61])

Trustworthy hadiths handed down from our Prophet Muhammad (pbuh) clearly show the value attached to women in Islam. Some of these hadiths read as follows:

Only noble and honorable people value women. And only evil and base people despise them... (Ibn al-Asakir)

The best of you is he who treats women best. (Ibn al-Asakir)

Do not distress your women. They are entrusted to you by Almighty God. Be gentle with them and treat them well! (Muslim)

Almighty God will love and increase the sustenance of people who treat their women well and laugh with them. (Ibn al-Lal)

The most superior believer is the virtuous who treats his wife the best and most generously. (Tirmidhi)

The best Muslim is he who treats his wife best. Of you all, I am the one who treats his wife best. (an-Nasai)

Someone who smiles at his wife earns as much merit as someone who frees a slave. (R. Nasihin)

189

Someone who beats his wife has rebelled against God and His Messenger. I will be his enemy in the hereafter. (R. Nasihin)

Someone who reads the Koran will immediately see various references in its verses to women's intelligence and ability to think deeply and see detail. For example, the Koran speaks of Balqis, the Queen of Sheba. Balqis was a head of state of her time. God thus shows us that a woman can be a head of state and govern that state.

Women who rebel against God and who are hypocritical and exhibit poor moral values are criticized not for being "women" but for their rebellion against God and their wickedness. The judgment on this subject is the same for women as for men: It is also the same in all of the Divinely revealed faiths. In the same way that a state cannot be called "hostile to women" for imprisoning female anarchists who seek to destroy it, so it is wrong to address the same accusation against an entire faith due to the presence of hypocritical and non-believing women.

Men in Islam are protectors and caretakers of women, not their rulers

Various people today, and particularly Christians, claim that men are described as "having sovereignty" over women in Islamic sources and evaluate the mistaken policies adopted toward women by certain fanatics in the light of that logic. The verse they foolishly cite as supposed evidence for this reads:

> **Men are the protectors and maintainers of women, because God has given the one more than the other, and because they support them from their means... (Koran, 4:34)**

The Arabic word *"qawwam"* used in this verse means "protector, maintainer, caretaker." Therefore, the meaning of this verse is fully in agreement with what we have been saying above. God has charged men with protecting women against troubles and difficulties and with watching over them. This, as we have already seen, **stems not from women being weak or helpless, but from their being valuable blessings.** It is clear that the reference to one being given more than the other emphasizes how men and women are created differently. Of course men and women have physical differences but a woman's physical features do not make her more naïve than a man nor less valuable than him in society. Of course there are women with great physical strength and abilities but generally speaking, it is obvious that men enjoy a physical superiority to enable them to undertake hard and difficult work. However, this physical difference in their creation is no indicator of any superiority in terms of moral values, intelligence or psychological characteristics. On the contrary, it is essential if men are to discharge their duties of protecting women.

The Koran says nothing about man ruling over woman. According to the Koran, neither man nor woman can establish dominion over the other. Both are created in such a way as to complement one another, and with equal rights and responsibilities before God. The fact that women are protected and watched over by men is due to the superior value bestowed on women by God.

Superiority lies in piety, not gender

Through the verses of the Koran, God has placed women under protection as delights and blessings. However, He also holds Muslim men and Muslim women equal in terms of service to Islam. Both have a duty to worship God, to live by the moral values of the Koran, to tell people to do good and avoid evil and to obey all the commandments and advice revealed in the Koran. In the verse **"You who believe! If you have fear of God, He will give you discrimination and erase your bad actions from you and forgive you. God's favor is indeed immense."** (Koran, 8:29) God promises that He will give everyone who fears Him discrimination, the ability to distinguish between right and wrong.

191

It makes no difference if the person is a man or a woman. In return for sincerity, purity and faith, God will lead a person onto the true path in every sphere of his life and give him the intelligence with which to take accurate decisions and to behave in a proper manner. Intelligence therefore comes about on the basis of sincere devotion and proximity to and fear of God, rather than of a person's gender.

The sole measure of superiority among male and female Muslims who wage an intellectual campaign against irreligious trends in the name of God **is piety.** In one verse our Lord says:

> **Mankind! We created you from a male and female, and made you into peoples and tribes so that you might come to know each other. The noblest among you in God's Sight is the one with the most piety. God is All-Knowing, All-Aware. (Koran, 49:13)**

This verse is the finest answer to the fundamentalists described above. Those who supposedly point to the Koran as evidence for regarding men as superior to women **are lying; they are trying to deceive people with invented superstitions. Examination of the verses of the Koran and the life of our Prophet (pbuh) will suffice to show that this has nothing to do with the true Islam.**

Almighty God speaks of male and female believers in several verses. **Men and women are not kept separate in the Koran.** In speaking of believers, God stresses that they must be people of piety, not whether they are men or women. The distinction in terms of superiority in the Koran is between believers who do good works and hypocrites and unbelievers, not between men and women. Everyone who acts in the light of the wisdom bestowed by faith, whether male or female, can achieve success in all areas of life and move ahead of a great many other people. This is entirely dependent on a person's ambition, wishes and enthusiasm. As stipulated by the moral values of Islam, believers never regard themselves as sufficient on any matter. They always strive to be wiser, more talented, more responsible and of better character and morals.

Almighty God reveals in verses that there is no distinction among Muslims between men and women and that any superiority among them lies solely in faith, sincerity, purity and fear of God, in other words in piety:

> The men and women of the believers are friends of one another. They command what is right and forbid what is wrong, and perform their prayers and pay alms, and obey God and His Messenger. They are the people on whom God will have mercy. God is Almighty, All-Wise. God has promised the men and women of the believers Gardens with rivers flowing under them, remaining in them timelessly, forever, and fine dwellings in the Gardens of Eden. And God's good pleasure is even greater. That is the great victory. (Koran, 9:71-72)

> Men and women who are Muslims, men and women who are believers, men and women who are obedient, men and women who are truthful, men and women who are steadfast, men and women who are humble, men and women who give alms, men and women who fast, men and women who guard their private parts, men and women who remember God much: God has prepared forgiveness for them and an immense reward. (Koran, 33:35)

As is quite clear from this verse, women and men are equal in their responsibilities to God. Equality between men and women can be seen from the way that God recognizes equal rights for men and women during the test in the life of this world.

Through the verses **"We made everything on the Earth adornment for it so that We could test them to see whose actions are the best."** (Koran, 18:7) and **"Every self will taste death. We test you with both good and evil as a trial. And you will be returned to Us."** (Koran, 21:35), God reveals that men and women are tested in order to reveal who will behave best. In another verse, God says **"We will test you with a certain amount of fear and hunger and loss of wealth and life and fruits. But**

193

give good news to the steadfast" (Koran, 2:155), thus revealing that men and women will be tested through various events up to the end of their lives, and that those who can exhibit fortitude in the face of them will receive His mercy.

God ordains the course of life for men and women. He holds them both responsible for the Koran. He has given them both a conscience to inspire them to do what is right at all moments of their lives and has made their lower selves and satan enemies of them both. God has also revealed that as a requirement of the test in the life of this world, if a man or a woman exhibits good moral values and does good deeds, then they will enjoy the finest reward in this world and the hereafter:

> **Anyone, <u>male or female</u>, who does right actions and is a believer, will enter the Garden. They will not be wronged by so much as the tiniest speck. (Koran, 4:124)**

Women's rights are always protected in the Koran

Through the moral values of the Koran which establish peace and justice among people all a woman's rights in both social life and the family are placed under protection; this is without doubt a great mercy, comfort and blessing. When people act in the light of the moral values revealed by God, women will not be left in difficulties and their futures and comfort will be guaranteed.

In the following section, we shall be looking at some of the verses that discuss women and guarantee their social rights and revealing the value and prestige bestowed on women under Islamic moral values.

194

Women must be contented and satisfied in the event of divorce

For some people who live according to their earthly desires, divorce means the end of all relations based on self-interest with the other party. These people believe that once these self-interested relations have ended, there is no longer any need to respect or esteem the other side. Most of the time, since they have lost all respect and affection for the person they have left, they act solely in such a way as to protect their own interests and may ignore such matters as the other party being in want or facing difficulties. The fact is, however, that in the Koran our Almighty Lord describes how women should be treated with affection and compassion, and treated well, after divorce:

> **When you divorce women and they are near the end of their dowry, then either retain them with correctness and courtesy or release them with correctness and courtesy.... (Koran, 2:231)**

> **You who have faith! When you marry believing women and then divorce them before you have touched them, there is no dowry for you to calculate for them, so give them a gift and let them go with kindness. (Koran, 33:49)**

The kindness, respect, care, compassion and protection that a man needs to show a woman during and after divorce are commanded by the Koran. Such a morality can only be lived by adherence to the Koran. The greatest value is clearly placed on woman in Islam. In order to see that, one should look at the verses of the Koran and the policies of our Prophet (pbuh), not at the deceptions of those who fabricate superstitions.

195

Women must be given financial security after divorce

Islam commands that women must be provided with material security after divorce. The Koran forbids a divorced woman being left abandoned, unprotected and financially unsupported. If someone is a pure believer who abides by the Koran, then he has an obligation to adhere to these commands set out by God in the Koran. Such a person will in any case do this willingly and punctiliously out of his love of God.

Verses from the Koran setting out the obligation to give financial security to divorced women read as follows:

> **Divorced women should receive maintenance given with correctness and courtesy: a duty for all who have fear of God.** (Koran, 2:241)

> **But give them a gift** – he who is wealthy according to his means and he who is less well-off according to his means – a gift to be given with correctness and courtesy: **a duty for all good-doers.** (Koran, 2:236)

> **He who has plenty should spend out from his plenty, but he whose provision is restricted should spend from what God has given him.** God does not demand from any self more than He has given it. God will appoint after difficulty, ease. (Koran, 65:7)

As these verses show, whether rich or someone of limited means, a believer is held responsible for protecting his divorced wife. Even if he never sees her again, and even if he stands to gain nothing from her, he still has a responsibility to ensure the financial security of the wife he has divorced and to treat her with kindness. Almighty God also reveals in verses the need to do this willingly and sincerely, without reluctance:

> **Give women their dowry willingly. But if they are happy to give you some of it, make use of it with pleasure and goodwill.** (Koran, 4:4)

Goods given to women must not be taken back after divorce

Our Almighty Lord also reveals in verses that in the event of divorce the man must not take back those things he gave his wife during their marriage:

If you desire to exchange one wife for another and have given your original wife a large amount, do not take any of it. Would you take it by means of slander and outright crime? How could you take it when you have been intimate with one another and they have made a binding contract with you? (Koran, 4:20-21)

... It is not lawful for you to keep anything you have given them [the women]... (Koran, 2:229)

God recalls in verses that with marriage, a man has given the woman a promise and a guarantee. And because of that promise, he must not ask to take anything back, no matter how much he has given her. He who has faith, fears God and seeks to attain His approval in all he does knows that this promise is made before God. He will therefore be most scrupulous to discharge his obligation on the subject. This is a very lofty moral value, but one that is acted on almost nowhere in the world. This is one of the greatest errors of the fundamentalists who fail to realize the depth of the Koran and its conception of love and affection, and of those who make the mistake of regarding such people as the true representatives of Islam. The only place where women are valued as they deserve is the Koran.

Some Christians wonder why these commands are not acted on at the moment in Islamic countries and generally approach the matter with suspicion. The reason, of course, is that people do not live by the real moral values of the Koran in Islamic countries, and that superstitions fabricated by fundamentalists prevail in many of them. Otherwise, every Muslim who acts in the light of the Koran will abide by these commands with a peaceful heart and happiness.

Women must be found accommodation after divorce

The verses of the Koran hold a man responsible for the security and comfort of his wife even after they divorce. A woman who until that time had all her needs met by her husband or the circumstances prevailing in the marriage may find herself in all manner of difficulties after divorce. The moral values of a believer require that under such circumstances a person should be as understanding and helpful as possible, considering the other person's needs in as much detail as if they were his own needs. That is why our Lord has set out in verses the precautions that need to be taken and the moral virtues that need to be exhibited in conditions, especially such as divorce, in which a woman may suffer great difficulties. Almighty God advises the man to keep the woman close by him during the divorce so that she should not experience difficulties and to ensure that she is sufficiently protected. Indeed, He says that this means that he should watch out for her in times of danger. Making appropriate facilities available for her after divorce until she can find a place of her own to live and ensuring that no harm comes to her is an important responsibility for a believer:

> **Let them [the women that you have divorced] live where you live, according to your means. Do not put pressure on them, so as to harass them. If they are pregnant, maintain them until they give birth. If they are suckling for you, give them their wages and consult together with correctness and courtesy. But if you make things difficult for one another, another woman should do the suckling for you. (Koran, 65:6)**

The importance of this needs to be reiterated: these protective measures cited in the verses do not, of course, mean that a woman is too weak to fend for herself; that is simply one of the fabrications spread by prejudiced people in order to attack Islam. The aforementioned verses speak of a superior moral value. The subject here is a kindly moral value attaching superiority and value to women. It is a question of watching out for the woman and making her feel she is a valued and respected person. It means translating the importance that God bestows on women and His protection of them into reality.

Women must not be inherited by force

One of the obligations in terms of the protection of women is that they should not be inherited by force. God says in one verse:

> **You who believe! It is not lawful for you to inherit women by force. Nor may you treat them harshly so that you can make off with part of what you have given them, unless they commit an act of flagrant indecency. Live together with them correctly and courteously...** (Koran, 4:19)

Through this verse, God forbids any pressure being placed on women and any measure that might make things difficult for them in material terms.

The importance attached to mothers

The station of motherhood is exalted in the Koran. Respect for one's parents, treating them well and watching over and protecting them in their elderly years, and at all other times, are responsibilities particularly imposed on devout believers in the Koran, and there are several verses on the subject. Some of these are as follows:

> **We have instructed man to honor his parents,...** (Koran, 29:8)

Muslims are advised in the Koran to respect their parents and treat them well. But mothers are shown a particular respect. As God reveals in verses:

We have instructed <u>man concerning his parents.</u> <u>Bearing him caused his mother great debility</u> and the period of his weaning was two years: <u>"Give thanks to Me and to your parents. I am your final destination."</u> (Koran, 31:14)

<u>We have instructed man to be good to his parents. His mother bore him with difficulty and with difficulty gave birth to him; and his bearing and weaning take thirty months.</u> Then when he achieves his full strength and reaches forty, he says, "My Lord, <u>keep me thankful for the blessing You bestowed on me and on my parents</u>, and keep me acting rightly, pleasing You. And make my descendants righteous. I have repented to You and I am truly one of the Muslims." (Koran, 46:15)

Every mother makes great sacrifices for months in order to bring her child into the world, and that is simply the matter of pregnancy; it goes without saying that every mother makes great sacrifice for her child throughout her life. As God reveals in the verse, she carries her baby inside her, putting up with immense difficulties, and then brings it into the world with more great difficulty. Then afterward she engages in more great self-sacrifice to ensure its comfort in all respects and to ensure that it is protected. Moreover, she expects no reward for doing all this, and relegates her own needs to a secondary status. God reminds us of these truths and tells us that mothers are highly valuable people.

Even though the importance and value placed on women in the Koran is made clear with such explicit statements, and even though women are protected in all ways, some Christians still presume to claim that women are despised in Islam and to criticize those true Muslims who live by the Koran by pointing to evidence from those who fabricate nonsense. What these people need to do is to read these verses with care and reflect upon them without prejudice. It is also quite amazing how these people insist on criticizing the Koran while ignoring certain statements regarding women that appear in the Torah and the Gospel.

Some Misguided Statements Regarding Women in the Torah and the Gospel

Misconceptions regarding the Islamic view of women are frequently brought up by some Christian groups, particularly as of late. The fact is, however, that as we have seen in detail, the Koranic view of women is based on love, affection, compassion and justice.

The way that some Christian groups who produce these criticisms of Islam **never mention certain statements that appear in the Torah and the Gospel is grounds for suspicion. When we look at the Torah and the Gospel we see that some very terrible things are said in regard to women.**

For example, in the Torah, which Christians also regard as a holy book and one of their own scriptures, the punishment for an adulteress is to be **stoned to death.** Contrary to the practice in certain Islamic countries, stoning to death appears absolutely nowhere in the Koran itself. But it does in the Torah. Passages on the subject read as follows:

> If a man is found lying with a married woman, _both the woman and the man_ lying with her shall be put to death. You shall thus rid Israel of evil. (Deuteronomy, 22: 22)

> [This is the law] where a virgin girl is betrothed to one man, and another man comes across her in the city and has intercourse with her. _Both of them_ shall be brought to the gates of that city, and _they shall be put to death by stoning._ [The penalty shall be imposed on] the girl because she did not cry out [even though she was] in the city, and on the man, because he violated his neighbor's wife. You shall thus rid yourselves of evil. (Deuteronomy, 22: 23-24)

If the accusation is true, however, and the girl does not have evidence of her innocence, then they shall take her out to the door of her father's house, and the people of her city shall put her to death by stoning. (Deuteronomy, 22: 20-21)

If a man commits adultery with a married woman, [and] she is the wife of a fellow [Israelite], both the adulterer and adulteress shall be put to death. (Leviticus, 20:10)

If a man has intercourse with his father's wife, he has committed a sexual offense against his father. Therefore, both of them shall be put to death by stoning. (Leviticus, 20:11)

If a man has intercourse with his daughter-in-law, both of them shall be put to death. Since they have committed an utterly detestable perversion, they shall be stoned to death. (Leviticus, 20:12)

If a man marries a woman and her mother, it is a perversion, and both he and they shall be burned with fire. (Leviticus, 20:14)

In the Koran, on the other hand, someone who accuses another person of adultery has to produce **four eyewitnesses to the event.** A person can only be convicted of adultery in the presence of four witnesses and if those witnesses were present and actually saw the event with their own eyes.

After conviction, the punishment is a hundred strokes (Koran, 24:2-8). The sentence is clearly intended as a deterrent because the presence of four eyewitnesses during the commission of adultery is impossible in practice.

Verses also say that **if four witnesses cannot be produced the charges are to be rejected:**

And the punishment is removed from her if she testifies four times by God that he [her husband] is lying. (Koran, 24:8)

In the Torah, however, the punishment for adultery is **stoning to death**. In addition, there is no need to produce eyewitnesses; mere allegation is enough for conviction. Some Christians criticize Islam on this subject but say nothing about this command in the Torah. Such a cruel and blatant rule could be laid at the door of all Jews and Christians if one so wished. These matters could lead to the emergence of very peculiar ideas about Christians and Jews. But Muslims regard the rule here **as intended to be a deterrent, one that could never be applied in practice, and their view of Christians and Jews develops accordingly.**

Another example concerns female prisoners in towns under siege. All captives, male or female are placed under protection in the Koran, which commands that they should be released at the end of hostilities. But according to the Torah, **women and children** in a besieged town are the **"property of the enemy" and "can be pillaged"**:

> *If they reject your peace offer and declare war, you shall lay siege to [the city]. When God your Lord gives it over into your hand, <u>you shall then strike down its [adult] males by the sword. However, the women, children, animals, and all the goods in the city, you shall take as your spoils.</u> You shall thus consume the spoils that God your Lord gives you from your enemies. (Deuteronomy, 20:12-14)*

Furthermore, in some circumstances, women and even children and babies in besieged towns must **be put to death:**

> *However, Moses was angry at the generals and captains, who were the officers returning from the military campaign. <u>"Why have you kept all the women alive?"</u> demanded Moses. "These are exactly the ones who were involved with the Israelites at Balaam's instigation, causing them to be unfaithful to God in the Peor incident, and bringing a plague on God's community. Now <u>kill every male child, as well as every woman who has been involved intimately with a man</u>. However, all the young girls who*

have not been involved intimately with a man, you may keep alive for yourselves." (Numbers, 31: 14-18)

"Now this is what the Sovereign Lord says: Bring an army against them and hand them over to be terrorized and plundered. For their enemies will stone them and kill them with swords. They will butcher their sons and daughters and burn their homes. (Ezekiel, 23: 46-47)

... I will shatter men and women, old people and children, young men and maidens. (Jeremiah, 51: 22)

Every one that is found shall be thrust through; and every one that is joined unto them shall fall by the sword. Their children also shall be dashed to pieces before their eyes; their houses shall be spoiled, and their wives ravished.. And their bows shall dash the young men in pieces; and they shall have no pity on the fruit of the womb; their eye shall not spare children. (Isaiah, 13: 15-18)

And to the others He said in my hearing, "Pass through the city after him, and strike. Your eye shall not spare, and you shall show no pity. Kill old men outright, young men and maidens, little children and women ..." (Ezekiel, 9: 5-6)

Now go and smite Amalek, and utterly destroy all that they have, and spare them not; but slay both man and woman, infant and suckling, ox and sheep, camel and ass. (1st Samuel, 15: 3)

We destroyed [these cities] just as we had done to those of Sichon, king of Cheshbon, annihilating every man, woman and child. (Deuteronomy, 3:6)

God our Lord gave him over to us, so that we killed him along with his sons and all his troops. We then captured all his cities, and we annihilated every city, including the men, women and children, not leaving any survivors. (Deuteronomy, 2: 33-34)

The need **to leave nothing alive, not even women and children,** is another of the laws in the Torah:

204

That is what you must do to the cities that are very far from you, and which do not belong to the nations that are here. However, when dealing with the cities of these nations, which God your Lord is giving you as hereditary territory, <u>you shall not allow any people to remain alive.</u> Where the Hittites, Amorites, Canaanites, Perizites, Hivites, and Yebusites are involved, <u>you must wipe them out completely,</u> as God your Lord commanded you. (Deuteronomy, 20:15-17)

As verses make clear, the penalty for theft in Islam is the severing of the hand in order to prevent repeated acts. But if a person repents of the crime he has committed, then the penalty is not enforced (Koran, 5:38-39). Nobody will renounce the blessing of repentance and forgiveness in the knowledge that they will suffer such a deterrent penalty. Therefore, **the rule here is intended merely to act as a deterrent, not to be enforced.**

Christians who criticize Muslims because of this rule should really have a look at the Torah. The penalty of loss of a hand **appears in the Torah on some interesting pretexts. The penalty is also intended to be enforced, and there is no question of having pity:**

If a man is fighting with his brother, and the wife of one comes to defend her husband, grabbing his attacker by his private parts, <u>you must cut off her hand</u> and not have any pity. (Deuteronomy, 25: 11-12)

Another of the interesting rules regarding women in the Torah is this:

If a woman presents herself to an animal and allows it to mate with her, you shall kill both the woman and the animal. <u>They shall be put to death by stoning.</u> (Leviticus, 20: 16)

The same thing applies to the Gospel. Some Christians accuse Muslims of regarding women as second-class citizens. Yet **when one looks at the Gospel, there are striking statements in it placing women in the position of second-class citizens and**

205

about men being created to have dominion over them. Passages from the Gospel along these lines are:

> For *the husband is the head of the wife*, even as Christ is the head of the church:. *(Ephesians, 5:23)*

> Let your women keep silence in the churches: for *it is not permitted unto them to speak;* but they are commanded to be under obedience, as also saith the law. *(Corinthians, 14: 34-35)*

> But I suffer *not a woman to teach, nor to busurp authority over the man,* but to be in silence. For Adam was first formed, then Eve. And Adam was not deceived, but the woman being deceived was in the transgression. *(Timothy, 2:12-14)*

> *Neither was the man created for the woman; but the woman for the man.* *(Corinthinas, 11: 9)*

While, as we have seen, there are such statements intended to degrade women in Judaism and Christianity, it is inconceivable how some people choose to close their eyes to them and try to blacken the name of Islam. There is no explanation for the way that these people presume to target Islam because of rules that in any case do not appear in the Koran. If Muslims do not look at Christians and Jews in that way and know that there are some fanatics who despise women among Jews and Christians but do not ascribe their views to those two faiths, then Christians should likewise not adopt a false view of Muslims, pointing to nonsense with no place in the Koran and the fanatics who abide by it as supposed evidence.

The Real Enemies of Women Are Fundamentalists, Hypocrites, Darwinists,

Materialists, Communists and Fascists

Treating women as second-class people, denigrating them at every opportunity, refusing to regard them as blessings and, in short, hating them, are all characteristics of Darwinists, materialists, communists, fascists and fundamentalists. In the same way that these people take no pleasure from any beauty and have no understanding of art, beauty, pleasant scents, animals, plants or music, so they are unable to understand the value of women, who are created as blessings. That is largely because they are themselves spiritually uneasy and live lives devoid of cleanliness and loveliness; they are unable to appreciate beauty. Their lives are full of troubles rather than pleasures, for which reason they approach blessings with rage and hatred.

Under fundamentalism, the person who most despises women and treats them as second-class people is held up as a role model. This sad truth goes for the fundamentalists of all three faiths. Yet the fact is that the fundamentalists who appear in the name of Islam act in total contravention of the Koran and live lifestyles that have no place in the verses of the Koran and the practices of our Prophet (pbuh). It is senseless to ascribe the ideas of these people, who abide by a superstitious faith and nonsense of their own creation, rather than by Islam, to Islam.

The perverse logic with regard to women of course has its roots in Darwinism, the main cause of irreligion. Darwin had no qualms whatsoever about expressing views that blatantly despised women. In his book, *The Descent of Man,* he says that with regard to women's ability to reason, understand and mimic, they possess the characteristics of "inferior races" and therefore **they possess an outdated and inferior civilization.** (John R. Durant, "The Ascent of Nature in Darwin's Descent of Man" in *The Darwinian Heritage*, Ed. by David Kohn, Princeton, NJ: Princeton University Press, 1985, p. 295). It is immediately apparent what kind of terrifying lifestyle such a mindset that regards women as an inferior race still in the process of evolving represents. Darwin, who did possess such a bigoted mindset, described women's place in marriage in these unbelievable words:

> *... a constant companion, (friend in old age) who will feel interested in one, an object to be beloved and played with—better than a dog anyhow—... (Charles Darwin, The Autobiography of Charles Darwin 1809-1882, Edited by Nora Barlow, W. W. Norton & Company Inc., New York, 1958, pp. 232-233)*

Fundamentalists, hypocrites, communists, fascists and atheists have maintained this terrifying view of Darwin's. The foul and fanatical Darwinist mentality maintains this attitude toward women. **This is the prevailing logic in all communist societies. It is the mindset of some Darwinist religious teachers** who appear in the name of Islam. **It is the fundamentalists who kill their baby daughters as soon as they are born** – even though female infanticide is explicitly prohibited in the Koran – **and regard themselves as humiliated by having daughters.** The Koran is always on the side of women and stresses the importance of protecting them, while with Darwinists, fundamentalists and hypocrites, the whole system is predicated on protecting men and the general oppression of women. This perverse mentality that despises women is therefore that of Darwin and the radicals, not of Islam.

Women are today treated as second-class people in all societies that do not live as the moral values of Islam require. The community that attaches the greatest value to women is that of Muslims who fully abide by the moral values of Islam and the practices of our Prophet (pbuh). That is why those people who seek to give the impression that the foul ideas of societies that are irreligious or live by nonsense instead of the Koran, actually stem from Islam are gravely mistaken. Islam attaches the highest value to women and is the only faith that recognizes all their rights, protects their lives and values them as they deserve.

SECTION 3
There is no compulsion in the religion. This is an absolute rule of the Koran.

The Koran's commandment is an explicit one: **There is no compulsion in the religion.** This is revealed as follows in verses:

> <u>There is no compulsion where the religion is concerned.</u> **Right guidance has become clearly distinct from error. Anyone who rejects false gods and has faith in God has grasped the Firmest Handhold, which will never give way. God is All-Hearing, All-Knowing. (Koran, 2:256)**

> **If your Lord had willed, all the people on the Earth would have had faith.** <u>**Do you think you can force people to be believers?**</u> **(Koran, 10:99)**

> **He said, "My people! What do you think? If I were to have clear evidence from my Lord and He had given me a mercy direct from Him, but you were blind to it,** <u>**could we force it on you if you were unwilling?"**</u> **(Koran, 11:28)**

> **Say: "Unbelievers! I do not worship what you worship and you do not worship what I worship. Nor will I worship what you worship nor will you worship what I worship. You have your religion and I have my religion." (Koran, 109:1-6)**

Believers obey God's command to **"command what is lawful and forbid what is unlawful"** and call people to the path of God with gentle words. However, it is God Who bestows guidance (Koran, 28:56), and all Muslims who read and comprehend the Koran know this full well. Therefore, the duty of a Muslim is to tell people about the Koran and to invite them to it, to preach, in other words. Only people who find guidance will heed this call, while those without will reject it. This means that no matter how hard you work at it, someone who has not found guidance will never become a true Muslim. It is therefore unlawful in the eyes of the Koran to compel such people, and compulsion produces no results.

Islam means submission. In order for someone to enter Islam, find true guidance and become a true Muslim, he must genuinely submit himself to God and the Koran.

But what happens if someone is forced to become a Muslim?

If someone is forced to convert to Islam, he will be a hypocrite, not a Muslim. He will worship and pray through compulsion, as a result of which he will most likely become a hypocrite full of rage and hatred. He will detest Islam and Muslims and, while appearing to be a Muslim, he will spend his life trying to lead Muslims into traps.

The hypocrite is Muslims' worst enemy, and the lowest form of life on Earth. God regards hypocrites as deserving of the lowest level of hell. These base creatures constantly seek to harm Muslims. Therefore, to go against God's command and try to compel someone to become a Muslim merely results in generating hypocrites and ends in harm. This is one of the last things Muslims should ever want.

Forcing someone to be a Muslim is also against the general spirit of the Koran. There is a conception of justice set out in the Koran, according to which all ideas and opinions are as free as possible. God makes this clear in the verse **"You have your religion and I have my religion,"** (Koran, 109:6) addressed to the unbelievers. This means full democracy, freedom of religion and belief. In other words, freedom of belief and democracy have their origins in the Koran. When this conception enshrined in the Koran spreads across the world, then we will have complete democracy and liberty. This system of justice is a law of humanity that includes all communities, the whole world and all beliefs: It is the law of God. The commandments of the Koran are created so as to bring people material and psychological comfort.

There is absolutely no commandment in the verses of the Koran that can offend anyone or make them uneasy. Islam was sent down so that people could live in happiness and tranquility. A Muslim has a responsibility to pray for others, even idolators to find happiness, to treat them with compassion and to protect and watch over them. God has given Muslims a responsibility even to protect unbelievers as they go from one place to another. Muslims are charged with protecting unbelievers even at the cost of their own lives. One verse on the subject reads:

If any of the idolators ask you for protection, give them protection until they have heard the words of God. <u>Then convey them to a place where they are safe.</u> That is because they are a people who do not know. (Koran, 9:6)

Islam is a religion built on love, affection, understanding and respect. Those who engage in other practices are unacquainted with and do not live by the moral values of Islam.

Fundamentalists are Dissimulating When They Say, "There Is No Compulsion in the Religion"

Some people point to various Muslims who initially say "there is no compulsion in the religion" but later employ stealthy and compulsive tactics to impose it, and suggest that Muslims are employing dissimulation on this matter. First of all, these people need to make a careful distinction between true Muslims and extremists who live by superstitions rather than by the Koran. A fundamentalist is a radical who has failed to fully grasp the goodness and wisdom in the commandments that God has revealed in the Koran, who has failed to properly understand the spirit of the Koran and who is therefore not convinced that the Koran is the one true Book. He, in his own eyes, imagines that if he resorts to force and compulsion, despite God's clear command and the verses of the Koran, then some people can become Muslims. Yet this

211

blatantly flies in the face of our Lord's commands. The result, as we have already seen, is hypocrites, enemies of Islam and people who regard the faith as one of compulsion and force.

When Islam is properly and fully applied, as in the time of our Prophet (pbuh), when people fully live by the verses of the Koran, only then will people be living by the real Islam. Nothing else is Islam. People who regard even a single verse of the Koran as insufficient have abandoned the faith. Things done by such people in the name of Islam, that have no place in the faith, cannot be attributed to Islam, in exactly the same way that **fanatics who kill and burn mosques and copies of the Koran cannot be attributed to Christianity.**

If a practice is incompatible with verses of the Koran, then it is not Islamic. Therefore, if Christians wish to learn the essence of and truth about Islam, they must look to the Koran alone.

The Koran Declares War on Fundamentalism

The Koran has declared war on all forms of affliction caused by fundamentalism; unhappiness, oppression, lovelessness, anger and bloodshed. The Islam based on the Koran is the exact opposite of fundamentalism.

Islam advises love, peace and friendship. It encourages unity, exalting the name of God together, brotherhood and the establishment of peace and security in the world.

Fundamentalism cannot be eliminated by declaring war on Islam

Those who mistakenly equate fundamentalism with Islam itself and wish to eliminate this extremist system are generally making a major error in adopting a hostile attitude toward Islam. Some elements of the atheist, materialist and Darwinist press, think tanks and other circles influential in global politics are attempting to spread this false perspective. The people in question deliberately misrepresent what it is to be a Muslim and incite hostility toward Islam and Muslims by saying, **"This is what Muslims are like, they deny you the right to exist, so you must destroy them before they destroy you."**

Under the influence of this conditioning, some Christians maintain the need for a fight against the Koran and Islam in order to eradicate the wrongful practices that the extremist system brings with it (surely Islam and the Koran are beyond that). But this, which is a violation of reason and good conscience, **simply leads to the further encouragement and growth of extremism. All attacks on the Koran and true Islam merely strengthen the extremist system that believes in the need for violence against all those who think differently from it.** The only way to eradicate the bloody system that these extremists espouse **is to bring the Koran and the true Islam into the foreground** and to make them a reality again, as in the Age of Bliss.

The joyful, extroverted, modern and progressive lives of true Muslims, built on love, affection, friendship and brotherhood cause extremists a great deal of unhappiness and discomfort. Therefore, our Christian brothers should therefore support true Muslims and act together with them against the extremist mindset, which is opposed to Christians and Jews as well as Muslims.

Combating extremism is a religious observance for Muslims because striving against those who ascribe equals to God is one of the commandments of the Koran. Extremist is another term for the word "idolaters" in the Koran. Almighty God speaks in verses of the hypocrites and unbelievers and those with sickness in their hearts; these are all idolaters. They are the enemies of the Age of Bliss, <u>**people who declare war on the Koran in the name of the Koran**</u>.

This struggle has to be an intellectual one, an ideological struggle, of course. Extremists are generally uneducated and ill-informed people who are unacquainted with the Koran for various reasons. These people therefore need to be educated if the fundamentalist threat is to be done away with. Once they are educated and understand the true Islam as described in the Koran, they will of course see the illogicality of the fundamentalist mindset.

The perverse school that is loveless, unaffectionate, ruthless, unintelligent, uncultured and ill-mannered, that dislikes art and science, that is unable to think deeply, that is all show, that seeks to make religion unnecessarily complex and that wants to invent its own religion on the basis of constant fabrications and superstitions is properly referred to as "fundamentalism," or the "school of the idolaters." **An extremist system that has been developed in complete opposition to the Koran, that does not regard the Koran sufficient and that applies the exact opposite of what is commanded in the Koran is one against which Muslims must wage an intellectual struggle.**

The solution to extremism is to advocate the Islam of the Age of Bliss and true Koranic moral values and to educate people who have fallen into the clutches of fundamentalism. Our Prophet (pbuh) was against extremists and applied the blessings of democracy, love, respect and liberty brought with it by Islam in the most perfect manner.

Christians and Jews will also be at ease when people live by the moral values of the true Islam

It is very important for our Christian brothers to regard the explanations regarding concepts such as love, peace, democracy, freedom, happiness and modernity set out in this book as being made with the very best of intentions. These are not personal opinions: **They are the essence of the Koran.** These are what conform to the spirit of the Koran, to all the examples we see in the Prophet Muhammad (pbuh) and to the approval of God, the Compassionate and Merciful. This is how these rulings of the

Koran were applied in the time of our Prophet. Bloodshed exists only in the superstitions of the fundamentalists. People with a fundamentalist mindset under the influence of the antichrist have depicted Islam as bloodthirsty by striving to spread it across the world and have thus deceived vast masses of people.

It is of the utmost importance for Christians to see the true and essential message of the Koran. Our Prophet and the Koran are both sources of light for all the people in the world. Everything that makes people happy and illuminates the world is in the Koran. Everyone who looks with the eyes of good conscience and faith will clearly see this. Living by the Koran as in the time of the Age of Bliss will bring comfort and beauty to the entire world. Muslims applying the Koran in this way will also bring peace, happiness and comfort to Christians and Jews. As a result, an exceedingly happy life will prevail throughout the world. That is in any case what is in people's nature, and the seeds of joy that have disappeared under the influence of the antichrist will return. Joy will return to people. Art will expand and artists who create true art will appear. The architecture that has vanished under the influence of the antichrist will be restored to life. Peace, happiness, security, friendship, brotherhood and, most important of all, love of God, will spread across the world. Once the love of God is in people's hearts, art and joy, happiness and science will come to that society, in other words, all beauty and delight. The Koran is built upon a Muslim having affection, compassion, love and intelligence, behaving in a balanced way, thinking rationally, being altruistic, thinking the best of events and seeing goodness in all things. A world in which Islam spreads in this form will also be an extraordinarily beautiful place for Christians and Jews.

What Christians need to oppose and wage an intellectual struggle against is extremism, Darwinism and materialism; a major threat to all three faiths. What they need to support and espouse is people living by Islam as described in the Koran and the system of the Mahdi that will bring this about in our day. When they support this, all fundamentalism, Darwinism and materialism will disappear, a great joy will descend on the world and everything

215

and everywhere will be illuminated. Fundamentalism will be eliminated through the proper education of people who have fallen under the influence of Darwinist and materialist ideologies. As revealed in verses of the Koran, churches and synagogues are under the protection of God. Our Christian and Jewish brothers will be able to worship as they wish and will enjoy the comfort and security they desire. Muslims will live in brotherhood and love with Christians and Jews, wars will come to an end, there will be no more bloodshed and the world will become a place of peace where people live in well-being and tranquility. This is God's promise. It will definitely come true. But God wants us to make effort for it.

Our Prophet's (pbuh) Affectionate, Protective and Loving Attitude toward the People of the Book

During a Visit by the Christians of Najran our Prophet (pbuh) spread his robe out for them to sit on

There are a great many accounts of our Prophet (pbuh) attending weddings of the People of the Book, visiting them when they were sick and giving them gifts. Indeed, when the Christians of Najran visited the Prophet Muhammad he spread his robe out on the ground and invited his Christian guests to sit on it.

Our Prophet (pbuh) Said that the People of the Book Are under the Protection of Muslims

In the peace treaty he had drawn up with the Christian ibn Kharis ibn Ka'b, the Prophet Muhammad said: **"The faith, churches, honor and property of all Christians living in the east and west are under the protection of God, the Prophet and all believers.** None of those who live by Christianity shall be forced to convert to Islam against their will. If any Christian is killed or exposed to any injustice, **Muslims have a duty to come to his assistance."** *(Ibn Hisham, Abu Muhammad Abdulmalik, As-Siratu'n-Nabawiyya, Daru at-Turasi al-Arabiyla, Beirut, 1396/1971, II/141-150)*

Our Prophet (pbuh) Opened the Houses of the Companions for Visiting People of the Book to Stay in

Envoys and delegations would visit Medina in groups in the time of our Prophet. Delegations, including those of the People of the Book, might sometimes stay longer than 10 days, and the houses of Abdurrahman ibn Avf, Mughire ibn Shubea, Abu Ayyub al-Ansari and **some members of the al-Ansar would be made available for them.** In addition, accommodation used by the people of the Suffa studying around the Masjid al-Nabawi and a tent set up near the mosque would be prepared for visitors.

Our Prophet would give official documents, written commands discussing rights and privileges bestowed on certain individuals and groups and documents setting out agreements with foreigners, to some of those who came to meet him. These would set out the places set aside for them. He would appoint governors from among them to some regions. The Prophet would send alms officials to Muslims and collectors of the tax on non-Muslims to those who remained Christians. These official delegations that arrived were

217

evidence that the prophethood and sovereignty of the Prophet were recognized in the entire Arabian peninsula. *(Sarıçam, Hz. Muhammed ve Evrensel Mesajı [The Prophet Muhammad and His Universal Message], p. 356)*

Our Prophet (pbuh) Followed the Behavior of the People of the Book Rather than That of the Pagans of Mecca Regarding Some Matters Not Clarified by Revelation

The Messenger of God acted according to the **behavior of the People of the Book,** in opposition to the pagans of Mecca, on matters not clarified by revelation. *(Bukhari, Libas 70; Muslim, Fedail 90)*

Our Prophet (pbuh) sent Companions on Hegira to the Christian Najashi

The first Christian country to interest our Prophet before the hegira, and to which he wished Muslims to migrate, was Abyssinia. The Messenger of God desired the Muslims of Mecca to migrate to Abyssinia because of the ruthless persecution on the part of the pagans of Mecca. He expressed his feelings as follows:

If you wish and if it is possible, seek refuge in Abyssinia. Because nobody can be persecuted in the lands of the king who rules there. That is a safe and sure place, so remain there until God makes matters easier. (Hamidullah, al-Wasaiku as- Siyasiya, [trans. Vecdi Akyüz], Istanbul 1997, p.115; Hamidullah, İslam Peygamberi [The Prophet of Islam], vol. I, 297)

Our Prophet (pbuh) Rose to His Feet When the Funeral Cortège of a Jew Passed by

Jabir ibn Abdullah relates:

A funeral cortège passed by us. Our Prophet immediately rose to his feet for it. We followed him and also rose to our feet and said: "O Messenger of God, this is the funeral of a Jewish woman." Our Prophet replied: "... Rise to your feet at once when you see a funeral procession." (Muslim, Janaiz, 78, Hadith no: 1593)

Ibn Abu Layla narrates in an account from Qays ibn Sa'd'in:

A funeral procession passed by Qays ibn Sa'd and Sahl ibn Hunaif when they were in Qadisiyye. They rose to their feet. They were told that the funeral was that of one of the local people (a non-Muslim, in other words). Qays and Sahl said: A funeral procession passed by the Messenger of God. The Messenger of God rose to his feet. When he was told it was the funeral of a Jew, he said: "Is he not also a human being?" (Muslim, Janaiz, 78, Hadith no: 1596)

Our Prophet (pbuh) Commanded that Non-Muslims Should Not Be Oppressed

In one hadith our Prophet said, *"Whoever oppresses a non-Muslim, I will be his enemy."*

Our Prophet (pbuh) Spoke with Christians When the Prophethood Came to Him

When our Prophet (pbuh) began preaching with the title of Messenger of God, **he first met with various Christians** from Mecca. In the first days, when revelation began coming to him, it was Waraka bin Nawfel, a Christian with handwritten copies of the Gospel, who spoke with the Prophet and Hazrat Khadija. *(Bukhari, Bedu al-Vahy 3)*

Our Prophet (pbuh) Never Permitted Any Interference in Anyone's Religion

In 630 our Prophet who applied the verse *"La iqraha fi'd-dîn* **(There is no compulsion in the religion)"** (Koran, 2:256), an expression of the freedom to choose one's own religion, issued the following command to the envoys who arrived at Medina from the ruler of Khimyar to announce that they had become Muslims:

> *If a Jew or a Christian becomes a Muslim, they are then one of the believers (equal with them under the law).* ***But there can be no interference with anyone who wishes to remain in Judaism or Christianity.*** *(Ibn Hisham, as-Sira, vol.II, 586)*

Our Prophet (pbuh) Personally Did Business with Jews

One of the values on which the Messenger of God based his relations with other people is honesty. The fact that someone in whom he saw this virtue was a member of another faith did not stop him entering into business relations with them. **He personally received foodstuffs from Jews of Medina.**

The Affection that Our Prophet (pbuh) Showed to the Jews in the Time of the Capture of Khaibar

Among the booty secured after the capture of Khaibar were copies of the Torah in scroll form. **Our Prophet had these scrolls removed from the booty and ordered that they be returned to the Jews.**

Again after the capture of Khaibar, Muslim troops began eating from the orchards and date groves belonging to Jews. The Jews complained to the Prophet. **Our Prophet commanded that the goods, orchards and gardens belonging to the people of the region should not be touched.**

Through the Constitution of Medina Our Prophet (pbuh) Commanded that There Should Be No Interference with the Faiths of Jews and Christians

The **Constitution of Medina** that our Prophet signed with Christian, Jewish and pagan communities is a most important example of justice. One of the articles of the constitution reads as follows:

> *The Jews of the Bnai Awf are the same community as the believers, **the Jews have their own faith and the Muslims have their own faith.***

Article 16 of the Constitution says, **"The Jews who follow us will enjoy the right to our help and support, with no injustice being inflicted on them and with no succor for their enemies."**

After our Prophet (pbuh), the Companion remained loyal to this rule that he had placed in the Constitution, and also applied it to the **Berbers, Buddhists, Brahmans and holders of similar beliefs.**

221

In the Protection Treaty He Gave to the People of Najran Our Prophet (pbuh) Said They Were under the Protection of Muslims

The freedoms our Prophet gave to the People of the Book from Edruh, Makna, Khaibar, Najran and Aqaba show that **the lives and property of the People of the Book were placed under the protection of Muslims and that they recognized their freedom of belief and worship.** These articles on the agreement our Prophet made with the people of Najran are particularly striking:

The lives, belongings, religion, assets, families, churches and everything else belonging to the people of Najran and their associates will be placed under the protection of God and the Prophet of God.

No bishop or monk will be forced from his church or monastery and no priest will be forced to abandon the life of the priesthood. ***No oppression or contempt will be shown them and their lands will not be invaded by our armies.*** *If anyone makes a rightful demand, a just ruling will be made in Najran...*

Their duty is to strive on loyalty and responsibilities. They will suffer no persecution or oppression.

An alliance between believers is obligatory

What belief in God, justice and good conscience demand is an intellectual struggle against the opponents of belief in God and the demolition of their ideological infrastructure by exposing all the evils in the world. The actions of those who foolishly seek to misuse the great religion of Islam in acts of violence, of ignorant people who bear the name of Muslim, or who are in fact atheists, and take part in actions which are incompatible with Islam and the verses of the Koran must be exposed.

It is impossible for a sincere believer to be taken in by the plans of the supporters of the antichrist by ignoring the true essence of Islam. Because of this covert and systematic conditioning, some Christians keep their distance from Muslims and even form a front of opposition against them. By doing this, under the influence of some people who portray themselves as Evangelical Christians but who in fact are opponents of the faith, they encourage feelings of hatred and anger toward Muslims. Instead of forming the necessary alliance, as people who truly love God, with the friends of God they, intentionally or not, follow the path of a stealthy organization in the vanguard of a Darwinist and terrorist system. They fail to see the dreadful harm that this erroneous belief does to both themselves and to all the believers in the world.

By God's leave, **the name and the word of God will emerge victorious and rule the world.** This is God's promise to all true believers. But in order to be instrumental in this, we still need to make use of natural causes and to establish a great union of faith across the world. If genuine Evangelical Christians can see the cunning plans of evangelical followers of the antichrist and become aware of the grave danger approaching and form an alliance with genuine and devout Muslims, then it will be possible to build a world in which everyone can live in peace and tranquility and in which wars and conflicts come to an end. As a blessing from God, they will live more peaceful, easier and pleasanter lives.

When they become better aware of the dimensions of the true danger being pioneered by atheist fanatics –in other words, the danger of atheism, Darwinism, materialism, Marxism and communism– then they will oppose all these perverse systems that have declared war on belief in God, and will wage the real struggle in the company of all other believers. By Almighty God's leave, the time of the coming of Jesus (pbuh) and Hazrat Mahdi (pbuh), awaited with great excitement by the members of all three faiths, is

223

imminent. According to the Koran, as required by God's promise, all Christians at that time will, of their own volition, heed Jesus' call for peace and unity. According to the Koran, when Jesus returns, nobody from the People of the Book (Christians and Jews) will refuse to believe in him before his death. (Koran, 4:159) Then, by permission of our Almighty Lord, they will realize that what really needs to be done is to constitute a powerful union of love and alliance between believers. The really essential thing, now that the time of the coming of Jesus and Hazrat Mahdi is so imminent, is to be aware of this and **to prepare a climate in which these blessed individuals can work easily by preparing the requisite intellectual environment for them.** It is of course an absolute fact that God has no need of anything in order to bring about the reign of Islamic moral values, peace, justice and love. (Surely God is beyond that.) However, God has also bestowed the blessing of prayer and reward on all believers. **A powerful alliance among sincere believers is equivalent to a prayer for irreligion to vanish from the world and for the name of our Almighty Lord to be remembered across the world as the One and Only.**

224

CHAPTER 8
JESUS (PBUH) HAS COME

Jesus (pbuh) and Hazrat Mahdi (pbuh) Are in the World Now

The great coming that Christians have been awaiting for 2,000 years and Muslims for 1,400 years has taken place: Jesus (pbuh) is in the world now. The time we are living in is the End Times. The two blessed individuals of the End Times who will be instrumental in the salvation of the world, Jesus and Hazrat Mahdi, are in the world now. They are continuing their work among us right now. The most important time in the world, after the Age of Bliss, is happening today. These are great and exciting tidings for believers.

We can see from the hadiths handed down from our Prophet (pbuh) and from the words of the Torah and the Gospel that the final times of the world are imminent and that we are living in the time of Jesus and Hazrat Mahdi. [For more detail, please see *Jesus (pbuh) and Hazrat Mahdi (pbuh) Will Come in This Century,* by Harun Yahya]

This is a blessed time, a glorious time. The turmoil the world is currently going through will come to an end with the activities of Jesus and Hazrat Mahdi. The world will embrace the Golden Age, when the joy, abundance, happiness and fervor of the Age of Bliss will arise again.

The Golden Age will be a happy time when all wars come to an end, when all people live in peace and tranquility, when there is no more crime, when scourges such as famine, poverty, fear and oppression no longer exist, when the prisons are all closed down and when guns and bombs and all the other weapons are melted down. There will be no wars and enmity, as some Christians imagine, in this blessed time. All religions will live together in brotherhood and friendship. The Golden Age will be a time when the whole world enjoys the greatest peace and ease.

When Jesus comes, he will personally tell Christians what a false belief the idea of the Trinity is. He will personally tell Christians that he is not the son of God, but just like all other people, a servant in need of Him. He will read and obey the Koran. He will call on all Christians to obey the Koran. And then all Christians will be definitively convinced of the truth of what he tells them. And, as God reveals in a verse, there will be nobody who does not believe in Jesus before he dies:

There is not one of the People of the Book who will not believe in him before he dies; and on the Day of Resurrection he will be a witness against them. (Koran, 4:159)

This book is a detailed and comprehensive clarification aimed at Christians who have fallen into the error of the Trinity. It is intended to invite them to the true path and the way of God with passages from the Koran and the Gospel. Christians are told of the most excellent tidings. God will show them, and all mankind of course, that fine, radiant and glorious face of Jesus. The dear Prophet Jesus, whom we will embrace again and welcome with joy after 2,000 years, is now on Earth. The days when he will appear to all mankind are close at hand.

The Events Leading up to the Appearance of Hazrat Mahdi (pbuh) in Torah and other Judaic Scriptures

The generation when the son of David [the Mahdi] comes... all the governments will be turned over to Minuth (will embrace the religion of the Minim [atheism]), and no preaching will avail... (Talmud, Sanhedrin 97a)

In the generation when the son of David [the Mahdi] comes... an evil man will be honored. (Talmud, Sanhedrin 97a)

In the footsteps of the Messiah [the Mahdi]... the government will turn to heresy, and there will be none [to offer them] reproof. (Talmud, Sotah 49b)

... In the seven-year cycle at the end of which the son of David [the Mahdi] will come... the arrows of hunger will be sent forth... a great famine, in the course of which men, women, and children, pious men and saints will die. (Talmud, Sanhedrin 97a)

In the generation when the son of David [the Mahdi] will come... multitudes of trouble and evil decrees will be promulgated anew, each new evil coming with haste before the other has ended... (Talmud, Sanhedrin 97a)

In the generation in which the son of David [the Mahdi] will come, the houses of assembly will be converted into houses of prostitution. (Talmud, Sanhedrin 97a)

In the footsteps of the Messiah [the Mahdi]... the dwellers on the frontier will go about [begging] from place to place without anyone to take pity on them... (Talmud, Sotah 49b)

I will gather all the nations... to fight... the houses ransacked, and the women raped. Half of the city will go into exile... (Zechariah, 14:2)

This is the plague with which the Lord will strike all the nations that fought... Their flesh shall consume away while they stand upon their feet, their eyes will rot in their sockets, and their tongues will rot in their mouths. (Zechariah, 14:12)

... All joy turns to gloom, all gaiety is banished from the earth. (Isaiah, 24:11)

... The foundations of the earth shake... The earth is thoroughly shaken... It sways like a hut in the wind... (Isaiah, 24:18-20)

The Lord of Armies will punish you with thunder, earthquakes, and loud noises, with windstorms, rainstorms, and fire storms. (Isaiah, 29:6)

An oracle concerning Babylon that Isaiah... They come from faraway lands, from the ends of the heavens... to destroy the whole country... Their wives [will be] ravished... Their houses will be looted... Their bows will strike down the young men; they will have no mercy on infants nor will they look with compassion on children. (Isaiah, 13:1, 5-16-18)

The Events Leading up to the Appearance of Hazrat Mahdi (pbuh) in the Gospel

As Jesus was sitting on the Mount of Olives, the disciples came to him privately. "Tell us," they said, "when will this happen, and what will be the sign of your coming and of the end of the age?" Jesus answered: "Watch out that no one deceives you. For many will come in my name, claiming, 'I am the Messiah,' and will deceive many. You will hear of wars and rumors of wars, but see to it that you are not alarmed. Such things must happen, but the end is still to come. Nation will rise against nation, and kingdom against kingdom. There will be famines and earthquakes in various places. All these are the beginning of birth pains. Then you will be handed over to be persecuted and put to death, and you will be hated by all nations because of me. At that time many will turn away from the faith and will betray and hate each other, and many false prophets will appear and deceive many people. Because of the increase of wickedness, the love of most will grow cold. But the one who stands firm to the end will be saved. And this gospel of the kingdom will be preached in the whole world as a testimony to all nations, and then the end will come." (Matthew, 24:3-14)

... [That day will not come] until the rebellion occurs... (2 Thessalonians, 2:3)

... You will be brought before kings and governors, and all on account of my name [the name of Jesus]... You will be betrayed even by parents, brothers, relatives and friends, and they will put some of you to death. All men will hate you because of me [Jesus]... By standing firm, you will gain life. [The Mahdi and his followers will be similarly oppressed.] (Luke, 21:12, 16, 17, 19)

When you hear of wars and revolutions, do not be frightened. These things must happen first, but the end will not come right away. Then he [Jesus] said to them: "Nation will rise against nation, and kingdom against kingdom. There will be great earthquakes, famines and pestilences in various places, and fearful events and great signs from heaven." (Luke, 21:9-11)

There will be signs in the Sun, Moon and stars. On the earth, nations will be in anguish and perplexity at the roaring and tossing of the sea. People will faint from

229

terror, apprehensive of what is coming on the world...
(Luke, 21:25-26)

It was the same in the days of Lot. People were eating and drinking, buying and selling, planting and building. But the day Lot left Sodom, fire and sulfur rained down from heaven and destroyed them all. It will be just like this on the day the Son of Man [Jesus] is revealed. (Luke, 17:28-30)

[It] was given power to take peace from the earth and to make men slay each other... (Revelation, 6:4)

Brother will betray brother to death, and a father his child. Children will rebel against their parents and have them put to death. (Mark, 13:12)

The merchants of the earth will weep and mourn over her [Babylon] because no one buys their cargoes any more— cargoes of gold, silver, precious stones and pearls; fine linen, purple, silk and scarlet cloth; every sort of citron wood, and articles of every kind made of ivory, costly wood, bronze, iron and marble; cargoes of cinnamon and spice, of incense, myrrh and frankincense... and olive oil, of fine flour and wheat; cattle and sheep; horses and carriages... They will say, "The fruit you longed for is gone from you. All your riches and splendor have vanished..." The merchants who sold these things and gained their wealth from her will stand far off, terrified at her torment... and cry out: "Woe! Woe to you, great city, dressed in fine linen, purple and scarlet, and glittering with gold, precious stones and pearls! In one hour such great wealth has been brought to ruin!" Every sea captain, and all who travel by ship, the sailors, and all who earn their living from the sea, will stand far off. When they see the smoke of her burning, they will exclaim, "Was there ever a city like this great city?" They will throw dust on their heads, and with weeping and mourning cry out: "Woe! Woe to you, great city, where all who had ships on the sea became rich through her wealth! In one hour she has been brought to ruin!"... With such violence the great city of Babylon will be thrown down... (Revelation, 18:11-21)

And then the lawless one [antichrist] will be revealed, whom... Jesus will overthrow with the breath of his mouth and destroy by the splendor of his coming. (2 Thessalonians, 2:8)

The Period of Hazrat Mahdi's (pbuh) Rule in the Gospel

Blessed are the meek, for they will inherit the earth. (Matthew, 5:5)

When these things begin to take place, stand up and lift up your heads, because your redemption is drawing near. He [Jesus] told them this parable: "Look at the fig tree and all the trees. When they sprout leaves, you can see for yourselves and know that summer is near. Even so, when you see these things happening, you know that the kingdom of God is near." (Luke, 21:28-31)

Now learn this lesson from the fig tree: As soon as its twigs get tender and its leaves come out, you know that summer is near. Even so, when you see all these things, you know that it [return of Jesus] is near, right at the door. (Matthew, 24:32-33)

... [From now on] the city does not need the Sun or the Moon to shine on it, for the Glory of God gives it light... There will be no more night. They will not need the light of a lamp or the light of the Sun, for the Lord God will give them light. And they will reign for ever and ever. (Revelation, 21:23-25; 22:5)

I will put My laws in their minds and write them on their hearts. No longer will a man teach his neighbor, or a man

231

his brother, saying, "Know the Lord,"—because they will all know Me, from the least of them to the greatest. (Hebrews, 8:10-11)

For as lightning that comes from the east is visible even in the west, so will be the coming of the Son of Man [Jesus]. [The light of faith will prevail the earth.] (Matthew, 24:27)

Even on My servants, both men and women, I will pour out My Spirit in those days and they will have morals like Prophets. (Acts, 2:18)

But mark this:... in the last days... [those who oppose the truth], men of depraved minds, who, as far as the faith is concerned, are rejected. But they will not get very far because... their folly will be clear to everyone. (2 Timothy, 3:8-9)

Has not God chosen those who are poor in the eyes of the world to be rich in faith and to inherit the kingdom He promised those who love Him? (James, 2:5)

He will wipe every tear from their eyes. There will be no more death or mourning or crying or pain... (Revelation, 21:4)

Now when he saw the crowds, he went up on a mountainside and sat down. His disciples came to him, and he began to teach them saying: "Blessed are the poor in spirit, for theirs is the kingdom of Heaven. Blessed are those who mourn for they will be comforted. Blessed are the meek, for they will inherit the earth. Blessed are those who hunger and thirst for righteousness, or they will be filled. Blessed are the merciful for they will be shown mercy. Blessed are the pure in heart, for they will see God. Blessed are the peacemakers, for they will be called servants of God. Blessed are those who are persecuted because of righteousness, for theirs is the kingdom of Heaven..." (Matthew, 5:1-11)

The nations will walk by its light, and the kings of the earth will bring their splendor into it. On no day will its gates ever be shut, for there will be no night there. The glory and honor of the nations will be brought into it. (Revelation, 21:24-26)

He has raised up a horn of salvation for us in the house of His servant David (as He said through His holy prophets of long ago), salvation from our enemies and from the hand of all who hate us. (Luke, 1:69-71)

... As it is written: "The deliverer [the Mahdi] will come... [and] he will turn godlessness away from Jacob." (Romans, 11:26)

He threw him [the antichrist] into the abyss, and locked and sealed it over him, to keep him from deceiving the nations anymore... (Revelation, 20:3)

... Through them you may participate in the Divine nature and escape the corruption in the world caused by evil desires. (2 Peter, 1:4)

Never again will they hunger; never again will they thirst... (Revelation, 7:16)

CHAPTER 9
THE DANGER IN SOME EVANGELICALS' IDEAS ABOUT THE ANTICHRIST

Since some present-day evangelicals misinterpret the description of the antichrist in the Gospel they wrongly equate the system of the antichrist with statements about Hazrat Mahdi (the King Messiah), who Muslims and Jews are awaiting as a savior and who will bring peace to the world. Due to this extremely dangerous perspective, they seek to portray the features of the Mahdi - who will bring peace to the world - as features of the antichrist (surely the Mahdi is beyond that). For that reason, they are also suspicious of those who speak of such concepts as peace, love and brotherhood. There are enormous errors in this perspective, involving dangerous ideas that can eliminate love and spread hatred across the world, even though that is nobody's desire.

It is a violation of good conscience to declare a whole

nation or society to be the antichrist

Evangelicals' Gospel-based description of the antichrist contains the claim that the reference to a savior who will bring peace actually points to the antichrist. What this odd claim means is that whoever speaks of peace, love and friendship is a potential antichrist or supporter of the antichrist. This false perspective is a dangerous one that might lead to nobody ever speaking of peace, nobody loving anyone else and, in particular, to a Muslim awaiting the coming of Hazrat Mahdi not speaking of peace and love. This way of thinking is a sickly attitude that makes the world's greatest need, that of an alliance between believers, impossible.

Certain evangelicals who make this claim target an entire nation or community from the countries around Israel, allege that such a community is referred to in the Bible, regard those people as the antichrist and have no hesitation in doing so.

But this is a form of behavior and a perspective that is incompatible with the essence of the holy book in which the Christians in question believe. It is a terrible violation of good conscience to harbor suspicions about a nation while ignoring all the devout, virtuous, innocent and well-intentioned people in it, then to regard them in advance as people who might follow the antichrist and to therefore oppose that society or incite hatred against it. There are good and bad people in all nations.

The supporters of the antichrist and the supporters of God are always distinguished from one another by their support of good or evil. Therefore, saying that a whole nation, no matter what its faith, is bad through and through, disregarding all the good and innocent people in it, has no place in God's religion. Such a description of the antichrist is a most ruthless one, devoid of compassion and love. Such descriptions encourage terror, oppression, corruption and hatred. Such descriptions encourage people to feel a groundless hatred for a society, and even to attack it or wage war on it. The people in question who do this are most likely unaware that they are, in fact, serving the antichrist.

Under normal conditions, someone who knows the essence of and lives by religion should not advocate such a view. They should live by and tell others of brotherhood, moral virtue and the beauty of treating people with affection and compassion. If someone possesses the kind of mind that can claim that a whole society is made up of the followers of satan, then that person is totally ignorant of the essence of the faith. All the Divine faiths advise that people be treated with love, affection and compassion. Again, all the faiths have described the antichrist, his system and his supporters. It is exceptionally easy to make out and identify the antichrist, the source of all evils. The relevant description goes:

Whoever wishes to shed blood and supports slaughter, killing and oppression, whoever that person may be, is a member of the army of the antichrist, and his servant. Of course there are irreligious people among them; there are also Jews and Christians and Muslims. But it is a huge mistake to say, "Muslims are the army of the antichrist." It is both a sin, and a violation of good conscience, not to mention seriously illogical, to regard all good things as portents of the antichrist and then ascribe this to an entire people. That means to suddenly ignore innocent children and innocent women and men, fine and true believers, who are part of that nation.

This is also a slander against their own holy scriptures. The Bible says nothing like that. The evangelicals in question are misleading the people around them by espousing such a perverse belief and may encourage those people to feel a mass hatred. This is a heavy responsibility to bear.

The Descriptions of the Antichrist in the Gospel Are an Exact Match for Darwinism

*... And **I saw a beast coming out of the sea**. It had ten horns and seven heads, with ten crowns on its horns, and on each head a blasphemous name. The beast I saw resembled a leopard, but had feet like those of a bear and a mouth like that of a lion. The dragon gave the beast his power and his throne and great authority. One of the heads of the beast seemed to have had a fatal wound, but the fatal wound had been healed. **The whole world was filled with wonder and followed the beast. People worshiped the dragon because he had given authority to the beast,** and they also worshiped the beast and asked, "Who is like the beast? Who can wage war against it?" The beast was given a mouth to utter proud words and blasphemies and to exercise its authority for forty-two months. It opened its mouth to blaspheme God, and to slander His name and His dwelling place and those who live in heaven. It was given power to wage war against God's holy people and to conquer them. And **it was given authority over every tribe, people, language and nation.** All inhabitants of the earth will worship the beast—all whose names have not been written in the Lamb's book of life, the Lamb who was slain from the creation of the world. Whoever has ears, let them hear. (Revelations, 13:1-9)*

"Beast with ten horns and seven heads coming out of the sea"

"And I saw a beast coming out of the sea. <u>It had ten horns and seven heads, with ten crowns on its horns, and on each head a blasphemous name.</u>"

237

The system of the antichrist that, according to Christians, will rise from the sea and spread across ten kingdoms - which are depicted by ten crowns - is regarded by some evangelicals as one country containing ten different peoples, and their description of the antichrist is based on this. However, this claim is as dangerous as it is illogical.

This passage from the Gospel is not referring to a country or a nation, but to an ideology that will spread across ten kingdoms, in other words, across a vast area. And this is Darwinism, which has brought disaster to the entire world and the destructive effects of which are still being felt today. Darwinism is a false ideology that started in Great Britain and then spread across the rest of the world. It seeks to disseminate the idea that life came into being by chance, by giving man the supposed status of an animal. By indoctrinating people with the lie that life requires the strong to crush the weak, it has caused tremendous afflictions, wars, slaughter and holocausts.

Darwinism that brought so much tragedy to the world in the 20th century and to this day perfectly matches the description of the antichrist that will appear in the End Times in which we are living. The evangelicals in question are both sinning by labeling various countries and nations as the antichrist and also engaging in a serious waste of time; while the real antichrist is continuing its impact, evangelicals are wasting time on misidentifications and failing to see the objective they should be opposing. In this way, the antichrist is distracting them, too.

Indeed, when we look at other passages from the Gospel it is very clear that what is being referred to is Darwinism:

"The whole world was filled with wonder and followed the beast."

The description of the antichrist in Revelations 13 refers to the beast in question spreading across the entire world. This disproves the evangelicals' idea of "a nation being the antichrist." And it also confirms that the antichrist in question will be a system of ideas that people will go along with. And even though Darwinism is a total and utter fraud, is based on no scientific evidence and is constantly being discredited by scientific experiments and discoveries, people are still going along with it.

The word "wonder" in the passage "The whole world was filled with wonder and followed the beast" is rather noteworthy. It means that people will follow the antichrist in a state of bafflement, without knowing what they are doing. Indeed, that is just how the spread of Darwinism happened. A theory devoid of any proof was launched using various fraudulent techniques and the whole world suddenly became its supporters, whether they really understood the ideology or not. Indeed, the Darwinist dictatorship now has all states, all universities, all educational institutions and all official bodies and the press under its control.

"People worshiped the dragon because he had given authority to the beast,"

The dragon that empowers the beast in the description is the science that has adopted Darwinism as its false god. People used - and are still using - the name of science to legitimize Darwinism. Even though science has refuted Darwinism it still claims to be scientific and, they replace God with science [Surely God is beyond that]. The headlines in various Darwinist publications that "Science is the New God" confirm that this prophecy has come about. (Surely God is beyond that)

"... they also worshiped the beast and asked, 'Who is like the beast? Who can wage war against it?'"

As a result of Darwinism being spread by various forces, its being brought to dominate the world and becoming "unquestionable" under the influence of the Darwinist dictatorship have meant that people have surrendered to this great ideology of the antichrist. It is now impossible for any professor, any statesman, a teacher, a student or a writer to say a word against Darwinism. Such people will immediately be fired, excluded from their social circles and lose their careers. Because of this domination on the part of the Darwinist dictatorship and this despotic and ruthless pressure, everyone has now submitted to Darwinism. Since a great many of them have been unable to resist the power of the Darwinist dictatorship, despite knowing the truth, they have surrendered rather than stand up and be counted. The description here squares exactly with our own day, describing some people's submission to the Darwinist dictatorship. This is the system of the antichrist.

"It opened its mouth to blaspheme God, and to slander His name and His dwelling place and those who live in heaven."

Exactly as the above passage describes, Darwinism is a theory developed in order to be able to reject belief in God (surely God is beyond that). Ever since the day it was announced, it has fed atheism across the world and has made believers in God and advocates of creation targets for the supporters of evolution. Darwinism is the basis for all atheist ideologies. This characteristic of Darwinism's also means that it exactly matches the description in the above passage.

"... it was given authority over every tribe, people, language and nation."

Today, there is not a single village or a single town anywhere in the world that Darwinism cannot reach. The foul ideology of the antichrist has spread everywhere.

It is perfectly clear from these statements that the antichrist described in the Gospel exactly matches Darwinism, which is spreading poison to all communities today. The descriptions of the antichrist in the Torah and the Koran also exactly match Darwinist ideology. The various descriptions in the holy scriptures all refer to the same antichrist. **The antichrist is not, as some evangelicals believe, a single country or nation: It is Darwinism, which has assumed control over societies, nations and countries.**

The false idea of dissimulation held by various evangelicals who fall into error on the definition of the antichrist

The dangerous aspect of those evangelicals discussed here is that they equate the supporters of goodness, love and beauty with the antichrist. According to this incorrect view, a person or a society that is not Christian is made up of potential antichrists, and if they espouse peace, brotherhood, friendship and love, then they are declaring themselves to be the antichrist. Evangelicals also misinterpret the description of the "savior Mahdi" in the Koran and the Torah, confusing him with the antichrist. This false conception of the antichrist they propose therefore indoctrinates people with the ideas that "You must not advocate peace," "You must not call people to brotherhood, joy and union" and that "You must be suspicious of people who call for friendship and brotherhood." Even though they may be unaware of it, or even unwilling for it to happen, they are doing precisely what the antichrist wants and are serving his purposes by depicting good as evil.

One of the incorrect beliefs that some evangelicals hold about Muslims is their explanation on the subject of dissimulation. The

Arabic word "taqiyya" means "caution or concealment." In the Koran God says, **"Those who reject God after having believed – except for someone forced to do it whose heart remains at rest in its belief – but as for those whose breasts become dilated with unbelief, anger from God will come down on them. They will have a terrible punishment."**

This verse describes how someone who is actually a believer can deny his faith, on a purely temporary basis, in the face of threats to his own life or that of others. To put it another way, it is permissible for him to dissimulate - to deny his faith in other words - in the face of threats to his life, property, family or country. That is all that the concept of dissimulation means.

However, a concept that is so completely transparent has been exposed to misinterpretation by various evangelicals and opponents of Islam. These people interpret this concept, which is set out so clearly in the Koran, according to their own lights to mean "Muslims who support peace build their whole lives around a lie and disseminate that lie in order to deceive people." In fact, far from being a misinterpretation, this is an outright slander. The people who make this claim are defaming Muslims by saying that "They advocate peace, but they will sooner or later reveal their true faces and engage in slaughter." Other opponents of Islam seek to distort the subject by saying, "They may seem to support peace and freedom of ideas and belief, but they will eventually seek to compel everyone to convert to Islam." This is a huge error and deception.

First and foremost, true Muslims believe in and practice unconditionally what God reveals in the Koran. And what is revealed in the Koran is love, peace, compassion and forgiveness. The sincerity that lies at the essence of Islam is for the heart and the tongue to be as one. Muslims therefore strongly avoid exhibiting any moral values outside those of the Koran. In accordance with God's commands, they always advocate peace, love, brotherhood and compassion.

As can be seen from the verse cited above, dissimulation means a person under pressure saying the words that he is not a believer for the purpose of escaping his predicament. It is most astonishing that such a concept, which applies only to one special situation, which a Muslim may never ever encounter, should be distorted and ascribed to a Muslim's entire life. People who fall into this error are ignorant of the true Islam and unaware that the moral values revealed in the Koran are based on sincerity and honesty. A Muslim cannot live a lie; that is unlawful. A Muslim lives his whole life with the honesty that comes from being a Muslim. He espouses peace and love, not out of dissimulation, but because that is what God commands in the Koran.

There is a grotesque logical error going on here. Imagine that someone devotes his entire life to peace and brotherhood and making people friends, all for God's sake. Then imagine that he one day decides to murder those people he brought together in a union of love by overcoming thousands of difficulties. First of all, this is a most illogical and perverse way of looking at things. If someone has satanic ideas and desires to kill people, then there is certainly no need to dissimulate, especially at a time when slaughter is so widespread in the world. He could act on this devilish idea under any circumstances. Indeed, we know that the supporters of the antichrist who imagine they can use religion as a tool do this today without batting an eyelid. These people appear in the name of religion, claim to be killers because "that is what the faith commands," and thus utter a terrible lie and falsehood against the faith. That is the true system of the antichrist.

Those who really serve the antichrist are the people who ban love, peace and affection

According to the mindset that says, "People who advocate peace are engaging in dissimulation," all those who support peace but who are not Christians must be labeled as the antichrist: All those who support love must be regarded as the antichrist. Everyone who wishes all people to come together, no matter what their religion, language, race, culture or nation, must be the antichrist. People who advocate affection are the antichrist. In short, they would prohibit a Muslim from exhibiting all the moral virtues that God praises in the Koran, the Torah and the Gospel because if a Muslim exhibits moral virtues, if he keeps peace and love alive, then he matches that evangelical description of the antichrist. It therefore appears impossible for true Muslims who seek to establish unity in this world and forge brotherhood and an inter-faith alliance to be friends with an evangelical because anyone who wants friendship is suspected of being the antichrist, while anyone who does not want friendship is an enemy. This wrongheaded logic literally prohibits people from being virtuous.

That way of thinking is by itself enough to inflict tragedy on the world. Under it, there would be no more peace in the world, no compassion and no forgiveness. World peace and people coming together in love would be impossible under such a perspective, because 23% of the world's population are believed to be the antichrist. Since it is impossible to forge an alliance with the supporters of the antichrist, then the false conclusion from this is that Muslims must always be avoided, that one must not be deceived by their calls for peace, and that if they speak of brotherhood, friendship, union and unity, one must not believe them; this is the highly dangerous and perverse logic that evangelicals put out and cause thousands of people to believe.

One important example of this is the perverse allegations that some radicals who portray themselves as Muslims make against Jews. They have also tried to have the perverse perspective described above applied against Jews by Muslims. They indoctrinate people with the idea that Jews must be hated and one must never be their friends. Although the radicals in question are working very hard on this, we, **as true believers who abide by the Koran**, are perfectly well aware that Muslims must never adopt such an attitude toward the Jews. We believe Jews who obey the profound commands of the Torah when they say, "We want to bring peace to the world, and this is what the Torah tells us." Because, just like us, they are advocating the essence of faith, in other words, peace and love.

The same thing also applies to Christians. Someone who claims to be a Muslim may believe that a Christian who says he is expecting the coming of Jesus (pbuh) is engaging in dissimulation and that this Christian will soon come and murder him. It might be quite easy to form such an impression when one looks at the attitude of some Christians toward Muslims. But no true Muslim would ever expect such a thing from a true Christian and he would never regard it as dissimulation. He knows that a true Christian who obeys the Gospel will be full of love and affection. The idea that "whoever loves what is good must be the antichrist" is both totally illogical and has no place in the true conception of religion created by God.

By making these claims, some evangelicals are in one sense attempting to prepare the way for further war and conflict which has brought disaster and terror to all mankind. Many of them may not realize it, but what they are doing is terribly harmful. They condition people to think that peace will never come and that scenes of terror will continue. They give rise to new communities of fear, and they turn these communities into ones far removed from the Gospel and filled with hatred and rage. They imagine that this is a service to the Gospel and Christianity. However, by doing this, they are wittingly or unwittingly serving the system of the antichrist that has come to dominate the world today. That is why it is essential for people to see what a huge danger is posed by this allegation, which has now become traditional and the subject of blind belief by many.

The Koran Tells Muslims to Feel Love and Affection for Jews and Christians. This is

what the Koran Commands, Not Dissimulation

People who say that, "Muslims are dissimulating when they say they want peace" are clearly not sufficiently well informed about what the Koran really commands. Jews and Christians are placed under the protection of Muslims in the Koran. A Muslim has a responsibility to show the People of the Book love and affection. **These commands exist, not so that people can dissimulate, but so that they can live by the love and friendship that form the basis of true Koranic morality.** Since a Muslim lives by the true moral values of the Koran, he will feel love and affection for the People of the Book.

In addition, according to the Koran, a Muslim can marry a woman from the People of the Book and eat their food. Can anyone suddenly decide one day to murder the person he married, the mother of his children, whom he addresses as "darling" or "beloved"? This is a terrible allegation to make; that after years of treating his wife well and making a family together, having children and treating her with love and respect, a Muslim man will suddenly reach for his gun and say, "I was only pretending all those years, and now I am going to kill you."

This is an insane belief and quite bluntly speaking, pathological paranoia. The evangelicals in question fail to comprehend the logical flaws inherent in it. Since they are ignorant of the commands of the Koran they are unable to make a proper analysis, and as a result a great many of them end up as ignorant enemies of Islam. Therefore, no permanent peace and friendship can be established.

Hazrat Mahdi (pbuh) will shed no blood and will never depart from that law

Some evangelicals maintain that Hazrat Mahdi will eventually be seen to have engaged in dissimulation. The Mahdi will supposedly abandon his peaceable policy and wreak terrible slaughter. The finest reply to this irrational claim comes from the hadiths of our Prophet (pbuh). Passages very similar to the hadiths can also be seen in the Torah.

The greatest quality of the Mahdi, in whom Muslims believe and who is described in considerable detail in hadiths, is that when he takes charge he will not permit one drop of blood to be shed. There is one very important point that needs to be emphasized here; the Mahdi's avoidance of bloodshed is the command of our Prophet: Our Prophet said this through the revelation bestowed on him. It is therefore impossible for Hazrat Mahdi to step outside that commandment. If someone does disobey that command and sheds blood, then he is no longer a Muslim. Hazrat Mahdi will implement our Prophet's command willingly, with love and with fervor. It is impossible for him to do anything else, and neither will he do so.

The qualities that a person must have in order to be Hazrat Mahdi are set out in detail in the hadiths. We are told that Hazrat Mahdi will emphasize love, peace, brotherhood and compassion and will wage an intellectual campaign to disseminate this and will be instrumental in people coming to have faith.

The Mahdi revealed in Islamic sources is the same person as the King Moshiach from Judaic sources and the Paraclete and the water bearer in the Gospels. We are now in the age of the way of the Mahdi. By the will of God, Hazrat Mahdi (pbuh) is alive and at work now, and we are simply awaiting his appearance. Therefore, since this is the age of the Mahdi, there will be no more wars after this; the great wars have come to an end. Rumors of war will persist for a while longer, but there will be no more real wars. This means that the expectations of war on the part of some evangelicals will not bear fruit.

Hazrat Mahdi (pbuh) will destroy all weapons and turn them into things that benefit mankind

One of the greatest qualities of Hazrat Mahdi in the eyes of Islam is that as soon as he takes charge he will eliminate all weaponry. This also appears in the Torah, which says that the King Moshiach (the Mahdi) will destroy all weaponry when he takes charge. All weapons will be melted down and benefit mankind by being used in industry. The fact that a small group of people still talk of war will not alter this lovely destiny that God has ordained for this world.

The destiny of this world is heading toward the Golden Age. Yes, prior to the coming of the Mahdi in our day there will be birth pains as also described in the Gospel, and these are currently happening; the turmoil in the world is an indicator of these birth pangs, but none of these will lead to a major world war. The hadiths tell us there will be talk of war, but no war will happen. The antichrist will be defeated by Hazrat Mahdi. However, this will not be through bloodshed and killing, as some evangelicals believe, but with compassion, friendship and knowledge.

Some Hadiths about Hazrat Mahdi (pbuh) Not Shedding Blood

*People will seek refuge in the Mahdi as honey bees cluster around their sovereign. He will fill the world that was once full of cruelty, with justice. His justice will be as such that **he will not wake a sleeping person, not even one drop of blood will be shed**. The Earth will return to the age of bliss. (Al-Qawl al-Mukthasar fi 'Alamat al-Mahdi al-Muntadhar, pp. 29, 48)*

*The Mahdi will follow the way of the Prophet (pbuh). **He will not wake a sleeping person or no blood will be shed**. (Al-Barzanji, Portents of Doomsday, p. 163)*

248

*He [the Mahdi] will **fill the Earth with justice**, just as people previously filled it with cruelty. (Sunan Ibn Majah, 10/348)*

*The Earth, which is full of cruelty and oppression, **will overflow with justice** after his [the Mahdi's] coming. (Ibn Hajar al-Haythami, Al-Qawl al-Mukhtasar fi `Alamat al-Mahdi al-Muntadhar, p. 20)*

*Like the cup fills with water **so will Earth fill with peace.** There will be **no enmity left between any people.** All **hostility, fighting and envy will surely disappear.** (Sahih Muslim, 1/136)*

... The good become even better, and even the wicked ones are treated well. (Al-Muttaqi al-Hindi, Al-Burhan fi Alamat al-Mahdi Akhir al-zaman, p. 17)

Hazrat Mahdi (pbuh) will cause people to forget war through his intellectual struggle and will establish a climate of peace and love

Since Hazrat Mahdi will allow no blood to be spilled and will destroy all weaponry, the claims made by some evangelicals are obviously untrue. Hazrat Mahdi's quality of not shedding blood will come about as the result of his intellectual struggle for peace over a period of many years. People will embrace one another as brothers and a climate of true love will emerge. Hazrat Mahdi will give messages of peace and friendship to all believers throughout his life in order for this climate to come about. The whole world will come to adopt the idea of peace. They will all be taught the beauty of love and will cast hatred aside. Therefore, while great efforts are being made, in the face of enormous difficulties, to sow the seeds of love at a time when the world is in intense turmoil and disorder, it is extraordinarily illogical and a violation of the hadiths and the Torah for the evangelicals in question to say that Hazrat

249

Mahdi will suddenly say, "All this was just dissimulation. I did it so I can now kill people."

Hazrat Mahdi will have eliminated all weapons, convinced people of the need for peace, made them love one another and installed justice. He will have achieved this in the face of various difficulties, slanders, false accusations and threats, through his intellectual struggle. How could he then suddenly decide to start killing people in the way some Christians allege? Hazrat Mahdi will never do that. Moreover, the climate will have changed in such a way as to not permit any wars. There will be supporters of peace everywhere, but not a single weapon. Weapons will have been melted down and eradicated. How, when according to the Koran everyone has been convinced of the need for peace, could they ever be convinced of the need for war again? People will have been shown evidence and verses from the Koran. They will have been taught how the Koran commands that peace must reign on Earth. They will have been told to treat Christians and Jews with love and affection. Everyone will have realized that this is God's command. So how will people be convinced of the opposite?

This is of course exceedingly illogical. It is through the presence of Hazrat Mahdi that people will be made to forget war. According to the Koran, the truth of the matter will come to people in the time of Hazrat Mahdi. Nobody can spoil the truth in any way. The age of the system of the Mahdi will be a glorious time when people live by the loving warmth of the Koran, in peace and tranquility.

All believers have a responsibility to make the world a place of beauty, love and peace

Although the evangelicals who make the claims we have been looking at in this section are people who love the Gospel, they have come to believe in a terrifying fantasy that we cannot see in the Gospel. What these people overlook is that the antichrist can have such a terrifying impact even on believers. Someone who espouses a faith that expects blood to rise as high as horses' manes is clearly living in a nightmare and causing his own followers to share that nightmare. The system of the antichrist immediately reveals itself here.

If someone is a true Muslim, he has an obligation to desire and advocate peace. He has a responsibility to build love and affection among people. If someone is a true Muslim he cannot feel any hatred for Christians or Jews; these things are unlawful for him. Indeed, a Muslim has a responsibility to protect even someone who does not believe, and even at the cost of his own life. This is an attribute of Muslims revealed in the Koran:

If any of the idolaters ask you for protection, give them protection until they have heard the words of God. Then convey them to a place where they are safe. That is because they are a people who do not know. (Koran, 9:6)

According to the Koran, a Muslim has an obligation to protect anyone who seeks his protection, no matter who they may be. If a Muslim departs from this moral value, then he is no longer a Muslim. This is a feature of the fine moral values he must maintain throughout his life. The hadiths also reveal that Muslims and Christians will forge an alliance against the antichrist. When Jesus (pbuh) comes, he will work together with Hazrat Mahdi (pbuh) and eliminate the antichrist through knowledge. It is of the greatest importance for members of these two faiths to form an alliance if the system of the antichrist is to be eliminated and peace is to rule the world.

When Hazrat Mahdi, who loves all faiths and all prophets, comes, God will also bring the beauty of that love to the world. The world will be a place of love and peace, of beauty and plenty. It is thus a matter of urgency for the evangelicals in question to free themselves from these false, pernicious and terrifying ideas and to live by the joy of the Messiah and the Mahdi and to prepare

251

the way for this climate of peace by spreading love and brotherhood. That is what God wants.

APPENDIX
THE DECEPTION OF
EVOLUTION

Darwinism, in other words the theory of evolution, was put forward with the aim of denying the fact of Creation, but is in truth nothing but failed, unscientific nonsense. This theory, which claims that life emerged by chance from inanimate matter, was invalidated by the scientific evidence of miraculous order in the universe and in living things, as well as by the discovery of more than 300 million fossils revealing that evolution never happened. In this way, science confirmed the fact that God created the universe and the living things in it. The propaganda carried out today in order to keep the theory of evolution alive is based solely on the distortion of the scientific facts, biased interpretation, and lies and falsehoods disguised as science.

Yet this propaganda cannot conceal the truth. The fact that the theory of evolution is the greatest deception in the history of science has been expressed more and more in the scientific world over the last 20-30 years. Research carried out after the 1980s in particular has revealed that the claims of Darwinism are totally unfounded, something that has been stated by a large number of scientists. In the United States in particular, many scientists from such different fields as biology, biochemistry and paleontology recognize the invalidity of Darwinism and employ the fact of Creation to account for the origin of life.

We have examined the collapse of the theory of evolution and the proofs of Creation in great scientific detail in many of our works, and are still continuing to do so. Given the enormous importance of this subject, it will be of great benefit to summarize it here.

The Scientific Collapse of Darwinism

As a pagan doctrine going back as far as ancient Greece, the theory of evolution was advanced extensively in the nineteenth century. The most important development that made it the top topic of the world of science was Charles Darwin's The Origin of Species, published in 1859. In this book, he opposed, in his own eyes, the fact that God created different living species on Earth separately, for he erroneously claimed that all living beings had a common ancestor and had diversified over time through small changes. Darwin's theory was not based on any concrete scientific finding; as he also accepted, it was just an "assumption." Moreover, as Darwin confessed in the long chapter of his book titled "Difficulties on Theory," the theory failed in the face of many critical questions.

Darwin invested all of his hopes in new scientific discoveries, which he expected to solve these difficulties. However, contrary to his expectations, scientific findings expanded the dimensions of these difficulties. The defeat of Darwinism in the face of science can be reviewed under three basic topics:

1) The theory cannot explain how life originated on Earth.

2) No scientific finding shows that the "evolutionary mechanisms" proposed by the theory have any evolutionary power at all.

3) The fossil record proves the exact opposite of what the theory suggests.

In this section, we will examine these three basic points in general outlines:

The First Insurmountable Step: The Origin of Life

The theory of evolution posits that all living species evolved from a single living cell that emerged on Earth 3.8 billion years ago, supposed to have happened as a result of coincidences. How a single cell could generate millions of complex living species and, if such an evolution really occurred, why traces of it cannot be observed in the fossil record are some of the questions that the theory cannot answer. However, first and foremost, we need to ask: **How did this "first cell" originate?**

Since the theory of evolution ignorantly denies Creation, it maintains that the "first cell" originated as a product of blind coincidences within the laws of nature, without any plan or arrangement. According to the theory, inanimate matter must have produced a living cell as a result of coincidences. Such a claim, however, is inconsistent with the most unassailable rules of biology.

"Life Comes From Life"

In his book, Darwin never referred to the origin of life. The primitive understanding of science in his time rested on the assumption that living beings had a very simple structure. Since medieval times, spontaneous generation, which asserts that non-living materials came together to form living organisms, had been widely accepted. It was commonly believed that insects came into being from food leftovers, and mice from wheat. Interesting experiments were conducted to prove this theory. Some wheat was placed on a dirty piece of cloth, and it was believed that mice would originate from it after a while.

Similarly, maggots developing in rotting meat was assumed to be evidence of spontaneous generation. However, **it was later understood that worms did not appear on meat spontaneously,** but were carried there by flies in the form of larvae, invisible to the naked eye.

Even when Darwin wrote *The Origin of Species*, the belief that bacteria could come into existence from non-living matter was widely accepted in the world of science.

However, **five years after the publication of Darwin's book, Louis Pasteur announced his results after long studies and experiments, that disproved spontaneous generation, a cornerstone of Darwin's theory.** In his triumphal lecture at the Sorbonne in 1864, **Pasteur said: "Never will the doctrine of spontaneous generation recover from the mortal blow struck by this simple experiment."** (Sidney Fox, Klaus Dose, *Molecular Evolution and The Origin of Life*, W. H. Freeman and Company, San Francisco, 1972, p. 4.)

For a long time, advocates of the theory of evolution resisted these findings. However, as the development of science unraveled the complex structure of the cell of a living being, the idea that life could come into being coincidentally faced an even greater impasse.

Inconclusive Efforts of the Twentieth Century

The first evolutionist who took up the subject of the origin of life in the twentieth century was the renowned Russian biologist Alexander Oparin. With various theses he advanced in the 1930s, he tried to prove that a living cell could originate by coincidence. These studies, however, were doomed to failure, and Oparin had to make the following confession:

> *Unfortunately, however, the problem of the origin of the cell is perhaps the most obscure point in the whole study of the evolution of organisms. (Alexander I. Oparin, Origin of Life, Dover Publications, New York, 1936, 1953 (reprint), p. 196.)*

Evolutionist followers of Oparin tried to carry out experiments to solve this problem. The best known experiment was carried out by the American chemist Stanley Miller in 1953. Combining the gases he alleged to have existed in the primordial Earth's atmosphere in an experiment set-up, and adding energy to the mixture, Miller synthesized several organic molecules (amino acids) present in the structure of proteins.

Barely a few years had passed before it was revealed that **this experiment, which was then presented as an important step in the name of evolution, was invalid, for the atmosphere used in the experiment was very different from the real Earth conditions.** ("New Evidence on Evolution of Early Atmosphere and Life," *Bulletin of the American Meteorological Society*, vol 63, November 1982, 1328-1330)

After a long silence, **Miller confessed that the atmosphere medium he used was unrealistic.** (Stanley Miller, *Molecular Evolution of Life: Current Status of the Prebiotic Synthesis of Small Molecules*, 1986, p. 7)

All the evolutionists' efforts throughout the twentieth century to explain the origin of life ended in failure. The geochemist Jeffrey Bada, from the San Diego Scripps Institute accepts this fact in an article published in *Earth* magazine in 1998:

> *Today as we leave the twentieth century, we still face the biggest unsolved problem that we had when we entered the twentieth century: How did life originate on Earth? (Jeffrey Bada, Earth, February 1998, p. 40)*

The Complex Structure of Life

The primary reason why evolutionists ended up in such a great impasse regarding the origin of life is that even those living organisms Darwinists deemed to be the simplest have outstandingly complex features. The cell of a living thing is more complex than all of our man-made technological products. **Today, even in the most developed laboratories of the world, no single**

protein of the cell, let alone a living cell itself, can be produced by bringing organic chemicals together.

The conditions required for the formation of a cell are too great in quantity to be explained away by coincidences. However, there is no need to explain the situation with these details. Evolutionists are at a dead-end even before reaching the stage of the cell. That is because the probability of just a single protein, an essential building block of the cell, coming into being by chance is mathematically "0."

The main reason for this is the need for other proteins to be present if one protein is to form, and this completely eradicates the possibility of chance formation. This fact by itself is sufficient to eliminate the evolutionist claim of chance right from the outset. To summarize,

Protein cannot be synthesized without enzymes, and enzymes are all proteins.

Around 100 proteins need to be present in order for a single protein to be synthesized. There therefore need to be proteins for proteins to exist.

DNA manufactures the protein-synthesizing enzymes. Protein cannot be synthesized without DNA. DNA is therefore also needed in order for proteins to form.

All the organelles in the cell have important tasks in protein synthesis. In other words, in order for proteins to form a perfect and fully functioning cell needs to exist together with all its organelles.

The DNA molecule, which is located in the nucleus of a cell and which stores genetic information, is a magnificent databank. If the information coded in DNA were written down, it would make a giant library consisting of an estimated 900 volumes of encyclopedias consisting of 500 pages each.

A very interesting dilemma emerges at this point: DNA can replicate itself only with the help of some specialized proteins (enzymes). However, the synthesis of these enzymes can be realized only by the information coded in DNA. As they both depend on each other, they have to exist at the same time for replication. This brings the scenario that life originated by itself to a deadlock. Prof. Leslie Orgel, an evolutionist of repute from the University of San Diego, California, confesses this fact in the September 1994 issue of the *Scientific American* magazine:

> *It is extremely improbable that proteins and nucleic acids, both of which are structurally complex, arose spontaneously in the same place at the same time. Yet it also seems impossible to have one without the other. And so, at first glance, one might have to conclude that life could never, in fact, have originated by chemical means. (Leslie E. Orgel, "The Origin of Life on Earth," Scientific American, vol. 271, October 1994, p. 78.)*

No doubt, if it is impossible for life to have originated spontaneously as a result of blind coincidences, then it has to be accepted that life was **created**. This fact explicitly invalidates the theory of evolution, whose main purpose is to deny Creation.

Imaginary Mechanism of Evolution

The second important point that negates Darwin's theory is that both concepts put forward by the theory as "evolutionary mechanisms" were understood to have, in reality, no evolutionary power.

Darwin based his evolution allegation entirely on the mechanism of "natural selection." The importance he placed on this mechanism was evident in the name of his book: *The Origin of Species, By Means of Natural Selection...*

Natural selection holds that those living things that are stronger and more suited to the natural conditions of their habitats will survive in the struggle for life. For example, in a deer herd under the threat of attack by wild animals, those that can run faster will survive. Therefore, the deer herd will be comprised of faster and stronger individuals. However, unquestionably, this mechanism will not cause deer to evolve and transform themselves into another living species, for instance, horses.

Therefore, *the mechanism of natural selection has no evolutionary power. Darwin was also aware of this fact* and had to state this in his book *The Origin of Species*:

> *Natural selection can do nothing until favourable individual differences or variations occur. (Charles Darwin, The Origin of Species by Means of Natural Selection, The Modern Library, New York, p. 127)*

Lamarck's Impact

So, how could these "favorable variations" occur? Darwin tried to answer this question from the standpoint of the primitive understanding of science at that time. According to the French biologist Chevalier de Lamarck (1744-1829), who lived before Darwin, living creatures passed on the traits they acquired during their lifetime to the next generation. He asserted that these traits, which accumulated from one generation to another, caused new species to be formed. For instance, he claimed that giraffes evolved from antelopes; as they struggled to eat the leaves of high trees, their necks were extended from generation to generation.

Darwin also gave similar examples. In his book *The Origin of Species*, for instance, he said that some bears going into water to find food transformed themselves into whales over time. (Charles Darwin, *The Origin of Species: A Facsimile of the First Edition*, Harvard University Press, 1964, p. 184.)

However, the laws of inheritance discovered by Gregor Mendel (1822-84) and verified by the science of genetics, which flourished in the twentieth century, utterly demolished the legend that acquired traits were passed on to subsequent generations. Thus, natural selection fell out of favor as an evolutionary mechanism.

Neo-Darwinism and Mutations

In order to find a solution, Darwinists advanced the "Modern Synthetic Theory," or as it is more commonly known, Neo-Darwinism, at the end of the 1930s. Neo-Darwinism added mutations, which are distortions formed in the genes of living beings due to such external factors as radiation or replication errors, as the "cause of favorable variations" in addition to natural mutation.

Today, the model that Darwinists espouse, despite their own awareness of its scientific invalidity, is neo-Darwinism. The theory maintains that millions of living beings formed as a result of a process whereby numerous complex organs of these organisms (e.g., ears, eyes, lungs, and wings) underwent "mutations," that is, genetic disorders. Yet, there is an outright scientific fact that totally undermines this theory: **Mutations do not cause living beings to develop; on the contrary, they are always harmful.**

The reason for this is very simple: **DNA has a very complex structure, and random effects can only harm it.** The American geneticist B. G. Ranganathan explains this as follows:

> *First, genuine mutations are very rare in nature. Secondly, most mutations are harmful since they are random, rather than orderly changes in the structure of genes; any random change in a highly ordered system will be for the worse, not for the better. For example, **if an earthquake were to shake a highly ordered structure such as a building, there would be a random change in the framework of the building which, in all probability, would not be an improvement.*** *(B. G. Ranganathan, Origins?, Pennsylvania: The Banner of Truth Trust, 1988, p. 7.)*

Not surprisingly, no mutation example, which is useful, that is, which is observed to develop the genetic code, has been observed so far. All mutations have proved to be harmful. It was understood

261

that mutation, which is presented as an "evolutionary mechanism," is actually a genetic occurrence that harms living things, and leaves them disabled. (The most common effect of mutation on human beings is cancer.) Of course, a destructive mechanism cannot be an "evolutionary mechanism." Natural selection, on the other hand, "can do nothing by itself," as Darwin also accepted. This fact shows us that **there is no "evolutionary mechanism" in nature.** Since no evolutionary mechanism exists, no such imaginary process called "evolution" could have taken place.

The Fossil Record: No Sign of Intermediate Forms

The clearest evidence that the scenario suggested by the theory of evolution did not take place is the fossil record.

According to the unscientific supposition of this theory, every living species has sprung from a predecessor. A previously existing species turned into something else over time and all species have come into being in this way. In other words, this transformation proceeds gradually over millions of years.

Had this been the case, numerous intermediary species should have existed and lived within this long transformation period.

For instance, some half-fish/half-reptiles should have lived in the past which had acquired some reptilian traits in addition to the fish traits they already had. Or there should have existed some reptile-birds, which acquired some bird traits in addition to the reptilian traits they already had. Since these would be in a transitional phase, they should be disabled, defective, crippled living beings. Evolutionists refer to these imaginary creatures, which they believe to have lived in the past, as "transitional forms."

If such animals ever really existed, there should be millions and even billions of them in number and variety. More importantly, the remains of these strange creatures should be

present in the fossil record. In *The Origin of Species*, Darwin explained:

> *If my theory be true, numberless intermediate varieties, linking most closely all of the species of the same group together must assuredly have existed... Consequently, evidence of their former existence could be found only amongst fossil remains. (Charles Darwin, The Origin of Species: A Facsimile of the First Edition, p. 179)*

However, **Darwin was well aware that no fossils of these intermediate forms had yet been found.** He regarded this as a major difficulty for his theory. In one chapter of his book titled "Difficulties on Theory," he wrote:

> *Why, if species have descended from other species by insensibly fine gradations, **do we not everywhere see innumerable transitional forms? Why is not all nature in confusion instead of the species being, as we see them, well defined?... But, as by this theory innumerable transitional forms must have existed, why do we not find them embedded in countless numbers in the crust of the earth?... Why then is not every geological formation and every stratum full of such intermediate links?** (Charles Darwin, The Origin of Species, p. 172)*

Darwin's Hopes Shattered

However, although evolutionists have been making strenuous efforts to find fossils since the middle of the nineteenth century all over the world, **no transitional forms have yet been uncovered.** All of the fossils, contrary to the evolutionists' expectations, show that **life appeared on Earth all of a sudden and fully-formed.**

One famous British paleontologist, Derek V. Ager, admits this fact, even though he is an evolutionist:

> *The point emerges that if we examine the fossil record in detail, whether at the level of orders or of species, **we find***

– over and over again – not gradual evolution, but the sudden explosion of one group at the expense of another. (Derek A. Ager, "The Nature of the Fossil Record," Proceedings of the British Geological Association, vol 87, 1976, p. 133.)

This means that in **the fossil record, all living species suddenly emerge as fully formed, without any intermediate forms in between.** This is just the opposite of Darwin's assumptions. Also, this is very strong evidence that **all living things are created.** The only explanation of a living species emerging suddenly and complete in every detail without any evolutionary ancestor is that it was created. This fact is admitted also by the widely known evolutionist biologist Douglas Futuyma:

Creation and evolution, between them, exhaust the possible explanations for the origin of living things. Organisms either appeared on the earth fully developed or they did not. If they did not, they must have developed from pre-existing species by some process of modification. If they did appear in a fully developed state, they must indeed have been created by some omnipotent intelligence. (Douglas J. Futuyma, *Science on Trial*, Pantheon Books, New York, 1983, p. 197)

Fossils show that living beings emerged fully developed and in a perfect state on the Earth. That means that "the origin of species," contrary to Darwin's supposition, is not evolution, but Creation.

The Tale of Human Evolution

The subject most often brought up by advocates of the theory of evolution is the subject of the origin of man. The Darwinist claim holds that man evolved from so-called ape-like creatures. During this alleged evolutionary process, which is supposed to have started 4-5 million years ago, some "transitional forms" between man and his imaginary ancestors are supposed to have existed. According to this completely imaginary scenario, four basic "categories" are listed:

1. Australopithecus

2. Homo habilis

3. Homo erectus

4. Homo sapiens

Evolutionists call man's so-called first ape-like ancestors *Australopithecus*, which means "South African ape." These living beings are actually nothing but an old ape species that has become extinct. Extensive research done on various *Australopithecus* specimens by two world famous anatomists from England and the USA, namely, Lord Solly Zuckerman and Prof. Charles Oxnard, shows that these apes belonged to an ordinary ape species that became extinct and bore no resemblance to humans. (Solly Zuckerman, *Beyond The Ivory Tower,* Toplinger Publications, New York, 1970, 75-14; Charles E. Oxnard, "The Place of Australopithecines in Human Evolution: Grounds for Doubt", Nature, vol 258, 389)

Evolutionists classify the next stage of human evolution as "homo," that is "man." According to their claim, the living beings in the Homo series are more developed than *Australopithecus*. Evolutionists devise a fanciful evolution scheme by arranging different fossils of these creatures in a particular order. This scheme is imaginary because it has never been proved that there is an evolutionary relation between these different classes. Ernst Mayr, one of the twentieth century's most important evolutionists, contends in his book One Long Argument that "particularly historical [puzzles] such as the origin of life or of Homo sapiens, are extremely difficult and may even resist a final, satisfying explanation." ("Could science be brought to an end by scientists' belief that they have final answers or by society's reluctance to pay the bills?" *Scientific American,* December 1992, p. 20)

By outlining the link chain as *Australopithecus > Homo habilis > Homo erectus > Homo sapiens,* evolutionists imply that each of these species is one another's ancestor. However, recent findings of paleoanthropologists have revealed that Australopithecus, Homo habilis, and Homo erectus lived at different parts of the world at the same time. (Alan Walker, *Science*, vol. 207, 7 March 1980, p. 1103; A. J. Kelso, Physical Antropology, 1st ed., J. B. Lipincott Co., New York, 1970, p. 221; M. D. Leakey, Olduvai Gorge, vol. 3, Cambridge University Press, Cambridge, 1971, p. 272.)

Moreover, a certain segment of humans classified as Homo erectus have lived up until very modern times. **Homo sapiens neandarthalensis and Homo sapiens sapiens (man) co-existed in the same region.** (Jeffrey Kluger, "Not So Extinct After All: The Primitive Homo Erectus May Have Survived Long Enough To Coexist With Modern Humans," *Time*, 23 December 1996)

This situation apparently indicates the invalidity of the claim that they are ancestors of one another. The late Stephen Jay Gould explained this deadlock of the theory of evolution although he was himself one of the leading advocates of evolution in the twentieth century:

> *What has become of our ladder if there are three coexisting lineages of hominids (A. africanus, the robust australopithecines, and H. habilis), none clearly derived from another? Moreover, none of the three display any evolutionary trends during their tenure on earth. (S. J. Gould, Natural History, vol. 85, 1976, p. 30)*

Put briefly, the scenario of human evolution, which is "upheld" with the help of various drawings of some "half ape, half human" creatures appearing in the media and course books, that is, frankly, by means of propaganda, is nothing but **a tale with no scientific foundation.**

Lord Solly Zuckerman, one of the most famous and respected scientists in the U.K., who carried out research on this subject for years and studied Australopithecus fossils for 15 years, finally concluded, despite being an evolutionist himself, **that there is, in**

fact, no such family tree branching out from ape-like creatures to man.

Zuckerman also made an interesting "spectrum of science" ranging from those he considered scientific to those he considered unscientific. According to Zuckerman's spectrum, the most "scientific"—that is, depending on concrete data—fields of science are chemistry and physics. After them come the biological sciences and then the social sciences. At the far end of the spectrum, which is the part considered to be most "unscientific," are "extra-sensory perception"—concepts such as telepathy and sixth sense—and finally "human evolution." Zuckerman explains his reasoning:

> We then move right off the register of objective truth into those fields of presumed biological science, like extrasensory perception or the interpretation of man's fossil history, where to the faithful [evolutionist] anything is possible – and where the ardent believer [in evolution] is sometimes able to believe several contradictory things at the same time. (Solly Zuckerman, Beyond the Ivory Tower, p. 19)

The tale of human evolution boils down to nothing but the prejudiced interpretations of some fossils unearthed by certain people, who blindly adhere to their theory.

Darwinian Formula!

Besides all the technical evidence we have dealt with so far, let us now for once, examine what kind of a superstition the evolutionists have with an example so simple as to be understood even by children:

The theory of evolution asserts that life is formed by chance. According to this irrational claim, lifeless and unconscious atoms came together to form the cell and then they somehow formed other living things, including man. Let us think about that. When we bring together the elements that are the building-blocks of life such as carbon, phosphorus, nitrogen and potassium, only a heap is formed. No matter what treatments it undergoes, this atomic heap cannot form even a single living being. If you like, let us formulate an "experiment" on this subject and let us examine on the behalf of evolutionists what they really claim without pronouncing loudly under the name **"Darwinian formula"**:

Let evolutionists put plenty of materials present in the composition of living things such as phosphorus, nitrogen, carbon, oxygen, iron, and magnesium into big barrels. Moreover, let them add in these barrels any material that does not exist under normal conditions, but they think as necessary. Let them add in this mixture as many amino acids and as many proteins as they like. Let them expose these mixtures to as much heat and moisture as they like. Let them stir these with whatever technologically developed device they like. Let them put the foremost scientists beside these barrels. Let these experts wait in turn beside these barrels for billions, and even trillions of years. Let them be free to use all kinds of conditions they believe to be necessary for a human's formation. **No matter what they do, they cannot produce from these barrels a human, say a professor that examines his cell structure under the electron microscope.** They cannot produce giraffes, lions, bees, canaries, horses, dolphins, roses, orchids, lilies, carnations, bananas, oranges, apples, dates, tomatoes, melons, watermelons, figs, olives, grapes, peaches, peafowls, pheasants, multicoloured butterflies, or millions of other living beings such as these. Indeed, they could not obtain even a single cell of any one of them.

Briefly, **unconscious atoms cannot form the cell** by coming together. They cannot take a new decision and divide this cell into two, then take other decisions and create the professors who first invent the electron microscope and then examine their own cell structure under that microscope. **Matter is an unconscious, lifeless heap, and it comes to life with God's superior creation.**

The theory of evolution, which claims the opposite, is a total fallacy completely contrary to reason. Thinking even a little bit on the claims of evolutionists discloses this reality, just as in the above example.

268

Technology in the Eye and the Ear

Another subject that remains unanswered by evolutionary theory is the excellent quality of perception in the eye and the ear.

Before passing on to the subject of the eye, let us briefly answer the question of how we see. Light rays coming from an object fall oppositely on the eye's retina. Here, these light rays are transmitted into electric signals by cells and reach a tiny spot at the back of the brain, the "center of vision." These electric signals are perceived in this center as an image after a series of processes. With this technical background, let us do some thinking.

The brain is insulated from light. That means that its inside is completely dark, and that no light reaches the place where it is located. Thus, the "center of vision" is never touched by light and may even be the darkest place you have ever known. However, you observe a luminous, bright world in this pitch darkness.

The image formed in the eye is so sharp and distinct that even the technology of the twentieth century has not been able to attain it. For instance, look at the book you are reading, your hands with which you are holding it, and then lift your head and look around you. Have you ever seen such a sharp and distinct image as this one at any other place? Even the most developed television screen produced by the greatest television producer in the world cannot provide such a sharp image for you. This is a three-dimensional, colored, and extremely sharp image. For more than 100 years, thousands of engineers have been trying to achieve this sharpness. Factories, huge premises were established, much research has been done, plans and designs have been made for this purpose. Again, look at a TV screen and the book you hold in your hands. You will see that there is a big difference in sharpness and distinction. Moreover, the TV screen shows you a two-dimensional image, whereas with your eyes, you watch a three-dimensional perspective with depth.

For many years, tens of thousands of engineers have tried to make a three-dimensional TV and achieve the vision quality of the eye. Yes, they have made a three-dimensional television system, but it is not possible to watch it without putting on special 3-D glasses; moreover, it is only an artificial three-dimension. The background is more blurred, the foreground appears like a paper setting. Never has it been possible to produce a sharp and distinct vision like that of the eye. In both the camera and the television, there is a loss of image quality.

Evolutionists claim that the mechanism producing this sharp and distinct image has been formed by chance. Now, if somebody told you that the television in your room was formed as a result of chance, that all of its atoms just happened to come together and make up this device that produces an image, what would you think? How can atoms do what thousands of people cannot?

If a device producing a more primitive image than **the eye could not have been formed by chance**, then it is very evident that the eye and the image seen by the eye could not have been formed by chance. The same situation applies to the ear. The outer ear picks up the available sounds by the auricle and directs them to the middle ear, the middle ear transmits the sound vibrations by intensifying them, and the inner ear sends these vibrations to the brain by translating them into electric signals. Just as with the eye, the act of hearing finalizes in the center of hearing in the brain.

The situation in the eye is also true for the ear. That is, **the brain is insulated from sound** just as it is from light. It does not let any sound in. Therefore, no matter how noisy is the outside, the inside of the brain is completely silent. Nevertheless, the sharpest sounds are perceived in the brain. In **your completely silent brain, you listen to symphonies, and hear all of the noises in a crowded place.** However, were the sound level in your brain measured by a precise device at that moment, complete silence would be found to be prevailing there.

As is the case with imagery, decades of effort have been spent in trying to generate and reproduce sound that is faithful to the original. The results of these efforts are sound recorders, high-fidelity systems, and systems for sensing sound. Despite all of this technology and the thousands of engineers and experts who have been working on this endeavor, no sound has yet been obtained that has the same sharpness and clarity as the sound perceived by the ear. Think of the highest-quality hi-fi systems produced by the largest company in the music industry. Even in these devices, when sound is recorded some of it is lost; or when you turn on a hi-fi you always hear a hissing sound before the music starts. However, the sounds that are the products of the human body's technology are extremely sharp and clear. A human ear never perceives a sound accompanied by a hissing sound or with atmospherics as does a hi-fi; rather, it perceives sound exactly as it is, sharp and clear. This is the way it has been since **the creation of man.**

So far, no man-made visual or recording apparatus has been as sensitive and successful in perceiving sensory data as are the eye and the ear. However, as far as seeing and hearing are concerned, a far greater truth lies beyond all this.

To Whom Does the Consciousness that Sees and Hears within the Brain Belong?

Who watches an alluring world in the brain, listens to symphonies and the twittering of birds, and smells the rose?

The stimulations coming from a person's eyes, ears, and nose travel to the brain as electro-chemical nerve impulses. In biology, physiology, and biochemistry books, you can find many details about how this image forms in the brain. However, you will never come across the most important fact: Who perceives these electro-chemical nerve impulses as images, sounds, odors, and sensory events in the brain? **There is a consciousness in the brain that perceives all this without feeling any need for an eye, an ear,**

271

and a nose. To whom does this consciousness belong? Of course it does not belong to the nerves, the fat layer, and neurons comprising the brain. This is why Darwinist-materialists, who believe that everything is comprised of matter, cannot answer these questions.

For **this consciousness is the spirit created by God**, which needs neither the eye to watch the images nor the ear to hear the sounds. Furthermore, it does not need the brain to think.

Everyone who reads this explicit and scientific fact should ponder on Almighty God, and fear and seek refuge in Him, for He squeezes the entire universe in a pitch-dark place of a few cubic centimeters in a three-dimensional, colored, shadowy, and luminous form.

A Materialist Faith

The information we have presented so far shows us that **the theory of evolution is incompatible with scientific findings.** The theory's claim regarding the origin of life is inconsistent with science, the evolutionary mechanisms it proposes have no evolutionary power, and fossils demonstrate that **the required intermediate forms have never existed.** So, it certainly follows that the theory of evolution should be pushed aside as an unscientific idea. This is how many ideas, such as the Earth-centered universe model, have been taken out of the agenda of science throughout history.

However, the theory of evolution is kept on the agenda of science. Some people even try to represent criticisms directed against it as an "attack on science." Why?

The reason is that this theory is an indispensable dogmatic belief for some circles. These circles are **blindly devoted** to materialist philosophy and adopt Darwinism because it is the only materialist explanation that can be put forward to explain the workings of nature.

Interestingly enough, they also confess this fact from time to time. A well-known geneticist and an outspoken evolutionist, Richard C. Lewontin from Harvard University, confesses that he is "first and foremost a materialist and then a scientist":

> *It is not that the methods and institutions of science somehow compel us accept a material explanation of the phenomenal world, but, on the contrary, that we are forced by our a priori adherence to material causes to create an apparatus of investigation and a set of concepts that produce material explanations, no matter how counter-intuitive, no matter how mystifying to the uninitiated. Moreover, that materialism is absolute, so we cannot allow a Divine [intervention]...(Richard Lewontin, "The Demon-Haunted World," The New York Review of Books, January 9, 1997, p. 28)*

These are explicit statements that **Darwinism is a dogma** kept alive just for the sake of adherence to materialism. This dogma maintains that there is no being save matter. Therefore, it argues that inanimate, unconscious matter brought life into being. It insists that millions of different living species (e.g., birds, fish, giraffes, tigers, insects, trees, flowers, whales, and human beings) originated as a result of the interactions between matter such as pouring rain, lightning flashes, and so on, out of inanimate matter. This is a precept contrary both to reason and science. Yet Darwinists continue to ignorantly defend it just so as not to acknowledge, in their own eyes, the evident existence of God.

Anyone who does not look at the origin of living beings with a materialist prejudice sees this evident truth: **All living beings are works of a Creator,** Who is All-Powerful, All-Wise, and All-Knowing. **This Creator is God**, Who created the whole universe from non-existence, in the most perfect form, and fashioned all living beings.

The Theory of Evolution: The Most Potent Spell in the World

Anyone free of prejudice and the influence of any particular ideology, who uses only his or her reason and logic, will clearly understand that belief in the theory of evolution, which brings to mind the superstitions of societies with no knowledge of science or civilization, is quite impossible.

As explained above, those who believe in the theory of evolution think that a few atoms and molecules thrown into a huge vat could produce thinking, reasoning professors and university students; such scientists as Einstein and Galileo; such artists as Humphrey Bogart, Frank Sinatra and Luciano Pavarotti; as well as antelopes, lemon trees, and carnations. Moreover, as the scientists and professors who believe in this nonsense are educated people, it is quite justifiable to speak of this theory as "the most potent spell in history." Never before has any other belief or idea so taken away peoples' powers of reason, refused to allow them to think intelligently and logically, and hidden the truth from them as if they had been blindfolded. This is an even worse and unbelievable blindness than the totem worship in some parts of Africa, the people of Saba worshipping the Sun, the tribe of the Prophet Abraham (pbuh) worshipping idols they had made with their own hands, or some among the people of the Prophet Moses (pbuh) worshipping the Golden Calf.

In fact, God has pointed to this lack of reason in the Qur'an. In many verses, He reveals that some peoples' minds will be closed and that they will be powerless to see the truth. Some of these verses are as follows:

> **As for those who do not believe, it makes no difference to them whether you warn them or do not warn them, they will not believe. God has sealed up their hearts and hearing and over their eyes is a blindfold. They will have a terrible punishment. (Koran, 2:6-7)**

274

... They have hearts with which they do not understand. They have eyes with which they do not see. They have ears with which they do not hear. Such people are like cattle. No, they are even further astray! They are the unaware. (Koran, 7:179)

Even if We opened up to them a door into heaven, and they spent the day ascending through it, they would only say: "Our eyesight is befuddled! Or rather we have been put under a spell!" (Koran, 15:14-15)

Words cannot express just how astonishing it is that this spell should hold such a wide community in thrall, keep people from the truth, and not be broken for 150 years. It is understandable that one or a few people might believe in impossible scenarios and claims full of stupidity and illogicality. However, "magic" is the only possible explanation for people from all over the world believing that unconscious and lifeless atoms suddenly decided to come together and form a universe that functions with a flawless system of organization, discipline, reason, and consciousness; a planet named Earth with all of its features so perfectly suited to life; and living things full of countless complex systems.

In fact, in the Qur'an God relates the incident of the Prophet Moses (pbuh) and Pharaoh to show that some people who support atheistic philosophies actually influence others by magic. When Pharaoh was told about the true religion, he told the Prophet Moses (pbuh) to meet with his own magicians. When the Prophet Moses (pbuh) did so, he told them to demonstrate their abilities first. The verses continue:

He said: "You throw." And when they threw, they cast a spell on the people's eyes and caused them to feel great fear of them. They produced an extremely powerful magic. (Koran, 7:116)

As we have seen, Pharaoh's magicians were able to deceive everyone, apart from the Prophet Moses (pbuh) and those who believed in him. However, his evidence broke the spell, or "swallowed up what they had forged," as revealed in the verse:

275

We revealed to Moses: "Throw down your staff." And it immediately swallowed up what they had forged. So the Truth took place and what they did was shown to be false. (Koran, 7:117-118)

As we can see, when people realized that a spell had been cast upon them and that what they saw was just an illusion, Pharaoh's magicians lost all credibility. In the present day too, unless those who, under the influence of a similar spell, believe in these ridiculous claims under their scientific disguise and spend their lives defending them, abandon their superstitious beliefs, they also will be humiliated when the full truth emerges and the spell is broken. In fact, world-renowned British writer and philosopher Malcolm Muggeridge, who was an atheist defending evolution for some 60 years, but who subsequently realized the truth, reveals the position in which the theory of evolution would find itself in the near future in these terms:

*I myself am convinced that **the theory of evolution**, especially the extent to which it's been applied, **will be one of the great jokes in the history books in the future.** Posterity will marvel that so very flimsy and dubious an hypothesis could be accepted with the incredible credulity that it has. (Malcolm Muggeridge, The End of Christendom, Grand Rapids: Eerdmans, 1980, p. 43)*

They said, 'Glory be to You! We have no knowledge except what You have taught us. You are the All-Knowing, the All-Wise.' (Koran, 2:32)

RESİM ALTI
YAZILARI

s.10

Not so! All who submit themselves completely to God and are good-doers will find their reward with their Lord. They will feel no fear and will know no sorrow. (Koran, 2:112)

s.21

Say, 'People of the Book! come to a proposition which is the same for us and you – that we should worship none but God and not associate any partners with Him and not take one another as lords besides God.' If they turn away, say, 'Bear witness that we are Muslims.' (Koran, 3:64)

s.25

He has sent down the Book to you with truth, confirming what was there before it. And He sent down the Torah and the Gospel, (Koran, 3:3)

s.26

Hagia Sofia Mosque.

All religions are built on love, friendship and brotherhood. The Koran was sent down to confirm all the previous books. Therefore, believing in the Koran does not deprive Christians of Christianity and Jesus (pbuh). On the contrary, it makes them more devout and draws them even closer to Jesus.

God is my Lord and your Lord so worship Him. That is a straight path. (Koran, 3:51)

s.35

This is the true account: there is no other god besides God. God – He is the Almighty, the All-Wise. (Koran, 3:62)

s.37

The House of Mary, a church in Bülbüldağı in Selçuk, Izmir, where Mary, mother of Jesus (pbuh), is believed to have spent her final years. This is a place of pilgrimage for Christians.

Her tomb is also thought to be in Bülbüldağı.

This is regarded as sacred by Muslims as well as Christians.

s.40

God is my Lord and your Lord so worship Him. That is a straight path. (Koran, 3:51)

s.41

Those who remember God, standing, sitting and lying on their sides, and reflect on the creation of the heavens and the Earth: 'Our Lord, You have not created this for nothing. Glory be to You! So safeguard us from the punishment of the Fire. (Koran, 3:191)

s.43

One of the many statues in front of the Basilica of St. Peter is that of Paul.

s.46

A drawing by Pedro Berruguete showing books considered heretical and being burned by order of the Inquisition and its courts.

s.48

That is God, your Lord. There is no god but Him, the Creator of everything. So worship Him. He is responsible for everything. (Koran, 6:102)

St. Patrick's Cathedral in New York

s.49

They believe in God and the Last Day, and enjoin the right and forbid the wrong, and compete in doing good. They are among the righteous. (Koran, 3:114)

s.52

The First Vatican Council, or Vatican I: 800 church leaders were called together by Pope Pius IX on June 29, 1868.

This council issued the final decision regarding the belief on the Trinity, which was made part of Christian dogma by church councils and for which there is no logical basis: "The Trinity is not a matter of reason and logic. There is no need for you to sit and think about it." In this way, the Trinity was made an article of faith without being understood, and those who refused to believe were excommunicated.

The Church of St. Peter

s.55

On the one hand, the Church stresses the unchanging nature of the Gospels. On the other hand, however, it has had no qualms about making various additions and subtractions so that the four Gospels would become compatible with one another.

s.68-69

And We sent 'Jesus son of Mary following in their footsteps, confirming the Torah that came before him. We gave him the Gospel containing guidance and light, confirming the Torah that came before it, and as guidance and admonition for those who have fear of God. (Koran, 5:46)

s.75

This is the path of your Lord – straight. We have made the Signs clear for people who remember.

They will have the Abode of Peace with their Lord. He is their Protector because of what they have done. (Koran, 6:126-127)

s.82

Celebrations to mark the 50th anniversary of Vatican II

s.84

Everything in the heavens and everything in the earth belongs to God. All matters return to God. (Koran, 3:109)

s.86

... God will certainly help those who help Him – God is All-Strong, Almighty. (Koran, 22:40)

s.90

The Church of Ludwig

The Gospel contains many passages referring to the Oneness of God. Belief in the Trinity was imposed by compulsion and is now a belief being kept alive by compulsion.

s.92

The nave of St. Peter's Basilica

The Presence of God, Who sees and knows all, is a blessing. The Presence of God, Who is with us at all times and answers our prayers, is a great blessing. The confusion of the Trinity deprives Christians of this great blessing. That is one of the reasons why this belief is so dangerous.

s.98

If their belief is the same as yours then they are guided. But if they turn away, they are in schism. God will be enough for you against them. He is the All-Hearing, the All-Knowing. (Koran, 2:137)

s.103

No, God is your Protector. And He is the best of helpers. (Koran, 3:150)

s.118

"The Last Supper" showing Jesus (pbuh) and his disciples

(Il Cenacolo or L'Ultima Cena)

s.133

Like everyone else, Jesus (pbuh) is a servant of God. The Gospel contains many passages to the effect that Jesus is a human being and that he fulfilled the duties of a servant. These passages from the Gospel therefore invalidate the idea of divinity ascribed to Jesus (surely God is beyond that).

s.138

Say: 'He is God, Absolute Oneness,

God, the Everlasting Sustainer of all.

He has not given birth and was not born.

And no one is comparable to Him.'

(Koran, 112:1-4)

s.150

A synagogue in Berlin

Supporters of the Trinity maintain that the belief originates from the Torah. Because Christian belief needs to be compatible with the Torah they seek to produce evidence from it, in their own eyes, and interpret some passages from the Torah in an incorrect manner. However, Judaic clergy have always rejected this specious claim made by the supporters of the Trinity. The Torah also rejects belief in the Trinity, just like the Gospel.

s.161

It is impossible for us to step outside the images in our brain and experience the original of matter. We watch merely the brightly colored and mobile world we are shown. Everything is therefore created as a phantom in our brains. So these are all images and manifestations created by God. This clarification of the subject of manifestation refutes the idea that "A manifestation of

God means the incarnation of God." Jesus (pbuh) is merely a fine manifestation of God, but he is not the incarnation of God.

s.162

HEARING

TASTE

s.163

TOUCH

SIGHT

SMELL

s.165

We perceive many things by the sea shore. The smell of the sea, the coolness of the breeze, the sound of the waves, the wetness of the pebbles, the distance of the horizon and all these things are only a collection of perceptions created in our brains. In fact, we can experience no real version of these objects outside our brains. There are only images, and these images are all manifestations of God. This means that God is closer to us than the pebbles we seem to feel in our hands.

s.169

Both East and West belong to God, so wherever you turn, the Face of God is there. God is All-Encompassing, All-Knowing. (Koran, 2:115)

s.174

He to Whom the kingdom of the heavens and the Earth belongs. He does not have a son and He has no partner in the Kingdom. He created everything and determined it most exactly. (Koran, 25:2)

s.181

God is my Lord and your Lord so worship Him. This is a straight path. (Koran, 19:36)

s.184-185

...and to warn those who say 'God has a son.'

They have no knowledge of this, neither they nor their fathers. It is a monstrous utterance which has issued from their mouths. What they say is nothing but a lie. (Koran, 18:4-5)

s.193

He [Jesus] said, 'I am the servant of God, He has given me the Book and made me a Prophet'. (Koran, 19:30)

s.205

Giuseppe Molteni's picture *La Confession*, 1838 (Fondazione Cariplo)

The belief that the Prophet Jesus (pbuh) died to expiate the sins of all Christians is a grave error. It is incompatible with God's justice for a person to assume the sins of another and then to be punished for them. A person is born without sin, but he only is responsible for the errors he makes throughout his life. There is always room for repentance and seeking the mercy of God in this world, of course.

s.225

Those who believe and those who are Jews and the Sabaeans and the Christians, all who believe in God and the Last Day and act rightly will feel no fear and will know no sorrow. (Koran, 6:69)

s.231

The 12th Century Church of St. Gabriel in Tarascon, France

s.232

God does not forgive anything being associated with Him but He forgives whoever He wills for anything other than that. Anyone who associates something with God has committed a terrible crime. (Koran, 4:48)

s.247

Those who believe, those who are Jews, and the Christians and Sabaeans, all who believe in God and the Last Day and act rightly, will have their reward with their Lord. They will feel no fear and will know no sorrow. (Koran, 2:62)

s.256

Iraq is weeping

Daily Türkiye, 23 March 2003

Iraq is in flames

Daily Zaman, 22 March 2003

Baghdad is burning

Daily Habertürk, 22 March 2003

Iraq is being divided into three

Daily Milliyet, 4 May 2003

Iraq will be divided into three

Daily Yeni Şafak, 4 November 2003

s.258
They have looted Baghdad worse than Hulagu

Daily Türkiye, 23 March 2003

Flight from hunger and death

Iraq is being swamped by debt

Daily Yeni Şafak, 30 March 2003

Daily Tercüman, 15 April 2003

The embargo is hitting only the Iraqi people

Daily Milli Gazete, 22 June 2003

s.261

ARMAGEDDON HAS LONG SINCE BEGUN AND IS STILL RAGING

s.263

... The noblest among you in God's Sight is the one with the most fear [of God]. God is All-Knowing, All-Aware. (Koran, 49:13)

s.276

Darwinism is the sole ideology of savagery adopted by communist and fascist leaders in order to shed blood. Darwinist logic lies behind terrorist attacks and savagery.

Marx

Lenin

Trotsky

Stalin

s.277

Hitler

Mussolini

Mao

s.278

The diary of the antichrist

Daily Radikal, 25 July 2011

"Cruelty is my business"

Daily Hürriyet, 27 July 2011

s.279

The fear of racist terror

Daily Türkiye, 25 July 2011

He was prepared for this slaughter for 5 years.

Daily Milliyet, 25 July 2011

s.307

We made everything on the Earth adornment for it so that We could test them to see whose actions are the best. (Koran, 18:7)

s.314

Mankind! worship your Lord, Who created you and those before you, so that hopefully you will have fear [of God]. (Koran, 2:21)

s.315

He is God in the heavens and in the Earth. He knows what you keep secret and what you make public and He knows what you earn. (Koran, 6:3)

s.336

THE HOLY KORAN

s.339

The People of the Book have a special place in Islam. Muslims have a duty to treat the People of the Book with love and respect, to protect them and to be their brothers.

s.356

Darwin appeared as declaring science to be his pseudo-idol and his dictatorship spread all over the world.

s.357

In this way, the system of the antichrist has cunningly led people into irreligion and disaster. In fact, the antichrist described in the Gospel and the sole source of the wars and degeneration in the world is Darwinism.

s.368

The money spent on wars and weaponry could instead be used for global regeneration, the total elimination of hunger, treating diseases such as cancer and Alzheimer's and for science and technology and new discoveries. There would be no more poor or hungry countries in the world. This money, enough to save the world, is instead being used so that people can kill each other, for the destruction of cities and for the crippling of millions. Hazrat Mahdi (pbuh) will eliminate this system, and there will be no more weaponry in the world, and not a drop of blood will be shed.

s.378

Those who do good will have the best and more! Neither dust nor debasement will darken their faces. They are the Companions of the Garden, remaining in it timelessly, forever. (Koran, 10:26)

s.379

He who brings the truth and he who confirms it –those are the people who have fear [of God].

They will have anything they wish for with their Lord. That is the recompense of the good-doers. (Koran, 39:33-34)

s.382

God will admit those who believe and do right actions into Gardens with rivers flowing under them. God does whatever He wishes. (Koran, 22:14)

s.383

"He picks out for His mercy whoever He wills. God's favor is indeed immense." (Koran, 3:74)

s.386

Charles Darwin

s.388

Louise Pasteur

s.389

As accepted also by the latest evolutionist theorists, the origin of life is still a great stumbling block for the theory of evolution.

s.390

Alexander Oparin's attempts to offer an evolutionist explanation for the origin of life ended in a great fiasco.

s.392

One of the facts nullifying the theory of evolution is the astonishingly complex structure of life. The DNA molecule located in the nucleus of cells of living beings is an example of this. The DNA is a sort of databank formed of the arrangement of four different molecules in different sequences. This databank contains the codes of all the physical traits of that living being. When the human DNA is put into writing, it is calculated that this would result in an encyclopedia made up of 900 volumes. Unquestionably, such extraordinary information definitively refutes the concept of coincidence.

s.396

antennae

eyes

mouth

leg

Since the beginning of the twentieth century, evolutionary biologists have sought examples of beneficial mutations by creating mutant flies. But these efforts have always resulted in sick and deformed creatures. The picture on the left shows the head of a normal fruit fly, and the picture on the right shows the head of a fruit fly with legs coming out of it, the result of mutation.

s.397

This fossil crocodile from the Cretaceous period is 65 million years old. It is identical to crocodiles living today.

This 50-million-year-old fossil plane-tree leaf was unearthed in the USA. Plane-tree leaves have remained unchanged for 50 million years, and have never evolved.

This mene unearthed in Italy is 54 to 37 million years old.

s.401

FALSE

There are no fossil remains that support the tale of human evolution. On the contrary, the fossil record shows that there is an insurmountable barrier between apes and men. In the face of this truth, evolutionists fixed their hopes on certain drawings and models. They randomly place masks on the fossil remains and fabricate imaginary half-ape, half-human faces.

s.405

Can life emerge if all the conditions stipulated by evolutionists are met? Of course not! In order to show why not, let us carry out the following experiment: Place all the enzymes, hormones and proteins—everything that evolutionists regard as essential for life to form—into a barrel such as that pictured on the left page. Then mix all these substances, using all possible physical and chemical techniques. But whatever you do, no matter how long you wait, not a single living cell will emerge from that barrel.

s.407

Signals from an object affect the brain by turning into electrical signals. When we say we see something, we are actually experiencing the effect of electrical signals in our brain. The brain is closed off to light. The interior of the brain is pitch black, and no light can enter where the brain is. The area known as the visual cortex is pitch black, somewhere that light can never reach, darker perhaps than anywhere you have ever seen. But you watch a brightly colored world in that pitch dark.

s.408

Compared to cameras and sound recording devices, the eye and ear are much more complex, much more successful and possess far superior features to these products of high technology.

s.414

In the same way that the beliefs of people who worshipped crocodiles now seem odd and unbelievable, so the beliefs of Darwinists are just as incredible. Darwinists regard chance and lifeless, unconscious atoms as a creative force, and are as devoted to that belief as if to a religion.

CPSIA information can be obtained
at www.ICGtesting.com
Printed in the USA
BVHW052335090223
658265BV00032B/672